I0759971

JEAN-MICHEL BASQUIAT:
THE MAKING OF AN ICON

JEAN-MICHEL BASQUIAT: THE MAKING OF AN ICON

DOUG WOODHAM

First published in the United States of America in 2025 by Thames & Hudson Inc.,
500 Fifth Avenue, New York, New York 10110

First published in the United Kingdom in 2025 by Thames & Hudson Ltd,
6–24 Britannia Street, London WC1X 9JD

Designed by BTDNYC

EU Authorized Representative: Interart S.A.R.L.
19 rue Charles Auray, 93500 Pantin, Paris, France
productsafety@thameshudson.co.uk
www.interart.fr

A CIP catalogue record for this book is available from the British Library

Library of Congress Control Number 2025936231

ISBN 978-0-500-03069-1

01

Printed and bound in China by Shenzhen Reliance Printing Co. Ltd

*A special thanks to my daughter Abby,
whose astute advice and encouragement
played a crucial role in my journey
writing this book.*

CONTENTS

INTRODUCTION

MY FASCINATION WITH JEAN-MICHEL BASQUIAT TOOK ROOT WHEN I MOVED TO NEW YORK CITY IN THE EARLY 1980S. Though his name was familiar to those of us who followed the contemporary art world, opportunities to see his work firsthand were scarce. I was delighted when his name appeared in a *New York Times* review of a group exhibition featuring four hundred artists. Eager to see his work, I visited the exhibition space—a sprawling, abandoned army depot in Brooklyn. But after wandering through the dystopian venue, I was unable to find any of his pieces. Frustrated, I returned to the entrance and asked the person at the front desk where the work was displayed. I was told that Basquiat's paintings had been removed due to concerns about theft, as his pieces had suddenly become highly sought after. While my plans to see his work that day were thwarted, my interest in his art only deepened.

Jean-Michel Basquiat, the Brooklyn-born artist who died of a drug overdose in 1988 at the age of twenty-seven, currently stands

Basquiat around the time he started working in the basement studio provided by Annina Nosei, 1981.

alongside a handful of others at the pinnacle of what a visual artist can hope to achieve in our world. When one of his paintings sold for $110.5 million at auction in 2017, he joined the exclusive "$100 million club," alongside luminaries such as Picasso, Modigliani, and Munch. The streets of Rio de Janeiro, Paris, and Singapore are filled with people of all ages wearing T-shirts, shoes, and accessories featuring his artwork or image. Some fans even express their admiration permanently through Basquiat-inspired tattoos, sharing their ink on social media with #basquiattattoo. His cultural impact is so far-reaching that he has become a frequent answer on *Jeopardy!*

But Basquiat's ascension into these parallel pantheons of fine art and pop culture was far from certain. Despite starting life with the gifts of a sharp intellect—his family recalled him reading articles in *The New York Times* by first grade—and a financially stable, middle-class home, he was sidetracked by profound early personal traumas. By his teenage years, he had dropped out of high school and was living on the streets. He was without any formal training as an artist and initially wanted to be a cartoonist. A shy and, in some ways, fragile young man, he also had to face down the challenge of penetrating the elitist contemporary art world of the early 1980s, where Black artists struggled to find recognition and acceptance.

So how did Basquiat's work overcome so many obstacles—both during his brief life and after his death—to achieve such critical and commercial acclaim? Like a deity with a broad scope of jurisdiction, he has become a patron saint to many: Basquiat the artistic visionary, Basquiat the truth-telling Black activist, Basquiat the outsider. Yet he was also a real person driven by relatable human motivations.

Since attending that Brooklyn exhibition, I've followed Basquiat's trajectory throughout my career—as a partner at a global management consulting firm; president of Christie's Americas, the international auction house; and an art advisor to collectors and institutions. What these roles have provided me with is an insider's view of the forces driving the blue-chip art market, a world often shrouded in opacity, as if its inner workings were best kept behind the canvas. Yet this labyrinthine and occasionally contentious system underscores a broader truth: Understanding how art is valued illuminates why certain artists rise to prominence. Whether one likes to think about it or not, the works that dominate attention and secure pride of place in leading museums and collections have all, at some point, passed a demanding market test.

As I delved deeper into this book, I also came to realize that while Basquiat and I have some of life's broadest experiences in common—middle-class upbringings in church-going households and a few years' difference in age—my real connection to him lies in my admiration for his insatiable curiosity, self-directed ambition, and relentless determination to carve out a place for himself in the world. Drawing on my own, albeit very different, experiences in an adjacent part of the art world, along with insights from over a hundred interviews with those connected to Basquiat—family members, friends, lovers, gallerists, collectors of all stripes, museum directors, auction house staff, academics, and artists—I have pieced together how Basquiat and his work achieved the level of recognition they enjoy today.

Since the publication of what was long considered the definitive biography of Basquiat over twenty-five years ago, much has changed with respect to his reputation and in the market for his work. In writing this book, I have drawn not only on the stories shared by those I interviewed, but also on newly available or previously difficult-to-access information about Basquiat's early life and brief career (including numerous photographs of him, some that have never been published before). These resources have helped uncover fresh insights into his life and art while correcting elements of what has become the accepted narrative. Unraveling the myth to connect with the gifted child, teenager, and young artist (who would have turned sixty-five this year) is the focus of the first part of this book.

Basquiat's personal biography ended tragically in 1988, and until now, that was largely where the story stopped. Therefore my other goal here is to present the biography of his work's survival and how, in the decades since his untimely death, both the artist and his work have attained an almost mythical status. The legacy of any great artist extends beyond their lifetime, often shaped by a small group of individuals who, motivated by varied interests, ensure the work continues to be seen, known, and experienced. For Basquiat, this was particularly true, given the significant obstacles his work had to overcome to secure the recognition it enjoys today. Additionally, his posthumous reputation was further strengthened by a shift among curators and academics toward examining art through the prism of identity—exploring how an artist's race, gender, and sexuality inform their engagement with themes such as oppression, discrimination, and inequality. Basquiat not only embodied this evolving paradigm of artistic relevance but also helped to define it. How these and other forces combined to elevate Basquiat's legacy—until now, the missing chapters of his story—are the focus of the second half of this book.

During his brief but prolific career, Basquiat produced approximately one thousand paintings and two thousand drawings. Many of his most celebrated works are readily accessible online through articles, websites, and Instagram posts. The Basquiat Estate has further capitalized on his legacy by licensing images for a wide array of consumer products, from shoes and underwear to candles and cosmetics. Yet this wave of commercialization masks a more complex and previously untold story—one tied to his highly accomplished but conservative accounting executive father, Gerard—which explains why this book does not include reproductions of Basquiat's art. Over decades, his father vigorously promoted his son's work while carefully curating Jean-Michel's narrative, suppressing elements he found uncomfortable or unacceptable: his traumatic childhood, his bisexuality, and the impact of his addictions on his art. These efforts profoundly influenced Basquiat's portrayal in exhibition catalogs and museum retrospectives over the past three decades. Ironically, for an artist whose work is so deeply entwined with personal identity, much of the scholarship has glossed over the very experiences that inspired many of his most celebrated creations.

The art world, like many creative industries, selects and elevates its luminaries in ways that can appear enigmatic, inscrutable, or even arbitrary. Yet its influence on our cultural landscape is profound. It is my hope that the stories I share about Jean-Michel Basquiat's against-all-odds journey from his Brooklyn childhood to the pinnacle of the art world, will help readers understand the surprising and often hidden reasons why his paintings, rather than another artist's, are on T-shirts worn by people around the world, on the walls of billionaires, and remain such a source of inspiration to creatives globally.

CHAPTER 1

EARLY YEARS (1960-1978)

JEAN-MICHEL BASQUIAT ARRIVED IN THE WORLD ON DECEMBER 22, 1960. While New York City, including Jean-Michel's native Brooklyn, was bustling with postwar confidence, it was also already wrestling with the social and economic tensions that would shape the coming decades. The city was flourishing as a hub of banking, media, and commerce, but it was also in the process of birthing America's counterculture, from the Beats and Dylan (who arrived in Greenwich Village the month after Basquiat's birth) to the Abstract Expressionists, with the work of such painters as Jackson Pollock and Willem de Kooning dominating the contemporary art scene. Meanwhile, the civil rights movement was gaining momentum across a teeming city, where cultural vibrancy existed alongside stark inequality.

Jean-Michel as a toddler, 1962.

Matilde Basquiat (right) with her mother Flora Andrades (left), late 1950s.

Jean-Michel's mother, Matilde Andrades, grew up in Brooklyn in a household shaped by resilience and ambition. Raised by parents who had immigrated from Puerto Rico, Matilde was encouraged to be strong and self-reliant. She attended Washington Irving High School, an all-girls public school near Gramercy Park, commuting to Manhattan for her education. After graduating, she secured a job at the local telephone company, eventually rising to a supervisory position. Matilde's youngest brother, Reuben Andrades Sr., described her as a sophisticated and articulate woman with a keen understanding of the world. "For being a Puerto Rican Black woman in those days," he noted, "she achieved a great deal and went pretty high up at New York Bell."[1]

Jean-Michel's father, Gerard Basquiat, immigrated to the United States from Haiti in 1955, leaving behind a privileged life disrupted by the Haitian revolution. At just twenty years old, he arrived alone, unemployed, and without knowledge of English.[2] Despite these challenges, he was determined to rebuild the stability and opportunities his family had once enjoyed in Haiti.

An attractive couple, Gerard and Matilde married in June 1959. At the time, Matilde was twenty-four and Gerard was twenty-three. It was Matilde's second marriage and Gerard's first.[3] Considering the traditional, patriarchal nature of Haitian culture, Gerard's choice to marry someone so independent and previously married was unconventional. Perhaps the large, supportive Andrades family in Brooklyn offered Gerard a sense of stability as he worked to build a new life and start a family. Matilde soon became pregnant with their first child, a boy, but miscarried. Their sorrow turned to hope when she became pregnant again, this time with Jean-Michel.

The young Basquiat family lived in a multigenerational household with Matilde's parents at 36 Covert Street in Bushwick, a working-class neighborhood in central Brooklyn. The house was warm and welcoming, with Jean-Michel's grandparents on the first floor, his immediate family on the second, and an uncle's family on the top floor. Occasionally, other relatives, including one of Gerard's brothers, also stayed with them.

These living arrangements made a lasting impression on Jean-Michel. Through his grandparents, he developed a deep love and appreciation for his Puerto Rican heritage. His maternal grandparents, John and Flora Andrades, had immigrated separately to the United States as young adults. By 1940, they were married with four children and living in what is now Dumbo, a Brooklyn neighborhood between the Brooklyn and Manhattan Bridges. The area attracted immigrants with its affordable rents and plentiful factory jobs along the waterfront. John worked at the Domino sugar factory, earning about $100 a month, while Flora was a homemaker. After the factory downsized, John found

The Andrades family town house in Bushwick, Brooklyn, where Jean-Michel lived as a young child.

work in a dry-cleaning business, specializing in sweater pressing. Through hard work, savings, and an inheritance Flora received from her parents, the couple purchased the Covert Street townhouse in 1956.[4] Because John and Flora insisted on speaking Spanish at home, their grandson upstairs became fluent in the language.

Jean-Michel was an intellectually gifted child. By the time he was in first grade, he was reading articles in *The New York Times*. The extensive literature on gifted children gives us some sense of how his mind likely worked.[5] Studies suggest that, in addition to a fascination with words and ideas, these children process new information quickly, identify patterns, and retain countless details over long periods of time. They pursue new interests passionately, with a tendency toward quick immersion. They also have the capacity to step back and view many sides of a question, which can help them be especially creative and inventive. Judging from accounts of those who knew him, Jean-Michel evidenced all these behaviors—a mind rich with information and ideas that he would later channel into his artwork.

Matilde was determined to invest whatever was required to help her brilliant young son reach his potential. At some point, she set aside her own career ambitions, leaving her job at New York Bell to focus on supporting Jean-Michel and Gerard. Meanwhile, Gerard balanced working during the day with pursuing an accounting degree at City College at night.

Jean-Michel's upbringing was steeped in religion, though he would later identify as an atheist. His grandmother Flora, a devout Christian, ensured that the family regularly worshipped at the First Spanish Presbyterian Church of Brooklyn. Yet Flora also had ties to another religious and ethnic identity through her ancestry. Her maternal lineage traced back to Spanish Jews, while her paternal lineage included a mix of Taínos—Indigenous people of the Caribbean—and Jews who had escaped the Spanish Inquisition. According to Jewish law, Jewish identity is passed through the maternal line, meaning Flora inherited her Jewish identity despite her embrace of Christianity. This identity, in turn, was transmitted to her daughter, Matilde, and then to Jean-Michel and his siblings. While Matilde also embraced Christianity, her Jewish lineage was a known topic of discussion within the family. Gerard Basquiat even mistakenly listed his wife as Jewish on a school enrollment form for Jean-Michel. Though it is unclear how fully Jean-Michel understood his Jewish heritage, he was likely aware of it and may have appreciated the paradox of his family identifying as Christian while being linked to the traditions of Judaism.

After about five years at the Covert Street residence, during which Jean-Michel gained a younger sister, Lisane, his parents purchased a two-story brownstone in East Flatbush, Brooklyn. The neighborhood was known for its vibrant and diverse immigrant community, particularly from the Caribbean.[6] Believing that education was paramount to the American dream, they enrolled Jean-Michel in Saint Ann's School, a prestigious private institution in Brooklyn Heights.[7] Matilde, an attentive and ambitious mother, helped Jean-Michel with his homework, engaged him in conversations about world events, and introduced him to the city's museums.

His seemingly happy childhood, however, was shattered by three traumatic events that occurred when he was seven years old, the first being a near-fatal car accident near his East Flatbush apartment. While playing with friends on a nearby stoop, he ran into the street and was struck by a car. His injuries required nearly a month in the hospital and multiple surgeries, including the removal of his spleen. During his recuperation, his mother gave him a copy of *Gray's Anatomy*, an illustrated reference book on human anatomy first published in 1858. By then, the book had been updated and revised more than twenty-five times, expanding to more than fourteen hundred pages. Though an unconventional gift for a sick child, it reflected the special bond between Matilde and her intellectually curious son. Basquiat cherished the book, using it to understand his broken arm and damaged internal organs. Later in life, Jean-Michel would repeatedly reference both this traumatic incident and what he had absorbed from *Gray's Anatomy* in his artworks.

The next blow came during the recuperation at home when his parents' marriage disintegrated. Matilde, suspecting Gerard of infidelity, confronted him, leading to a physical altercation in which she injured his legs. Gerard left the house and returned only sporadically, leaving Matilde to care for their children. Over the following months, the Andrades family rallied to support Matilde, but the stress became overwhelming, and she suffered a nervous breakdown. Her decline was fast and precipitous, and she was admitted to Kings County Hospital, in Brooklyn. Reuben Andrades Sr., Matilde's youngest brother, recalled taking her to the hospital while listening to her distressed cries of confusion and despair: "What's wrong with me; what's happening to me?" She remained hospitalized for several months. During this time, Gerard returned to the East Flatbush apartment to care for Jean-Michel, his four-year-old sister, Lisane, and their one-year-old sister, Jeanine.

As Matilde's release date approached, she told her family that she did not want her children to lack for anything but that men ruled the world. She was concerned that Gerard might drift away emotionally and financially if she kept the children. To safeguard against this, she asked Gerard to raise them, which he agreed to do. Matilde returned to her parents' home on Covert Street without her children—for Jean-Michel the third, and perhaps the most damaging, trauma suffered during his childhood.

The absence of his nurturing and supportive mother was a devastating loss. Matilde had been Jean-Michel's emotional anchor, and her departure left a profound void in his life. Although she received treatment and medication, she never fully recovered or returned to her previous self. Over the years, her mental illness would sometimes flare up, with occasional hospital readmissions. While her exact diagnosis is unclear, her younger brother believes it was likely schizophrenia, a complex condition characterized by symptoms such as hallucinations, delusions, and disordered thinking. Treatment usually involves lifelong medication and substantial family support. While Matilde received early intervention, the medications, especially those prescribed in the 1960s, often had the side effect of flattening her personality.

Jean-Michel was acutely aware of the changes in his world. The mother he adored, who continued to show him affection and appeared unchanged outwardly, was now grappling with a condition beyond his understanding. These early traumas had a profound effect on him. His cousin, Reuben Andrades Jr., remembers the day when Jean-Michel finally appreciated that his parents had separated and that he would no longer live with his mother: "He was a total wreck. I remember him crying and screaming to my grandmother about his family when he was visiting us at the Covert Street house. He was so hurt by the whole thing. His parents were no longer together, and his mom was sick with something serious. It didn't sit well with him for a very, very long time, if ever. I remember vividly the emotions, the drama, and my grandmother crying while she was trying to console Jean-Michel. But he just ran out of the house screaming."[8]

JEAN-MICHEL'S YOUNG LIFE had been upended: His parents were no longer together, he was being raised by his father, and his mother was struggling with significant mental health issues. Living with his dad was an especially stinging blow. By the norms of the day, he had been thrust into an acute state of otherness.

Despite his fractured family, Jean-Michel remained deeply attached to his mother. He regularly visited her at the Covert Street house, enduring an hour-long commute that required taking two subway trains. A few years later, those visits became easier when Gerard

The brownstone in Boerum Hill that became Jean-Michel's new home in 1972.

purchased a brownstone in the rapidly gentrifying Brooklyn neighborhood of Boerum Hill, closer to Matilde's location (and still owned by the Basquiat family, near the present-day Barclays Center).[9] At the time, Gerard worked as an accountant at Macmillan Inc., a diversified media company with interests in publishing, film, and education.[10]

Jean-Michel's visitation rhythm with his mom was disrupted when Gerard accepted a new position in San Juan, Puerto Rico, as the financial controller for the Latin American division of Berlitz, a language-training company owned by Macmillan. In March of 1974, when Jean-Michel was thirteen years old and in the eighth grade, Gerard and his three children relocated there.[11]

Jean-Michel was delighted to move to the warm tropical island his grandparents had often described. However, it meant he would rarely see his mother and had to face the challenge of starting a new school mid-year. Gerard enrolled him in the Episcopal Cathedral School, a private institution conveniently located near their new home. Classes were taught in English, sparing him the need to rely entirely on his Spanish-language skills. As part of the enrollment process, Jean-Michel filled out a questionnaire detailing his interests.[12] In neat penmanship, he wrote that he enjoyed books about movies and the history of comics, favored English, science, and social studies, but disliked mathematics. Looking to the future, he wrote that after graduating from high school, he wanted to study art, stating, "I hope to become a worldwide syndicated cartoonist or a commercial artist."

Shortly after arriving in Puerto Rico, Jean-Michel began to unravel. The first indication of trouble was his eighth-grade report card, which showed that he had failed math and was skating by in his other subjects. Gerard pivoted and transferred him to a different school for ninth grade: Academia San Jorge, a private Roman Catholic institution. Yet Jean-Michel failed four classes that year—Spanish, Latin American history, science, and algebra—managing to pass only creative writing. He would have to repeat most of that grade.

In addition to struggling academically, Jean-Michel began acting out, frequently skipping school and running away from home. His striking good looks and articulate manner allowed him to mingle with an older crowd, leading to early experiences with sex, drugs, and alcohol in San Juan's nightlife. He later confided in a girlfriend that he left home for a period and lived with a San Juan disc jockey, with whom he had his first homosexual relationship.[13] He also clandestinely returned to New York once to see his mother and escape from Gerard.

Jean-Michel during a clandestine trip home to see his mother in Brooklyn while he was living temporarily in Puerto Rico, 1975.

After spending a couple of years in Puerto Rico, the family moved back to Brooklyn. Jean-Michel returned a different person—fifteen years old, wild and uncontrollable, with a nihilism that terrified his extended family. Within weeks, he once again ran away, spending two weeks roaming the streets before eventually returning home. The school he was supposed to be attending suspended him.

The New York City school system offered a novel solution for dealing with a determined yet self-destructive teenager: a small Brooklyn high school designed specifically for at-risk kids. While such programs are now common nationwide, City-As-School was a pioneer. Instead of traditional classes, it used "community resources" as an alternative educational model. A health credit might involve working for the Red Cross during a blood drive, while an art credit could be earned by taking a class at the Museum of Modern Art. English or science requirements might be fulfilled at yet another institution. There were few rules and ample freedom. "We moved around like a loose herd," recalled one former student who attended with Jean-Michel, "seeing each other out on the street. It was very much a hippie school with a lot of sex and drugs for kids that couldn't make it in a conventional high school."

After starting at City-As-School, Jean-Michel met Al Diaz, a fellow student a year ahead of him. Their friendship led to the creation of SAMO, a graffiti tag short for "Same Old Shit," which brought them an early taste of fame and notoriety. Diaz commuted from his home on Manhattan's Lower East Side to attend City-As-School. The son of working-class Puerto Rican immigrants, Diaz grew up in a household shaped by his parents' determination to build a better life in the United States. He became involved with graffiti in the early 1970s, when he was twelve years old. A cousin who lived in Washington Heights—a hotbed for graffiti culture—introduced him to tagging. Diaz frequently took the subway there to meet his cousin, and together they roamed the city, tagging buildings and subway cars. "I became an early

Al Diaz (right), co-creator of the SAMO tag, with high school friends, 1975.

graffiti fanatic, bombing sites around town," Diaz recalled. "It was like a secret organization. I was deeply entrenched in it."[14] Drawn to art, Diaz enrolled in the High School of Art and Design, a magnet school in midtown Manhattan. However, after three years, he was expelled for repeatedly skipping school to spend time with fellow graffiti artists. He later enrolled at City-As-School.

In the 1970s, graffiti culture in New York City provoked fierce debate: Was it a sign of urban decline or a revolutionary form of expression? Norman Mailer, in his 1974 essay "The Faith of Graffiti," lauded graffiti as avant-garde art, drawing parallels between its creators and Abstract Expressionists. He framed graffiti as a raw and democratic assertion of identity, and a challenge to established notions of art and ownership. Similarly, writers at *The Village Voice* often celebrated the medium as a vibrant, rebellious art form, transforming subway cars and walls into public canvases. *The New York Times*, in contrast, largely took a more critical view. Much of its coverage depicted graffiti as a symptom of urban disorder, emphasizing its financial costs and damage to the city's image. Articles echoed the concerns of officials and property owners, casting graffiti as vandalism rather than art—an affront to order in a city beset by fiscal crises and rising crime.

The SAMO tag Diaz and Basquiat created started out as a joke. Jean-Michel wrote a satirical piece for the school newspaper about an imaginary religion he called SAMO. Diaz thought it would be fun to tag buildings with caustic, quasi-religious phrases that a leader of the SAMO religion might proclaim. Although Jean-Michel had never tagged anything before, he jumped on Diaz's idea.

They were soon spending time getting high and crafting nihilistic poems that possessed a distinctive style and rhythm:

- SAMO© AS AN END TO MINDWASH RELIGION, NOWHERE POLITICS, AND BOGUS PHILOSOPHY
- SAMO© AS A MEANS OF DRAWING ATTENTION TO INSIGNIFICANCE
- SAMO© AS AN ANTIDOTE TO NOUVEAU-WAVO BULLSHIT
- SAMO© AS AN ALTERNATIVE TO GOD

Using black spray paint and Magic Markers, Diaz and Basquiat produced hundreds of tags during 1978. What made them so noteworthy was that most were painted in SoHo and other downtown neighborhoods where they were sure to be seen by the creatives who lived and worked there. As a brand-building gesture, the Diaz-Basquiat duo was remarkably cunning and creative.

Spanning approximately fifty blocks between Houston and Canal Streets, and Crosby Street and West Broadway, SoHo was transitioning from light manufacturing into an artists' community of

Jean-Michel below a SAMO tag he created with Al Diaz, 1978.

studios and lofts in the spaces left behind. Galleries had established a presence in the area, with many along West Broadway, the main thoroughfare running north to south. Adventurous museums were bringing their trustees to the neighborhood to visit artists' studios. Smart restaurants and specialty food shops added to the allure of the area, like the inaugural Dean & DeLuca store, which stocked indulgent cheeses, exotic vinegars, and tins of caviar. The *SoHo Weekly News* diligently reported on the important comings and goings in the community. Despite not having a plan for how to fit into this chic and glamorous enclave, Jean-Michel yearned to be a part of it.

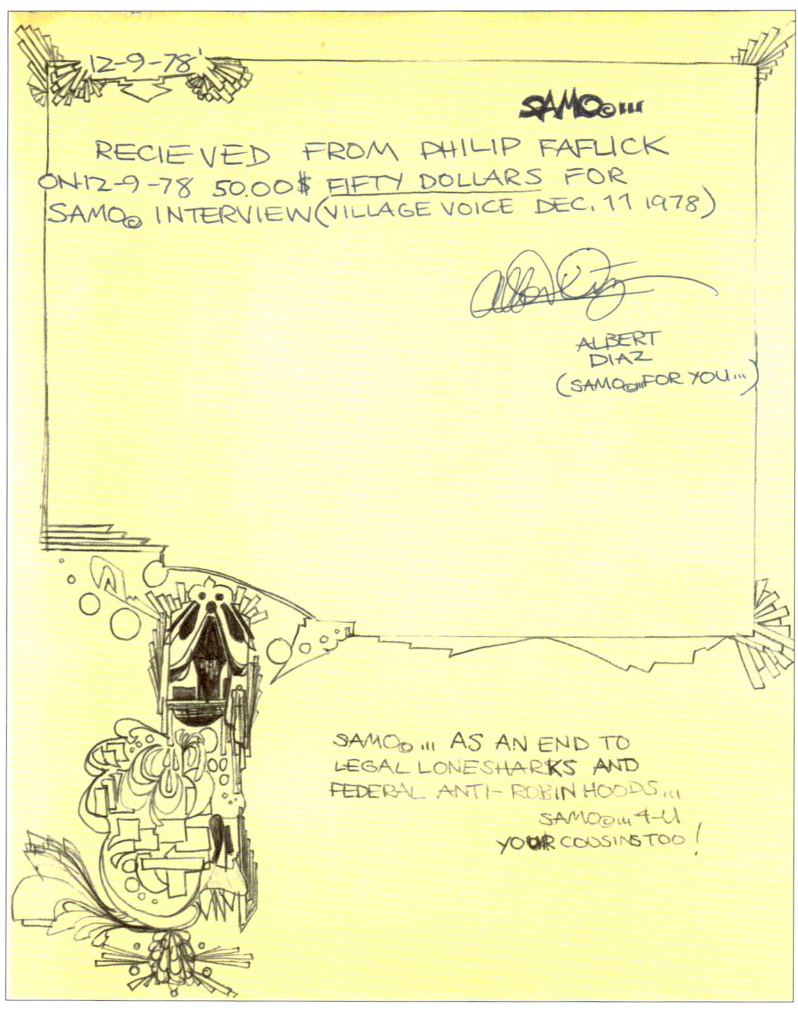
12-9-78'

SAMO©...

RECIEVED FROM PHILIP FAFLICK
ON 12-9-78 50.00$ FIFTY DOLLARS FOR
SAMO© INTERVIEW (VILLAGE VOICE DEC. 11 1978)

ALBERT
DIAZ
(SAMO©...FOR YOU...)

SAMO©... AS AN END TO
LEGAL LONESHARKS AND
FEDERAL ANTI-ROBIN HOODS...
SAMO©... 4-U
YOUR COUSINS TOO!

Diaz and Basquiat earned $100 for their Village Voice *interview. Diaz memorialized his share of it with this receipt, December 1978.*

During one of their daytime SoHo excursions, Diaz ran into Matilde. She stopped by a metalworking shop on Spring Street, a spot frequented by the SAMO duo. "She was medicated and kind of confused," Diaz recalled. "Jean-Michel was very loving to her, acting almost like a parent figure." While chatting with her, Jean-Michel casually mentioned that he occasionally worked at the shop, a fabrication intended to please her. Hearing this, Matilde told him, "I want you to get a regular job with the post office." For Diaz, it was the kind of stuff you would expect to hear from an attentive mom. "She wanted him to have a steady, solid job. It was very sweet, but it was also kind of sad because she was sort of out of it."

The duo's tags vied for attention amidst the sea of graffiti covering most SoHo buildings. Their distinctive word poems, however, stood out, earning mentions in the *SoHo Weekly News* and a more detailed feature in *The Village Voice*, titled "SAMO© Graffiti: BOOSH-WAH or CIA?" Drawing on interviews with Diaz and Basquiat, the article offered insights into the cryptic graffiti messages appearing across Lower Manhattan, while subtly hinting at the artists' identities without fully revealing their names. This early recognition gave Jean-Michel his first glimpse of how the world can quickly embrace and reward provocative acts by artists.

In addition to his SAMO tags, Jean-Michel liked to draw. One of his pieces was chosen to be on the cover of the City-As-School yearbook for 1978. The featured artwork depicted the head of a unicorn with a flowing mane composed of intricate curving lines, each terminating with a star. Several other pieces by Basquiat, sharing a similar aesthetic, were also included in the yearbook. These pleasant drawings seem to be inspired by Peter Max, a popular artist known at the time for his colorful counterculture-infused creations. Max's works were ubiquitous, appearing on *Time* magazine covers and posters sold in head shops, making him a favorite among high school students. During this period, Basquiat made other drawings, including some attempts at depicting the human body.[15] What distinguishes all these drawings is how little they foreshadow the work that would ultimately catapult him to worldwide fame. While intellectually gifted, Basquiat was by no means an early artistic prodigy.

Basquiat's time at City-As-School was short-lived. His disdain for authority soon made even its freewheeling environment feel stifling. During the senior graduation ceremony at the end of his junior year, he publicly humiliated the school principal, Fred Koury. As Koury addressed the audience, Jean-Michel lurched from the side of the stage, smashed a cream pie into his face, and then fled the hall. With countless bridges burned, Basquiat dropped out of high school. From his early days at the prestigious St. Ann's to his time at City-As-School, he attended at least eight different institutions. These frequent moves disrupted his education and repeatedly required him to rebuild his circle of friends.

After dropping out, Jean-Michel spent most of his time idle and stoned, which did not sit well with his father, who was also juggling the responsibilities of raising two daughters. Gerard's new girlfriend, Nora Fitzpatrick, a British woman of Irish descent, had also recently moved into the household. Arguments between Jean-Michel and Gerard grew increasingly heated. Gerard, having worked hard to build a life for himself after arriving in the United States alone and jobless, likely felt deeply frustrated by what he saw as Jean-Michel's disregard for the opportunities he had provided. Jean-Michel, however, viewed his father as an authoritarian menace who belittled and diminished him.[16] In an interview, he once claimed that he ran away from home because "I was smoking pot in my room and my father came in and he stabbed me in the ass with a knife. And then I thought I better go before he killed me."[17] Whether or not this account is true, it underscores the fraught nature of their relationship.

Jean-Michel left home in the summer of 1978. He began couch surfing with new acquaintances, sleeping on the street, and staying in homeless shelters. Odd jobs, panhandling, and tricks with men helped finance his itinerant life. Once he even landed in the hospital for a prolonged stay, due to a severe foot infection he contracted while living on the streets. His grandmother and cousin visited him there.

Gerard Basquiat and his partner, Nora Fitzpatrick, in the living room of their Boerum Hill brownstone, March 4, 1978.

"He had it really bad. It was a horrible situation," remembered Reuben Andrades Jr. "Trying to comfort him, I asked Jean-Michel, 'Why don't you pray with God?' And he looked at me and said, 'Religion is only for weak-minded people.'"

For someone so young, Jean-Michel no longer had any illusions left to lose. *Being a devout Christian won't prevent a nervous breakdown. Married life doesn't bring happiness. Racism is rampant. Intimate relationships with both men and women expose you to insults and danger. Morality is a farce.* These ideas helped shaped his worldview and would influence the artworks he would soon make.

CHAPTER 2

ART MAKING (1979–1982)

AFTER LEAVING HOME, BASQUIAT SLIPPED INTO THE DOWNTOWN SCENE. New York then was still recovering from near bankruptcy. Vast portions had fallen into gross disrepair but this decay had a bright spot: Downtown Manhattan was full of affordable living spaces and now it teemed with the creative energies of those who had flocked there from across the country and around the world, driven by a desire to be part of the scene. Their belief in the free exchange of ideas and the rejection of orthodox viewpoints gave rise to vibrant creative communities in fields such as art, music, and dance. At the time, there was no other place in the world like it: West Berlin was an isolated city surrounded by the Berlin Wall and East German territory, London was a place for bad food and Old Master paintings, while Paris remained focused on

Basquiat when he started frequenting the Mudd Club, January 1979.

the past. With so many creatives pursuing their passions downtown, the competition to distinguish oneself was fierce. By the late 1970s, other Downtown neighborhoods had emerged after SoHo, including the East Village, the Lower East Side, and TriBeCa, short for Triangle Below Canal Street.

For large stretches a dreary, industrial landscape, Downtown came alive at night when the clubs and bars opened, with the Mudd Club a top destination. It quickly gained a reputation for its wild and fabulous atmosphere after opening on Halloween night in 1978 in a six-story corner loft building on White Street in a desolate part of TriBeCa. Clubgoers danced to DJ'd music, smoked and snorted all kinds of drugs, and watched performances by a variety of up-and-coming bands. The club also hosted pop-up art exhibitions, screened foreign films, and featured readings by Beat Generation authors like William Burroughs and Allen Ginsberg. Cosplay events with titles like "The Joan Crawford Mother's Day Celebration" and "The Puberty Ball" were especially popular. Celebrities including Mick Jagger, Iggy Pop, and David Bowie frequented the grungy club, which added to its allure. One columnist writing about the place noted, "For sheer kinkiness,

A crowd gathered outside the entrance of the Mudd Club, 1979.

there has been nothing like it since the cabaret scene in 1920s Berlin."[1]

The Mudd Club was a popular spot for celebrities like Iggy Pop (left) and David Bowie (right).

Most evenings you could find Basquiat at the Mudd Club, along with a handful of other club kids. "We were on the grimier side, scrounging the floor of the club looking for loose change," remembered Hal Ludacer, an acquaintance of Basquiat's. "We ran around like modern-day versions of Fagin's larcenists and orphans."[2] Being downtown day and night exposed Basquiat to what leading-edge creatives were making and how their work was being promoted in clubs, art galleries, and nonprofit venues. This opened his mind up to what he too might create and what he would need to do to secure a spot in this hypercompetitive milieu. While he loved to draw, his vagabond lifestyle made it difficult to secure such basics as paper and pencils. He found another outlet for his creativity in the realm of music.

Always plugged in, Basquiat learned about a party called the Canal Zone, organized by a group of young tastemakers to showcase graffiti artists and rap music. At the helm were Michael Holman, a budding impresario, Fred Brathwaite, a graffiti artist otherwise known as Fab 5 Freddy, and Stan Peskett, a designer working for Fiorucci, a hip Italian fashion brand with a store on East Fifty-Ninth Street. Brathwaite asked Lee Quiñones, another street artist, to join him in creating colorful artworks on large sheets of clear plastic suspended from the ceiling of Peskett's TriBeCa loft. Holman and Peskett promoted the event as an opportunity for guests to meet the two artists and watch them create their works. Music and drinks provided the needed lubrication.

While the event was being set up, Basquiat arrived uninvited and asked if he could create something alongside Brathwaite and Quiñones. Holman remembers Basquiat's request: "He was so charming, handsome, and confident that you just surrendered to him instantly. So we put a big piece of paper on the wall for him, as we didn't have any more plastic sheets."[3] Basquiat then proceeded to make one of his SAMO poems. By this time, Basquiat and Al Diaz had already split, completing their final SAMO collaboration in early 1979, as Basquiat had decided to chase fame independently.[4]

As Holman watched Basquiat create his piece, it dawned on him that the creator of the word poems he had admired around town was standing right in front of him. His delight was soon matched when Basquiat learned that Holman had taken a year off from college to join the Tubes, an arena-filling band renowned for their theatrical stage performances and subversive humor. Holman had joined the group as a dancer after catching the attention of one of its members while dancing at a nightclub. For Holman, a premed major, it was like running away from home and joining the circus. After a year with the band, he returned to San Francisco, finished college, and made a beeline back to New York.

A fan of the Tubes, and recognizing an opportunity, Basquiat approached Holman near the end of the party and proposed starting a band together. "He probably felt, here's another Black guy on the scene who knows something about music, so let's do something together," Holman explained. While neither was musically trained, the very concept of what could be considered music had broadened considerably with the advent of punk, industrial, and no wave. Many artists and other Downtown creatives made room in their lives to join or form bands. Holman enthusiastically accepted Basquiat's proposal. "His magical, stellar, sophisticated genius was obvious the moment you met him," he recalled. "Everything about him screamed, 'I'm special, I'm significant, I'm someone who's going to be important'–from his SAMO poems, his weird, shaved head, to the way he dressed. I couldn't say yes fast enough." By starting a band, Basquiat was following in the musical footsteps of his maternal grandfather and

Michael Holman, co-founder of the band Gray with Basquiat.

uncle, both of whom played in local Puerto Rican bands and whose rehearsals in the basement of the 36 Covert Street home he had listened to as a child.

Holman and Basquiat began working together to create music that would fit the vibe at the Mudd Club: loud and dissonant yet delivered with great panache. "We approached music as if we were aliens given instruments they didn't know how to play but who could intuit how to use them to create sound sculptures," Holman explained. Their influences ranged from avant-garde composers like John Cage and Karlheinz Stockhausen to funk and soul. The band consisted of Holman on drums, Nick Taylor and Vincent Gallo on guitar, Wayne Clifford on keyboards, and Basquiat playing clarinet and the Wasp synthesizer.

Basquiat quickly emerged as the de facto leader of the group. The band cycled through various names, including Bad Rules, Test Pattern, and Channel Nine, before settling on Gray. "We were walking along the northern side of Washington Square Park," Holman recalled. "Jean-Michel said, 'I figured out the name of the band—Gray,' and we instantly were like, 'Yeah, that's it.' We liked its connection to machines, industrial sound, and rusted factories." The name also had an association with *Gray's Anatomy*, the guide to the human body that Basquiat's mother gave him after his car accident. "We all understood his history and how significant *Gray's Anatomy* was to him," Holman added. Gray's first performance took place at Hurrah, a well-known dance club on West Sixty-Second Street that showcased punk and no wave music. They went on to perform at other iconic Downtown venues such as CBGB and became part of the vibrant music scene.

Basquiat with some of his Gray bandmates before a performance at the nightclub Harrah. From left to right: Basquiat, Michael Holman, Wayne Clifford, Shannon Dawson, October 1979.

Basquiat's involvement in the band, along with his SAMO credentials and striking appearance, helped him build a network of friends in the Downtown scene. One individual who played a significant role in his transition to being an artist was Diego Cortez, an irrepressible hustler who was always short of cash. An artist, curator, and one of the three co-founders of the Mudd Club, Cortez knew everyone, and everyone had an opinion about him. Brian Eno, the influential British musician and producer, felt that, "like most interesting people, Diego was a tangle of contradictions; he had a deep natural kindness and affection which he disguised by a façade of mischievous cynicism and nonchalance."[5] Another friend described him as being "a rather shady character . . . living off the air and through his own ingenuity."[6]

Diego Cortez, a Mudd Club co-founder, began providing Basquiat with pocket money to buy art supplies.

Basquiat's dance moves caught Cortez's eye. "He looked very unusual; a Black guy with a blonde Mohawk—and he was dancing beautifully," Cortez later recalled.[7] It was not long before Cortez discovered that Basquiat was not only a talented dancer but also an aspiring artist, who was behind the SAMO tags. Around this time, Basquiat's work made its public debut at the *Times Square Show*, a scrappy, artist-organized exhibition held in a derelict massage parlor in June 1980. Featuring over a hundred emerging talents, the show embodied the raw, experimental ethos of New York's Downtown art scene. Basquiat's contribution, now lost, was displayed on the second floor in an area called the Fashion Lounge, though photographs suggest it was frequently obscured by racks of clothing—a fitting metaphor for the unpolished and chaotic energy of his early career.

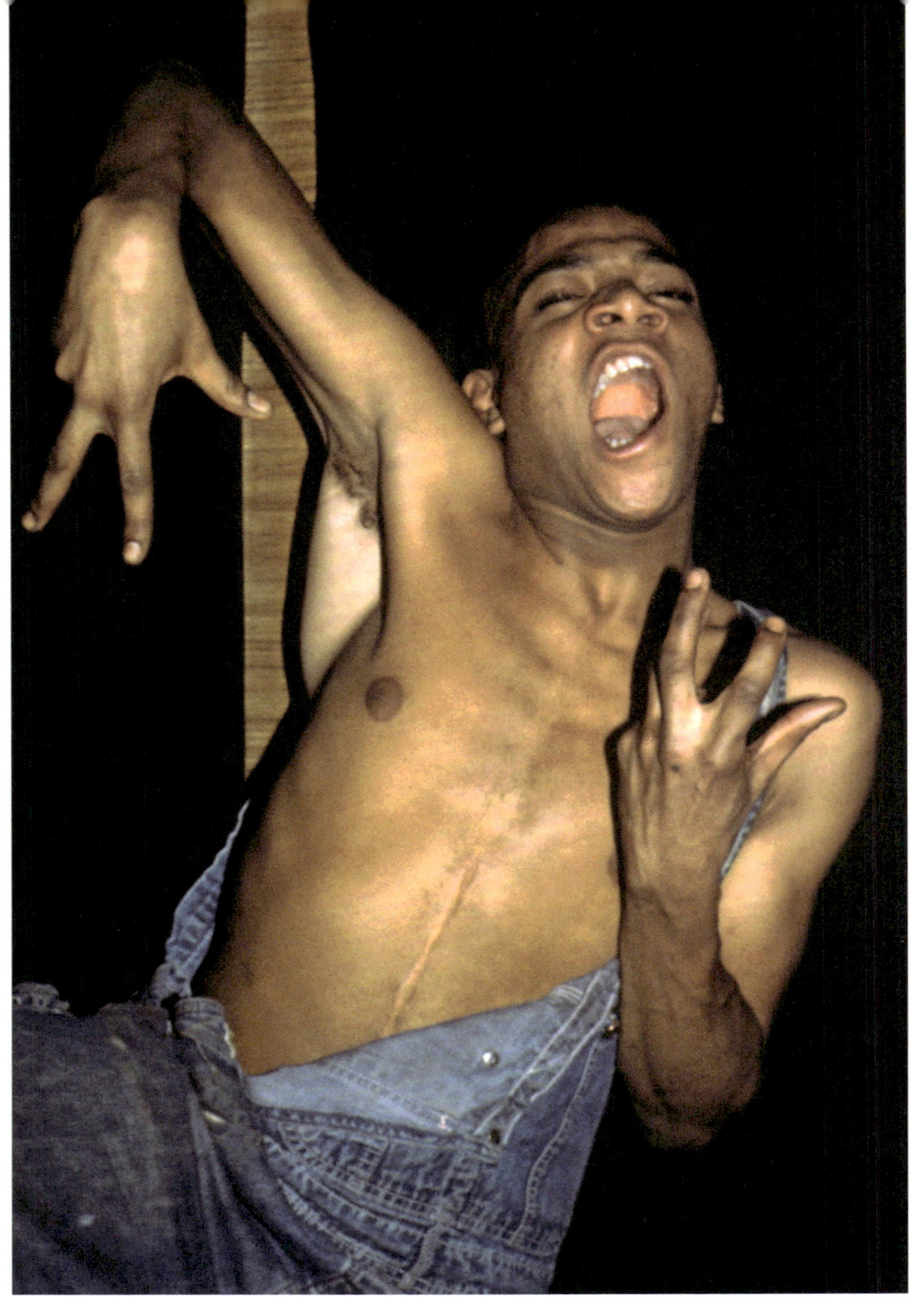

Basquiat dancing at the Mudd Club, February 1979.

Seeing potential, Cortez began giving Basquiat pocket money for art supplies, which he used to create drawings in the small East Village apartment he shared with his girlfriend, Suzanne Mallouk. By the end of 1980, Cortez was bringing visitors to the apartment, hoping they would purchase some of Basquiat's work. Although the market for experimental art like that featured at the *Time Square Show* was very limited, both Basquiat and Cortez needed the money.

Meanwhile, the more established contemporary art world was jolted when *The New York Times* ran a front-page article announcing that the Whitney Museum had acquired Jasper Johns's painting *Three Flags* for a staggering $1 million—the highest price ever paid for a work by a living artist. The Whitney's directors justified the purchase—from Burton and Emily Tremaine, a prominent collecting couple based in Connecticut—by emphasizing the painting's seminal role in launching the Pop Art movement, elevating it to the status of a masterpiece.

The publicity surrounding the sale underscored for many the extraordinary returns that early investments in artists' careers sometimes deliver. The *New York Times* article revealed that the Tremaines had bought the painting in 1959 for just $900, plus a $15 delivery fee, and even featured a photograph of the original purchase invoice. The story sparked widespread chatter about the art market as one of the rare arenas where $1,000 could grow into $1 million in a relatively short time. Soon, more people than ever before were heading downtown in search of works by emerging artists.

The opening of the Odeon restaurant in TriBeCa in October 1980 also helped mark the moment when downtown Manhattan began to capture the attention of the moneyed set. It quickly became a late-night hotspot for wealthy Upper East Side residents, showbiz personalities, and artists who lived nearby. The witty and acerbic restaurant critic for *New York Magazine*, Gael Greene, loved the place, noting, "There is a species of Manhattan snob who will insist he or she has never been south of 57th Street and thinks the Upper West Side is attached to New

Jersey. So what, pray tell, is going on down below the Holland Tunnel in the anonymous wastes of West Broadway? The giant red neon letters—Odeon—have become a beacon to the eclectic chic. The bachelor rogues of show biz. The art world. Fashion's precious babies of every sexual persuasion. Suburban squares. Punksters with tufts of apricot hair."[8] When Basquiat's artistic career began to take off, the Odeon became one of his favorite haunts.

Diego Cortez found success in selling Basquiat's drawings and soon told the young artist that he would include him in a museum exhibition he was curating. At that time, the boundaries between curators and art dealers were often blurred, as museums had vague or nonexistent policies to prevent conflicts of interest. This allowed curators like Cortez to use their positions to promote artists they represented, aiming to boost their reputations and market values. The exhibition, *New York/New Wave*, opened in February 1981 at PS1, a museum housed in a former public-school building across the Fifty-Ninth Street Bridge in Queens. Featuring work by more than one hundred artists, the show displayed art floor-to-ceiling across two floors. In the evening, live bands and performances transformed the space into a scene more reminiscent of the Mudd Club than a traditional museum—exactly the aesthetic Cortez intended.[9]

Cortez gave Basquiat a prominent space in the museum to showcase around twenty works, all labeled as being by SAMO. Ever the astute marketer, Basquiat saw no reason to abandon the recognizable brand name. Most of the works had an appealing messiness, featuring images of cars, faces, and buildings interspersed with text phrases, though lacking the finesse of Basquiat's later work. These early pieces feel more like intriguing student experiments—understandable, as Basquiat was only twenty years old at the time and working without a proper studio.

While critics were largely lukewarm about the PS1 show, it attracted many contemporary art collectors and members of the

Downtown demimonde.[10] Basquiat's work caught the attention of Emilio Mazzoli, an art gallery owner from Modena, a small city in northern Italy. According to Bruno Bischofberger, a gallerist who later played an enormous role in Basquiat's development, Sandro Chia, an Italian artist living in New York, and curator Achille Bonito Oliva encouraged Mazzoli to see Basquiat's work. Bonito Oliva, known for his interest in figurative art, had coined the term *Transavanguardia* to describe the work of artists like Sandro Chia, Francesco Clemente, and Enzo Cucchi during the 1970s.

Cortez drove Mazzoli and Bonito Oliva to the *New York/New Wave* exhibition and later to his apartment on West Thirty-Sixth Street, where he had stashed some of Basquiat's works for sale. Mazzoli bought five pieces for around $6,000. Shortly after, Basquiat and Cortez traveled to Modena with the sold artworks. These works, along with a few more created on-site, were featured in Basquiat's first solo exhibition, which Mazzoli billed as being by SAMO to tap into the Downtown graffiti culture.[11]

Basquiat returned to New York more self-assured than ever, with money in his pockets from art sales. With his artistic career now starting to percolate, he told his Gray bandmates that he would be leaving the group after their next gig. He was determined to find a New York gallery to represent him. While the Modena show was a nice start, it had taken place in a small if charming city that scarcely broke into the list of the top twenty most populous in Italy. Basquiat wanted more.

ANNINA NOSEI, an influential gallerist in SoHo, was perhaps the most important person in Basquiat's artistic life. Her sharp-witted intellect, aesthetic insights, and marketing methods helped turn an ambitious young man into a sensation.

Nosei grew up in an intellectual Roman family. After earning an advanced degree in art history from the University of Rome, she ventured to Paris and began working at the Sonnabend Gallery, a contemporary art hot spot. She was soon helping Robert Rauschenberg set up his show at the Venice Biennale in 1964, where he became the youngest artist and the first American to win the Golden Lion, the exhibition's top prize. A Fulbright fellowship brought Nosei to the United States, where she taught art history at the University of Michigan and, subsequently, at UCLA. While in Los Angeles, she met her future husband, a director at a gallery devoted to contemporary art. After relocating to New York City in 1968, Nosei taught at local universities and organized exhibitions of contemporary art. Over time, her focus shifted toward the commercial art world. By the late 1970s, she was drawing on her extensive personal and professional networks to deal privately in contemporary art, operating out of a SoHo loft she shared with Larry Gagosian, a private art dealer from Los Angeles also building his business in New York.

Confident in her potential, Nosei purchased the first floor and basement of a classic SoHo loft building at 100 Prince Street and opened her gallery in the fall of 1980. By year's end, the gallery had showcased a series of exhibitions featuring works by the rising Italian stars affectionately known as the Three C's (Francesco Clemente, Sandro Chia, and Enzo Cucchi), as well as notable young Americans like David Salle and Julian Schnabel. Without family wealth to support her, the divorced Nosei was determined to make her gallery a financial success.

Nosei was intrigued when she saw Basquiat's work in the *New York/New Wave* show. "I believed they were conveying something special about the Afro-Caribbean experience, which was an important part of urban life in New York City," she recalled.[12] She tried tracking Basquiat down but was unable to connect with him. They finally met at a gallery opening, where Basquiat invited her to see his latest work. A few days later, Nosei said, "I arrived at his girlfriend's apartment in the East Village to find it filled with beautiful drawings. I loved the work and agreed to include him in a group show scheduled for October 1981, but I told him it would have to be paintings rather than drawings."

Basquiat was elated with this turn of events, as no other New York gallery had expressed any interest whatsoever in showing his work following the PS1 show. Nosei was now his essential lifeline.

Annina Nosei, in 1982. The SoHo gallerist provided Basquiat with the support and encouragement he needed to grow as an artist.

Basquiat showed up at Nosei's gallery a few days later with two paintings he had created using supplies purchased with the $400 advance she had given him against future sales. Remembering the cramped space in which he worked, she offered him a temporary studio in the basement of her gallery. Basquiat jumped at the opportunity; it would be his first-ever dedicated workspace.

Accessing his new studio was easy. A door in the main gallery led to a staircase that descended to the lower level. This area housed a private viewing space, occasionally used to showcase artworks for clients, along with a storage area for art. Basquiat's studio was situated at the far end of the basement, behind its own door. The studio's size rivaled that of most two-bedroom apartments in Manhattan. Windows that looked out to the backyard provided some natural light.[13]

Basquiat took full advantage of his studio, arriving promptly at ten in the morning, when the gallery opened, often with a coffee and a croissant from the nearby Dean & DeLuca store. "If he got there at 10:15 A.M., he would apologize for being late," Nosei recalled. "I assured him he could come anytime during gallery hours, but he seemed to believe he needed to be there right when we opened." He would head downstairs and would play jazz and classical music while working. "He loved playing Maurice Ravel's *Boléro* over and over again, which," she confesses, "began to drive me crazy."

One visitor to the basement was Mick Jagger, whom Nosei escorted to the private viewing area to see a painting by Carlo Maria Mariani, an Italian artist known for his neoclassical imagery. Upon hearing Jagger's voice, Basquiat opened his studio door and introduced himself. "Mick seemed rather indifferent," Nosei recollected, "as we were discussing the painting and its price." After Jagger departed, Basquiat excitedly told her that this encounter confirmed that he should be with her gallery, because someone like Jagger was in her circle of friends. A stickler for details, Nosei corrected Basquiat, telling him that Jagger was not a friend but a client.

Basquiat and Nosei began spending time together discussing artists, art history, and his own work. "He was extremely bright and inquisitive," she remembered. "We'd flip through books together and analyze different artworks. We talked about European and American art history. He was also remarkably knowledgeable about literature beyond what you would have ever expected to see in someone his age. He always made me talk, as he never wanted to speak about himself or his past."

The studio space and discussions with Nosei had a profound impact on Basquiat's artistic output, leading to the creation of works that far surpassed anything he had exhibited at PS1. Excited by this new work, Nosei dedicated a room to them in the promised group show. The six other artists in the exhibition, including rising talents like Keith Haring, Jenny Holzer, and Barbara Kruger, had to share the remaining room in the gallery.[14] Basquiat signed these works with his own name for the first time, leaving his SAMO moniker behind. The opening was packed with clients and friends of the gallery. Nosei's extensive network ensured that Basquiat's work was seen by important buyers and influencers within the contemporary art world. All the pieces sold, along with many more in the following months.

Basquiat's father had, by this point, also reentered his life. The conflicts and resentment that had strained their relationship had subsided. Basquiat invited his father to the opening to share in his newfound success. Gerard and his longtime partner, Nora Fitzpatrick, arrived early at the event. They came from their tennis club dressed in their tennis whites, showcasing their nonchalant yet peculiar way of expressing their interest in being there.

Sales from the show meant that Basquiat could afford to rent his own studio, yet he chose to remain in the basement space. Joe La Placa, who worked part-time for Nosei, aided Basquiat there. His knowledge of materials and processes helped Basquiat achieve the painterly effects he was looking for. "I would buy large rolls of very heavy cotton duck canvas and lug them back to the studio," La Placa said.[15]

> We would then cut them up into various sizes, depending on what he wanted to work on. I prepared them with gesso or rabbit-skin glue, so paint would not seep into the weave of the fabric. Pearl Paint was a wonderful five-story mecca for art supplies on Canal Street. But I didn't want him to become completely reliant on the tyranny of commercially available paint colors. I said, "Let's try something new, given what you are trying to achieve." A place called Guerra Paint & Pigment had recently opened in the East Village. Art Guerra was an amazing guy who was importing industrial pigments from around the world. It was a system where, for example, you could buy the red that Maserati used in their sports cars. The colors were super vivid and could be manipulated to achieve incredible levels of lucidity, from very matte to very shiny. Richer-looking paintings can often be created when something very matte appears next to something shiny.
>
> I'd mix up some Art Guerra colors and paint the grounds on the prepared canvases with Jean-Michel directing me by saying, "Put some here, put some there." Then he would work on top of it. We painted everything on the floor, which is why there are footprints and handprints on many of these studio paintings. At some point he would want to mount a canvas so he could continue working on it. Whether it was stretched or nailed to the wall depended on what he wanted to do. There was a painting of a boxer which I think is really a self-portrait of him conquering the art world. We stapled it to the wall because he wanted to draw on it with black oil sticks. The more friction you apply to a piece of oil stick, the more it kind of melts onto the canvas. He then used his fingers to blend and manipulate that luxurious paint.
>
> Watching him work in the studio was like a miracle. He drew like you sign your signature, with that kind of familiarity. The way he processed information and how he could take things around him and

transform them. This kind of sublimation process was like nothing I've ever seen before or since.

After working in the studio, he'd sometimes come back to my loft on Greenwich Street. He'd hang out with me and my wife, along with our artist friends and writers that included Rene Ricard and Duncan Smith. I got to see the casual racism he experienced when trying to get a taxi in SoHo. They would drive past him when he was hailing a cab to take us down to Greenwich Street. They only stopped when he moved back onto the sidewalk and I raised my hand.

Continuing to use the basement studio allowed Basquiat to focus on creating work for his solo show at the Annina Nosei Gallery, planned for March of 1982. For Nosei, it provided opportunities to bring clients down to meet the rising young star. However, issues surrounding the basement space began to arise, particularly concerning Basquiat's drug habits. His clubbing friends would occasionally visit to trade cocaine for drawings. Additionally, newly formed friendships, including that with Perry Rubenstein, became problematic.

Rubenstein, a handsome man, had worked as a model in Paris and Milan after graduating from Pennsylvania State University in 1975. Despite not having grown up in an art-collecting family, he began using his substantial modeling earnings to buy contemporary art. One place he frequented was Emilio Mazzoli's gallery in Modena, not far from Milan. After spending six years in Europe, Rubenstein decided to relocate to New York in 1981. "I had no clear direction at the time," he related, "but I had two things: a heroin habit and an art collection with works by emerging Italian artists like Francesco Clemente, Sandro Chia, and Enzo Cucchi."[16] Learning of his move, Emilio Mazzoli encouraged him to meet specific people, including Diego Cortez and Basquiat, as well as two of the Italian artists he collected, Francesco Clemente and Sandro Chia, who were then residing in New York. Mazzoli made the necessary introductions.

Basquiat around the time he started working in the basement studio provided by Annina Nosei, 1981.

Rubenstein paid a visit to Basquiat's basement studio shortly after arriving in New York. "I brought along a nice flake of coke that we did together," Rubenstein recalled. "We became friends, and I visited him frequently." Eager to immerse himself in the New York art world, Rubenstein rented a space in a building on West Twenty-Third Street owned by Sandro Chia. This allowed him to sell artworks from his extensive collection, taking his first steps toward becoming a private art dealer.

During one of Rubenstein's subsequent visits to the basement studio, Nosei caught him trading cocaine for drawings. Outraged, and under the impression that Basquiat was still in his teens, she confronted him, exclaiming, "This is a teenager. What are you doing? I'll call the police." Rubenstein left; a few days later, he sent Nosei an apology letter along with a small wooden box as a gift. "I thought it was something for the bathroom," she recollected. "I opened it a few months later to find it filled with white talcum powder to mimic cocaine." It was Rubenstein's snarky way of mocking her.

Nosei's encounters with Rubenstein and Basquiat's questionable acquaintances reached a critical point a few months before his scheduled solo exhibition. She spoke with Basquiat about how he needed to address his dangerous drug habits and find a new studio. She assured him of her support and promised to help him locate a suitable place. A few weeks later, she secured a spacious loft at 101 Crosby Street, in SoHo. The third-floor space, roughly twice the size of the basement studio, rented for $1,400 a month. As Basquiat lacked a credit history, Nosei took responsibility for guaranteeing the lease, which ran from mid-February until November 1982. Basquiat, accompanied by his girlfriend, Suzanne Mallouk, moved into the loft.

The New York art world has long been rife with envy and gossip. Around the time Basquiat moved to his new loft, rumors circulated that Nosei had coerced him into working in the basement studio while relentlessly demanding more artworks. The economic relationship between a sought-after artist and their gallery often becomes tense, particularly regarding the pace of production and sales. Sometimes, it is the artist pushing for quick sales to boost their ego and bank account; other times, it is the gallery pressing for more inventory to cover expenses like rent and payroll. Nosei undoubtedly encouraged Basquiat to stay productive. Yet, given his well-documented disdain for authority, it is hard to imagine him tolerating any form of subjugation, especially since he had the financial resources to secure his own studio. This was a man, after all, who was acutely aware of his own agency. After relocating to his Crosby Street studio, an interviewer pressed Basquiat about the rumors. He set the record straight: "That just has a nasty edge to it. I was never locked anywhere. Ah, Christ. If I was white, they would just say 'artist in residence,' rather than say all of that other stuff."[17]

Unlike most artists, who struggle for years in the hopes of finding an audience, Jean-Michel Basquiat achieved unimaginable success in 1982. Annina Nosei was the pivotal figure who created the platform that allowed Basquiat to soar. His first solo exhibition in the United States, which opened at her gallery in March, sold out. She worked diligently to secure his inclusion in Documenta, an influential contemporary art exhibition held every five years in Kassel, Germany. When the exhibition opened in June, he was the youngest artist to ever be featured in it. Additionally, Nosei assisted in organizing two more exhibitions of his work that year: one at the new Larry Gagosian Gallery in Los Angeles and another at the Galerie Delta in Rotterdam.

Like exceptional music and film producers, gallerists can sometimes help artists discover their true potential. One of Basquiat's friends, Vincent Gallo, who went on to have a career as an artist, movie director, and musician, witnessed firsthand the impact Nosei had on Basquiat's trajectory.

Gallo and Basquiat initially met in 1978 when they were both living on the streets after escaping troubled family lives. They would soon perform together in the band Gray. Although they grew apart for a few years after Basquiat's career took off, they reconnected and grew close again toward the end of Basquiat's life. Gallo was well acquainted with Annina Nosei; he showed his own work at her gallery starting in 1983.

"I remember the day Jean met Annina; he was never the same again," Gallo said.[18] "He was able to transform his smaller, less ambitious works and grow and materialize it in one massive leap forward. It's not that Annina created the work. But if George Martin wasn't the

Basquiat in the Crosby Street loft that Annina Nosei secured for him, 1982.

Beatles' first producer, the music may not have been the same, grown as fast, and transformed to as high a level. Annina's intellect was beyond Jean's and beyond his understanding of his own work. I had a similar experience with her."

Vincent Gallo, a close friend of Basquiat's.

Comparing intellects is challenging, even when you know the people well, because it involves assessing their abilities to acquire, understand, and apply knowledge. However, it is certain that Nosei, who was in her forties, was vastly more insightful than a twenty-one-year-old. Her ability to perceive and understand the creative process stemmed from her years of experience developing and promoting artists, her formal education in art history, and her being extremely well read.

Gallo shared how Nosei helped advance that creative process:

> When you get a chance to work on a larger scale, and the person who's giving you that opportunity has an intellect that can really see your best potential, great things can happen. You not only have somebody who is thinking big, who's planning a show, who wants you to do great work. They also understand when that is happening, an artist's best work is better than them. It is transformational beyond the creator and beyond the creator's own understanding. The work is bigger than yourself. Annina would provide you with feedback and excitement about achieving that much higher level, which makes you aim higher.

When he started working with Nosei, Basquiat was driven by personal motivations and certain assumptions. "He wanted to show his father that he was worth something," Gallo explained, "to make a name for himself, and to be famous. He also had this premise of what success was like in the art world and how he could maneuver his way into it. How he could play the role. However, Annina made him realize that he was more than what he thought he was and that it wasn't a trick, that he didn't need to fool anybody, and that he had it. 'I will get these pieces sold and you'll be able to continue to work and focus on your art.' How was that not the most influential thing that someone could have done for him?"

BASQUIAT'S DISTINCTIVE PAINTING STYLE emerged from a myriad of influences, with his intellectual curiosity serving as a driving force. Fueled by an insatiable fascination with ideas, theories, and abstract concepts, he drew inspiration from diverse disciplines, including philosophy, literature, history, and science. His creativity was sparked by a variety of visual stimuli, from comic books and cereal box covers to the intricate drawings of Leonardo da Vinci. The forms, colors, and symbolic potential of these seemingly unrelated sources captivated him. He took great pleasure in integrating these elements into his artworks, rejecting conventional pairings and predictable juxtapositions to craft compositions that invited both contemplation and visceral engagement.

Basquiat had an astute eye for color and composition that he used to convey a raw, frenetic energy. Working swiftly, he would paint over elements or mark them with an X or jagged black lines when dissatisfied. Traces of earlier ideas often peeked through his paintings, a testament to his relentless experimentation. This impatience lent an important immediacy and vitality to his works.

Drawing was an abiding passion, although he rarely made preparatory sketches for paintings. Drawing and painting were seamlessly intertwined for him, with their distinction primarily lying in the scale of his creations. He would often paste his drawings, or photocopies of them, to a canvas and then continue to work over and around them. The images he drew were typically rendered as flat, two-dimensional objects, without the benefit of light and shadow or perspective. Like most self-taught artists, he never acquired the technical skills needed for realistic portraits or landscape paintings. However, he embraced his lack of technical prowess, confidently channeling his unique thought processes into artworks that defied established norms and conventions.

In addition to his distinctive artistic style, Basquiat's choice of subject matter also helped set him apart from other artists. One source of inspiration was the difficulty of his own life, his struggles and hardships. Consider, for example, *Dustheads*, a six-by-seven-foot painting that portrays two figures painted in lurid colors against a black background. The figure on the right, with raised arms and a blood-red body, features a ghoulish face defined by strokes of black and white paint. This figure's frenetic stance is mirrored on the left by a person with sunken eyes and a skeletal body. The painting draws inspiration from the destructive cycle of addiction experienced by angel dust users, colloquially called "dustheads," encompassing their journey from euphoria to desperation. Given Basquiat's own proclivity for drug use, this work can be seen as a disguised self-portrait.

Another vivid example of his personal experiences shaping his choice of subject matter is the life-threatening car accident he suffered when he was seven years old and the copy of *Gray's Anatomy* his mother gave him during his recovery. Basquiat used the book as a source for the bones, organs, and dissected limbs that appeared in many of his artworks. One striking example of its influence can be seen in *Masonic Lodge*. Having created a vivid indigo-blue background, Basquiat then filled the canvas with line drawings of a human skull depicted from different angles, resembling illustrations from *Gray's Anatomy*. At the center of the fragmented skull is an "evil eye" motif, which generally refers to a belief in various cultures that certain individuals possess a malevolent gaze or a supernatural ability to inflict harm or misfortune on others through their eyes. The destructive power of this eye becomes evident at the top of the composition, where Basquiat painted the phrase "PARANOID SCHIZOPHRENIA," only to subsequently scratch out most of the letters. The painting is a remarkably poignant yet intricately coded portrayal of Basquiat's mother's struggle with schizophrenia.

Basquiat took great pleasure in showcasing Black bodies. He once told an interviewer, "Black people are never portrayed realistically in . . . modern art enough, and I'm glad that I do that. I use the 'Black' as the protagonist because I am Black, and that's why I use it as the main character in all my paintings."[19] He made many self-portraits, including *Portrait of the Artist as a Young Derelict* and *Self Portrait as a Heel*. He regularly paid tribute to his Black male heroes, including jazz musician Charlie Parker, in *Charles the First,* and boxing legend Sugar Ray Robinson, in an eponymous painting. In addition, he made many works with anonymous Black protagonists, such as *Obnoxious Liberals*, *Mitchell Crew*, and *Irony of Negro Policeman.*

Basquiat frequently incorporated handwritten words, phrases, or even sentences directly into his paintings and drawings. These texts, which were rendered in uppercase letters similar to those in his SAMO tags, often appeared fragmented and disjointed, reflecting his stream-of-consciousness approach. The words and phrases could encompass poetry, politics, or fleeting personal memories. While he predominantly used English, he sometimes laced his artworks with Spanish words or phrases.

In addition to text, Basquiat incorporated a wide variety of symbols into his artwork. Many of them were sourced from Henry Dreyfuss's *Symbol Sourcebook: An Authoritative Guide to International Graphic Symbols*, a reference book that explored the visual language and cultural significance of symbols. Published in 1972, the book encompassed symbols from everyday life as well as more obscure ones, like the "hobo signs" used by vagabonds to signal to others about safe or treacherous areas. One remarkable example of Basquiat's obsession with this book can be seen in *Pegasus*, an immense black-and-white drawing filled with hundreds of meticulously rendered symbols.

A three-point crown is the symbol most associated with Basquiat. However, he rarely discussed his artistic influences or divulged the inspiration behind his frequent use of it. Al Diaz, Basquiat's SAMO-tagging partner, and Lee Quiñones, who participated in the Canal Zone party and was another prominent figure in the graffiti community, shared their perspectives on what the crown symbol meant to Basquiat.

In graffiti culture, artists did not sign their work with their given names, since they did not want to be accused of defacing property. They instead used aliases, such as Taki 183 or Coco 144; these often combined their nickname with the street number where they lived. Respect within the graffiti community was based on the quantity and quality of tags produced by a writer. Those at the top of the creative pyramid would sometimes incorporate a crown into their alias to symbolize their special status as kings in the community. Taggers further down the hierarchy, when encountering outstanding pieces by kings, would sometimes add a crown to the piece to show respect for the creator. In this context, crowns were always rendered without paint drips or splatter, since honor, rather than irony, was the motive.[20] Al Diaz's alias was Bomb 1. As a respected figure in the community, he would sometimes add a crown to his alias, especially when he had time to create an elaborate piece. Having grown up in the city and being friends with Diaz, Basquiat understood the role and significance of crowns in graffiti culture.

Lee Quiñones believes that "Jean-Michel was fascinated by society's complexities, contradictions, and hypocrisy. I think he was questioning what kingship really meant. Was it a symbol of privilege, respect for accomplishments, or anger toward those who exploited others to attain their status?"[21] Rather than the refined crowns preferred by street artists, Basquiat's were always crudely painted. Quiñones thought Basquiat intentionally made them this way to avoid being subservient to a crown. "If it was perfect, then he was a servant to the crown," Quiñones explained. "He instead wanted to challenge authority and ask who truly rises to the top and what does it take to stay there. I think he was making a powerful statement by taking something from graffiti culture and tweaking it to make it his own."

The Ruffians is an early example of Basquiat incorporating crowns into an artwork. The painting's background is filled with twenty photocopies of two simple drawings he made of cartoon-like characters. On this collaged surface, he then drew three large stick figures, each with a colorful, masklike face topped with a crudely drawn three-point crown.

Although history often fails to capture the interest of twenty-somethings, Basquiat created numerous paintings that reference important moments in human history, from great achievements to periods of subjugation. One such painting, often referred to as *The Nile* or *Untitled (History of the Black People)*, is filled with imagery related to humanity's long history with slavery. On the left side of this nearly six-by-twelve-foot artwork, two vividly painted African masks are situated below the word "NUBA." Basquiat is referencing the ancient Nubian people, who inhabited the region along the Nile that today sits between southern Egypt and northern Sudan. Many Nubians were enslaved as part of the trans-Saharan slave trade and forced to work elsewhere in northern Africa. A slave ship heading north to the Egyptian city of Memphis is depicted in the center panel, and the city of Thebes (now part of Luxor), which had its own history of slavery, is referenced as well. Basquiat included the names of these towns at the bottom of the right panel, below a Black figure on whom he painted and subsequently scratched out the words "SLAVE, "ESCLAVO," and

"ESCLAVA," the last two words being the masculine and feminine nouns for "slave" in Spanish. To bring the painting into the present day, Basquiat added the word "TENNESEE" in the right panel.

Basquiat's other history paintings touch on a wide range of topics, including the toppling of oppressive regimes in eighteenth-century Haiti and fifteenth-century Italy (*Toussaint L'Ouverture Versus Savonarola*), the history of trade and private property (*Notary*), the Roman Empire's eventual conquest by the Goths (*Speaks for Itself*), and colonial oppression (*Native Carrying Some Guns, Bibles, Amorites on Safari*).

Lastly, Basquiat enjoyed making portraits of friends and family members. Two notable works are the stylized portraits of his parents, titled *Mater* and *Pater*, after the Latin words for "mother" and "father." These seven-by-six-foot works feature Basquiat's signature expressionist style. However, rather than depicting his parents as clothed, as one would expect, he painted them as naked figures. While artists throughout the ages have made nude portraits of friends and lovers, instances of artists creating naked portraits of their parents are extraordinarily rare in art history. In the painting of Matilde, her muscular body faces the viewer. Her breasts are painted red, and her triangular pubic area is defined with white paint against a black background. Her grasping outstretched arms create a sense of dynamic energy. Basquiat painted a circle with lines emanating from it around her head. Given Matilde's passionate Christian beliefs, it was his way of deifying her with a halo. In contrast, Basquiat's portrait of his father is far less flattering. Gerard has a goofy look on his face. However, what makes this painting so lewd is the crude depiction of Gerard's genitalia as dangling "cock and balls," reminiscent of bathroom-wall graffiti. It is the opposite of deification and hard not to see the effect Basquiat was after: to have viewers laugh at his father. This raw portrait serves as a reminder of the complicated relationship Basquiat had with his father—and, for that matter, with any authority figure.

The works Basquiat created from the middle of 1981 to the end of 1982 are among the finest of his short seven-year career as an artist. His confidence and ambition shine through in the scale at which he worked. Many of the approximately two hundred paintings he produced in just 1982 were life-sized or larger. If laid side by side, they would easily cover a basketball court. Nothing quite like them had been made before. As the famous trumpeter Miles Davis once noted, "Sometimes it takes a long time to learn how to play like yourself." Basquiat was a rare instance of someone who found his distinctive voice when still in his early twenties.

BASQUIAT'S REMARKABLE FOUR-YEAR JOURNEY, from leaving home to becoming a sought-after young artist, stands as a testament to his relentless pursuit of success. Underpinning this drive were two important personality traits: an insistent desire for new experiences and an unyielding urge to express his creativity without constraints or limitations. Within the Downtown scene, these qualities made him an alluring figure, both captivating as a friend and enticing as a lover. This enabled him to cultivate a network of friends and partners who encouraged his artistic endeavors. However, as he moved from being a penniless unknown to earning fame as a young star, his callous treatment of those who supported him became yet another defining characteristic.

One person who sought to meet Basquiat early on was Glenn O'Brien, a freelance writer with a regular column in *Interview* magazine. Founded by Andy Warhol, *Interview* served as a cultural barometer, blending celebrity profiles with candid interviews and striking photography. O'Brien's column, "Glenn O'Brien's Beat," offered a sharp mix of commentary, humor, and insights into the downtown New York art, music, and fashion scenes. In 1979, while researching an article on graffiti for *High Times* magazine, O'Brien arranged to meet Basquiat.

O'Brien was struck by the artist's intelligence and distinctive presence, and the two quickly became close friends. "He had a sort of silver Mohawk that was shaved in the front and he was wearing a paint-covered army surplus jump suit and old black dress shoes that looked like they came off a dead man," O'Brien later recalled. "He looked young but he had the presence of an adult. He wasn't afraid; in fact he was polite, articulate, and well spoken but quietly fierce."[22]

After the interview, O'Brien invited Basquiat to appear on *TV Party*, a late-night talk show he hosted on a public-access cable channel. Launched in 1978 by O'Brien and Chris Stein, co-founder and guitarist of Blondie, it served as a weekly, MTV-style house party for the East Village crowd. Basquiat became a frequent guest, which allowed him to forge connections with other Downtown creatives, including Debbie Harry, Blondie's lead singer. These introductions helped Basquiat inject himself into the heart of the Downtown scene.

O'Brien also played a key role in casting the then-unknown Basquiat in a film he wrote about the Downtown art and music scene, which began production in December 1980. Directed by Edo Bertoglio, the movie follows an unnamed young artist (played by Basquiat) as he roams the desolate Lower East Side, with a central focus being on

Glenn O'Brien interviewing Jean-Michel Basquiat on the set of his weekly cable TV show, April 24, 1979.

music performances by Downtown groups such as Kid Creole and the Coconuts. Although the film was never completed during Basquiat's lifetime, it stands as another example of how Basquiat became intertwined with the creative energy of the Downtown scene.[23]

Another early friend was David Bowes, an artist who lived with his girlfriend in the back of a SoHo loft owned by another artist, on a mattress they had thrown on the floor. "Before I met Jean-Michel, I remember seeing him dancing at the Mudd Club and talking at the bar with his friend John Lurie," reminisced Bowes.[24] "The two of them were so quick-witted and clever, with a wickedly funny repartee." One late evening toward the end of 1979, as David was walking back to his SoHo crash pad, someone emerged from the shadows and asked for a match. It was Basquiat. They strolled around Downtown until the early hours of the morning, becoming close friends. It was Bowes who provided Basquiat with the money he needed to purchase, from a pawnshop, the clarinet he would play in Gray. "He was already 'all there' when I met him," Bowes recalled. "He was already very focused, with an incredible bag of tricks. Nothing that happened later surprised me. It was clear to me everything that was going to happen. It was very strange. It was like being hit by an overwhelming wave, witnessing the train of destiny barreling toward him–that it would be great, but that it would also be awful."

Basquiat shared with Bowes stories of his childhood traumas and his experiences while living on the street. "He knew violence and he knew that he was fragile, but he never dwelled on it," Bowes said. The foot infections Basquiat endured when he was homeless were horrible, he added, "but I can imagine his sense of humor about those things, given his ravenous appetite for new experiences. Perhaps he had too much courage to explore the gritty aspects of city life."

Bowes and Basquiat's friendship eventually blossomed into a brief, intimate relationship, around the middle of 1980. While Bowes was apartment sitting, Basquiat became a frequent guest. "In the milieu we lived in, it was very ordinary to be adventurous in that way," Bowes explained. "At the same time, we were aware that this was kind of new territory. It was a unique experience for me. For Jean-Michel, it was a completely natural part of his character, yet his circumstances and society in general made it difficult and complicating for him."

Suzanne Mallouk, one of Basquiat's girlfriends, offered an interesting perspective on his sexuality. Mallouk arrived in New York City in early 1980, seeking refuge from an emotionally and physically abusive family in Canada.[25] Later that year, while working as a bartender at Night Birds, an East Village dive bar, she met Basquiat. He soon moved in with her, at an apartment she was sharing with friends. What began as a temporary crash pad evolved into an intense, drug-fueled relationship that developed in fits and starts until the middle of 1982, when she moved out of Basquiat's Crosby Street loft.

Mallouk subsequently beat her drug addictions and went to college and medical school; she currently works in New York City as an addiction psychiatrist and psychotherapist focused on treating artists. In her memoir, which she wrote with a friend, she discussed Basquiat's pansexual inclinations:

> It was clear that his sexual interest was not monochromatic. It did not rely on visual stimulation, such as a pretty girl. It was a very rich multichromatic sexuality. He was attracted to people for all different reasons. They could be boys, girls, thin, fat, pretty, ugly. It was, I think, driven by intelligence. He was attracted to intelligence more than anything and to pain. He was very attracted to people who silently bore some sort of inner pain as he did, and he loved people who were one of a kind, people who had a unique vision of things.[26]

Basquiat's insatiable thirst for experiences and experimentation knew few bounds. According to one of his friends, in the early 1980s, "he basically did everything: he ate everything, he drank everything, he did every drug. He could take more heroin than anyone else and was proud of it. He could snort or freebase more coke than anyone. He had the constitution of an elephant. Like a lot of drug addicts, he would also encourage you to do drugs with him and then be mad when you declined."[27]

Many individuals tried to discourage Basquiat's drug habits, including Madonna. They began dating in the second half of 1982, when she was an up-and-coming singer recording her debut album. Suzanne Mallouk, furious with this turn of events, got into a fight with Madonna after spotting her at a nightclub. Basquiat memorialized their clash in a painting titled *A Panel of Experts*, now housed in the collection of the Montreal Museum of Fine Arts.

After living together for a period in the Crosby Street loft, Madonna could no longer tolerate Basquiat's drug use. She broke up with him around the time her album was released, in July 1983. "He was an amazing man and deeply talented. I loved him," she revealed during a 2015 interview with Howard Stern.[28] Enraged by her decision to leave, Basquiat demanded that she return the paintings he

David Bowes, an artist and close friend of Basquiat's.

had given her. He then proceeded to wreck them by smearing them with black paint. "It's difficult to watch people destroy themselves," Madonna recalled. "We always think we can fix people and we can't. They have to do it for themselves."

Basquiat enjoyed his status as a rising art star and the financial rewards it brought. He began splurging on expensive wines, lavish dinners, and large parties for his friends, and hired a new studio assistant, Stephen Torton. Seeking to further distinguish himself in the Downtown scene, he began wearing paint-splattered designer suits to events–a performative flourish that may have been his way of trying to outshine Julian Schnabel, a more established and commercially successful artist known for attending parties in pajamas.

Basquiat took great pleasure in reminding his Downtown friends that he was now a star and making a lot of money–unlike them. One of his close friends, John Lurie, experienced this scorn firsthand. Lurie, an artist and musician who later formed the Lounge Lizards, an eclectic, jazz-infused band, became friends with Basquiat after meeting him at the Mudd Club. Eight years older than Basquiat, Lurie was the brother figure Basquiat never had. "He most certainly had a cruel streak," Lurie wrote in his memoir, describing how their relationship soured. "I was poor. Really poor," Lurie recalled. "And now to be a poor artist was not cool. Just like that, money was the thing, and Jean-Michel had tons of it. You would go over to his place and there would be stacks of hundred dollar bills lying everywhere. Flaunt it, why don't you." As Basquiat's wealth and fame grew, his circle of friends shifted. "He started surrounding himself with an entourage who told him his every thought was genius, and I was not having it. The stacks of hundred dollar bills were constantly being nibbled on by his idolaters."[29]

Loving cash, Basquiat became quite promiscuous regarding the people to whom he would sell his artworks. After he moved to the Crosby Street studio, word spread among certain circles that one could visit his studio and purchase works directly from him for cash. One buyer shared their experience, recounting how "I would go there with cash to buy paintings and Jean-Michel's drug dealer would be hanging around. There was always a huge mound of coke on a table that he would be using while I was there."[30] Over the course of 1982, Basquiat became increasingly volatile and unpredictable, with drugs playing a part. But he also knew that as a hot, in-demand artist, he could be abusive and callous with little fear of immediate consequences.

About a year into their relationship, Basquiat told Annina Nosei he was leaving her gallery to be represented by Galerie Bruno Bischofberger in Zurich, Switzerland. Bischofberger, a respected and successful contemporary art dealer, was known for representing Andy Warhol globally. Warhol was the one artist Basquiat was determined to get to know. From a purely business perspective, moving to Bischofberger's gallery may have been a logical decision for the ambitious Basquiat. However, for Nosei, who had done so much for him, it was a bitter pill to swallow.

Basquiat's departure from Nosei's gallery was marred by an odd incident. While she was in Europe, a drug-addled Basquiat and a companion showed up at her gallery and went down to the basement. They rifled through her storage area and pulled out a few Basquiat paintings. They proceeded to cut them up, leaving the pieces on the basement floor. When Nosei returned from Italy and questioned him about his actions, he cobbled together a feeble excuse, claiming that he needed to destroy unfinished paintings to release the hidden "ghosts" trapped within them.

Despite their fraught parting, Nosei and Basquiat eventually reconciled, their shared achievements proving too significant to ignore. Basquiat would occasionally visit her gallery to view exhibitions by artists she represented, while Nosei, in turn, visited his studio to discuss his latest creations, continuing this dialogue until shortly before he died. After Basquiat's death, Gerard Basquiat invited Nosei to join an authentication committee he established, recognizing her pivotal role in shaping his son's early career and her intimate knowledge of his working methods.

ROLF
BENZ

CHAPTER 3

EARLY COLLECTORS (1981-1982)

BASQUIAT POSSESSED AN EXTRAORDINARY LEVEL OF SELF-CONFIDENCE FOR SOMEONE IN HIS EARLY TWENTIES. His intelligence and soft-spoken charisma allowed him to comfortably navigate different social circles, encompassing people of various ages, races, sexual orientations, and economic backgrounds. He dressed and behaved in a way that would attract attention, having learned from his Mudd Club experiences that standing out as an artist in the bustling downtown scene required both artistic distinctiveness and a memorable persona. Basquiat relished his uniqueness, which also

Basquiat thrived in SoHo, where he connected with early collectors who helped launch his career.

meant often being the sole Black or Hispanic person in a room filled with collectors.

As ambitious young artists know, you are only as good as the first collectors who buy your work. The initial buyers of Basquiat's work during his formative years, 1981 and 1982, were mostly serious collectors with well-trained eyes, who were on the hunt for the fresh and new—and these collectors, primarily wealthy, white, and middle-aged, saw glimmers of great promise in Basquiat's work. Because it was relatively inexpensive, they often purchased multiple pieces. Their early endorsement encouraged others to take Basquiat's audacious work seriously and to consider adding him to their collections.

Five early buyers of Basquiat's work stand out: three from the New York City area and two from Los Angeles. They each came to appreciate Basquiat in ways that reflected their personal backgrounds and the inner workings of the early 1980s art world. Some even developed close relationships with the artist, which helped boost his self-confidence. All five collectors became passionate believers in Basquiat's work, collectively buying more than sixty pieces.

APPEARANCES CAN BE DECEIVING. Jim Dorment was a partner in a New Jersey law firm, where he specialized in corporate law, an especially tradition-bound area of the legal profession. A devout Catholic, he graduated from the University of Notre Dame and Fordham University's School of Law, two institutions with close ties to the Catholic Church. He and his wife lived in a bedroom community where the weekend attire tilted toward Lilly Pulitzer clothes in shades of pink and green. However, beneath this seemingly conventional exterior, Jim harbored an unwavering passion for collecting art, eventually leading him to discover Basquiat.

Collecting was an important part of his life before he married his younger wife, Maureen, in the early 1970s. Jim Dorment's tastes then were for more traditional modern artists. Before having children, the couple routinely spent weekends in New York City, going to museums and exploring art galleries uptown. A decade later, they had five children and a home that was now filled with works by emerging contemporary stars.

"He had this bug to move on to what was new," Maureen said.[1] By the late 1970s, "he wanted to break with older artists and move into more contemporary things. He became very immersed in contemporary culture, including film, theater, ballet, and fine art. He was a voracious reader who was obsessed with learning. He subscribed to every art magazine and became very well-schooled in art theory." Lunch with his law firm colleagues gradually transformed into quick trips on the PATH train, which connects New Jersey to Manhattan, to go gallery-hopping in SoHo. As his eye developed, he began buying works by rising contemporary artists such as David Salle, Julian Schnabel, and Sandro Chia.

Annina Nosei's gallery became a regular stop on Jim's SoHo sojourns. The first Basquiat painting he acquired depicted a boxer with raised hands against a white backdrop filled with graffiti-like scrawls. Basquiat made many paintings inspired by boxers. The monumentally scaled painting Dorment bought, *Untitled (Boxer)*, is among the artist's finest works. It hung on the first floor of the Dorments' New Jersey home, amid a sea of children's toys.

Loving the work, Jim wanted more. He asked Maureen to accompany him on a Saturday SoHo visit to meet the artist and see more paintings. With numerous athletic events already on the children's schedules, Maureen agreed to rearrange things. Their seven-year-old daughter, Maura, joined them, while the other children were looked after by a babysitter. After lunch at a favorite SoHo spot, they headed over to Nosei's gallery.

"We went downstairs and there he was, painting on the floor," recollected Maureen. "Some canvases were propped up against the walls. Jean-Michel spoke briefly with Jim but was extremely rude to me. I thought, 'Okay, so maybe he has contempt for collectors. I get it.' But he was very sweet to my daughter. He made a point of asking Maura if she liked to paint, which was very, very sweet." Jim bought two paintings that day; others would follow.

As they left the basement, Maureen remembers Jim turning to Maura and proclaiming, "You have just met the person who is going to be the greatest American painter of the second half of the twentieth century. You should write this down, because you are going to be able to tell your children and your grandchildren about this day."

Back upstairs, as they prepared to leave, Jim reminded his daughter that Basquiat was a great artist. Yet she was distracted by something else and turned to her mom, asking, "Do you see that little girl over there? Why does she have that big purse?" Maureen turned to see what Maura was referring to and then told her that the person she was looking at was not a little girl but, rather, a dwarf. "I tried to explain that some people are born small and remain that way."

During the drive home, Jim continued to remind Maura that Basquiat was a great artist. When they got home, the other kids were enjoying a pizza dinner. Jim addressed all of them, saying, "I want you to listen. Maura, tell them what you saw today." This moment remains etched in Maureen's memory. "Maura looked at her brothers and sisters and excitedly told them, 'I saw a dwarf today.' It was just what you would expect a seven-year-old to say, yet the obsessive-compulsive collector that resided in Jim's brain was crestfallen. His mind was just in a different spot than the rest of the family."

Jim Dorment continued to acquire great works by emerging artists, always seeking to enter the scene early, when their work was still affordable. He loved researching new talent, exchanging ideas with art dealers, and spending time downtown looking at art. That was his passion, his mode of collecting. He would inevitably find new artists to collect, which sometimes led him to sell pieces to fund new acquisitions or to cover household expenses. Educating five kids, after all, was an expensive responsibility.

In 2017, Jim passed away. At his memorial service, one of his sons spoke on behalf of the family, saying, "My father was always so interested in what was going to happen next. He was always glancing around corners, looking for the next great artist or searching for a new TV show or finishing the book that everyone else would be reading in six months, and more than anyone I've ever met, he loved the *possibilities* of life—the excitement of what was going to happen next. There was no end to the wonders this shy, curious man showed us."

MANHATTAN WAS HOME to many collectors, including Barbara and Gene Schwartz, a cosmopolitan couple living on the Upper East Side. Gene was an advertising copywriter and the author of popular instructional books, such as *How to Double Your Child's Grades in School* and *How to Double Your Power to Learn*. Barbara was a partner in a prominent interior design and decorating firm.

Their real passion, however, lay in assembling a major collection of works by the best contemporary artists of their day. They did not have great wealth but found ways to achieve their goal through dogged determination. At times, they sold pieces from their collection to buy more art or, simply to remain current on household bills. They also frequently donated works to museums, viewing themselves as temporary stewards until the pieces found their permanent homes.

Their journey into the art world began in the late 1950s when they started taking art history classes at New York University and the New School. They quickly decided that collecting was their thing, but they could afford only contemporary art. European Modernists such as Joan Miró, Wassily Kandinsky, and Pablo Picasso were exorbitantly priced and beyond their means. The first significant piece they bought was by Hans Hofmann, a noted Abstract Expressionist painter. It cost

$20,000, which was a princely sum at the time. They worked out a deal with the gallery to pay for it over time. Barbara remembers, "We sent the monthly check to the gallery before paying the psychiatrists, which is what we really needed, and before the rent and anything else."[2]

The young, attractive couple developed a reputation for always paying on time. Gallerists, in turn, became comfortable offering them great works, instead of reserving those pieces for their wealthier clients who could pay immediately. Most of their major acquisitions were made through installment plans. The noted art dealer Leo Castelli, after seeing their collection, once quipped to Barbara, "It's pretty amazing what you can do on $1,000 a month."

In late 1981, Gene Schwartz got a cold call from Diego Cortez, who excitedly told him about this young artist he had featured in his PS 1 show. Cortez told Schwartz he was inviting a select group of collectors to come to his apartment on West Thirty-Sixth Street to see works he had available for sale. Intrigued by the pitch, Gene decided to go and was gobsmacked by what he saw. That night, he returned home with the couple's first Basquiat—a two-panel window frame that Basquiat had found on the street. He had painted the glass panes blue, embellishing the left panel with a masklike face adorned with a three-point crown. The right panel was filled with scratchy strokes of white paint surrounding a rectangle bearing a capital *K*, which likely stood for "King."

Cortez gave Schwartz a typewritten receipt for the purchase:

> Sold to Eugene and Barbara Schwartz ONE Artwork by JEAN MICHEL BASQUIAT [Painting on Tenement WINDOW—with "K" in right half of work] for the AMOUNT of $1500.00. I have today received $400.00 in CASH and a check for the remainder of $1,100.00 which I have deposited to my account.

Excited about their new acquisition, Barbara and Gene wanted more of Basquiat's works. They soon visited Annina Nosei's gallery and bought one of Basquiat's captivating boxer paintings. The figure in this six-foot-square painting oscillates between claiming victory and succumbing to defeat, depending on the viewer's perspective. It cost them $3,150.

By the year's end, the tenement window and boxer paintings were hanging in the Schwartzes' Manhattan apartment, along with a third work, which they had bought from yet another gallery. "Everybody thought we were absolutely crazy for living with such raw works," remembers Barbara. "But we knew that he was a great artist."

In the new year, Gene was disappointed to learn that Basquiat had not received his share for the tenement window painting from Diego Cortez. Concerned about maintaining his reputation for timely payments, he sent Basquiat a letter:

> 3/8/82
>
> Dear Jean Michel,
>
> It seems now that Diego played a rotten trick on you, and a rotten trick on me, at the same time. I like it even less than you do. All you have to lose is money, while I have the chance of losing my reputation, which is worth far more than money to me.
>
> Here's the half of the money you didn't get on the sale of that painting. If you get the money back from Diego, send me my share. If you don't, I feel outraged for you . . . but now it's your problem and his problem, but no longer mine.
>
> You are an excellent artist. My family and myself are proud to own your work.
>
> Best,
>
> Gene Schwartz

Gene never received a response from Basquiat, so he considered the matter closed.[3]

Gene and Barbara Schwartz, early collectors of Basquiat's work, who lived in Manhattan.

The Schwartzes continued their tradition of donating artworks to museums; in 1984, they gave the wonderful boxer painting to the Israel Museum, in Jerusalem. Interestingly, it was the second Basquiat to enter the museum's collection. Back in late 1982, a young curator from the museum had bought *Agony of the Feet* from the Annina Nosei Gallery for $9,000.[4] It was the first Basquiat work to be included in a museum collection worldwide. The painting depicted a disembodied foot alongside a masklike face, with the title suggesting Basquiat's own struggles with his severe infections in both feet when he was homeless after leaving his father's residence. There is a certain poetic justice to the Israel Museum, unaware of Basquiat's Jewish heritage, becoming the first institution to own multiple works by him.

Two decades later, the Israel Museum approached Barbara Schwartz, seeking permission to sell the donated painting. The museum wanted to establish an endowment to support the acquisition of contemporary art. Barbara, believing that museums should have the flexibility to sell works periodically to support new additions to the collection, granted their request. On May 15, 2007, the painting sold for a record-breaking $14.6 million at Sotheby's. The proceeds from the sale have since enabled the museum to acquire many important pieces of contemporary art.[5]

IN ADDITION TO NEW JERSEY, where Jim Dorment and his wife lived, and Manhattan, home to Barbara and Gene Schwartz, the suburbs north of the city also housed many collectors. Herb and Lenore Schorr epitomized a wealthy couple living in a prosperous suburban community. Herb, a senior IBM executive with a PhD in electrical engineering from Princeton University, and Lenore, a homemaker raising their three sons, began their collection with prints by artists such as Pablo Picasso. Over time, their interests evolved, leading them to acquire paintings and drawings by Abstract Expressionist luminaries like Willem de Kooning. However, in the early 1980s, their focus shifted toward collecting works by younger artists.[6]

Their introduction to Basquiat came via an article in *Artforum*, a leading contemporary art magazine. Titled "The Radiant Child" and written by Rene Ricard, a Downtown scenester who survived on his wits as a writer for various art publications, the piece highlighted the emergence of graffiti-inspired artists like Basquiat, Keith Haring, and Judy Rifka in SoHo galleries. The title referred to a motif associated with Keith Haring: a crawling baby encircled by a halo of spiky lines. Intrigued by the article, they visited the Annina Nosei Gallery to see Basquiat's work in person. During their visit, the Schorrs purchased *Poison Oasis*, a large painting depicting a nude Black man with a spiky halo, standing in a lurid yellow landscape alongside a coiled snake and the skeleton of a cow—bold imagery that likely perplexed Herb's IBM colleagues.

Basquiat was working in the basement studio when the Schorrs visited the gallery. While Basquiat was often rude to visitors, he hit it off with the Schorrs. They began coming by regularly to see his latest work and to talk about his inspirations. In addition to breaking bread with him, they were soon helping him run errands, as he did not have a driver's license or a car. According to a person familiar with their relationship, there was an immense bond of love and respect among them. The Schorrs were perhaps the surrogate parents Basquiat yearned for.

The Schorrs became enthusiastic Basquiat collectors. They bought work from various galleries, in addition to acquiring it from the artist directly. Their frequent interactions with him and their intimate understanding of his art led them to believe they possessed a special "decoder ring" that enabled them to appreciate and comprehend his work more profoundly than other collectors and curators. By the time of Basquiat's death, the Schorrs owned more than twenty-five paintings and drawings by him.[7]

IN THE EARLY 1980s, despite the tremendous wealth generated by the local entertainment and petrochemical industries, Los Angeles had few collectors and even fewer art galleries. However, the nascent art scene included two collectors who, after discovering Basquiat's work in 1982, began buying it in depth. Like many Southern California residents, these collectors were not natives but had relocated there later in life.

Stéphane Janssen, the great-great-grandson of Ernest Solvay, a Belgian entrepreneur whose namesake chemical company laid the foundation for dynastic family wealth, grew up in a small town near Brussels. After a stint in the family business, in 1965 he shifted gears and opened an art gallery in Brussels that focused on artists associated with the avant-garde CoBrA movement. The CoBrA artists were known for their vibrant and colorful works, often inspired by children's drawings and Norse mythology. The name CoBrA was derived from the initials of the capital cities in the founding members' home countries: Copenhagen, Brussels, and Amsterdam.

After eleven years in the art world, Janssen decided to close the gallery. No longer wanting to live a life of lies and deceptions, he left his wife and children in Belgium to start a new life in Los Angeles as a gay man. In 1981, he met the love of his life and settled with his partner in a spacious Beverly Hills home, which provided ample wall space for his existing art collection from Belgium and the new acquisitions the couple fervently pursued.

In early 1982, Janssen came across a review in the *Los Angeles Times* about a young artist having his first show in the city. Intrigued, he visited the recently established Larry Gagosian Gallery to view the exhibition and instantly fell in love with the work. He bought a painting of a life-sized Black man standing next to the scales of justice; it cost $8,500.[8]

Janssen saw elements of other great twentieth-century artists in Basquiat's work, but he also recognized something that felt fresh and innovative. The painting he bought that day was the first of thirteen Basquiat works he would acquire through the Gagosian Gallery by the end of 1985. "It was exactly the kind of work that I love, which tends to be brutally tough work. After seeing my collection, a psychologist once told me that I must be a very peaceful man because only murderers buy Renoir and flower paintings."[9]

Stéphane Janssen, an LA-based collector, acquired thirteen Basquiat paintings.

After acquiring his first painting and learning that Basquiat was in Los Angeles, Janssen invited Basquiat and

Larry Gagosian to his Beverly Hills home for lunch. When he took the artist on a tour of his collection, which included great works by twentieth-century artists such as Jean Dubuffet, Pierre Alechinsky, and Karel Appel, Basquiat repeatedly muttered, "That's shit, that's shit too, so is that." The only items that garnered his admiration were drawings by Hergé, the celebrated Belgian cartoonist best known for a series of books titled *The Adventures of Tintin*. Basquiat was delighted to see them, telling his host that he had read all the Hergé books during his elementary school days in Brooklyn.

Janssen realized that Basquiat was on a quest to shock him that day. "He was smoking a joint the size of an ice cream cone when he arrived," Janssen recalled. "I'd never seen anything like it. I didn't use drugs; nor did I like being around people who were using them." But Basquiat's indiscretions had no impact on him. Having been a contemporary art dealer, he was all too familiar with the antics of those looking to provoke.

Later that year, when Janssen and his partner were in New York, Larry Gagosian invited them to visit Basquiat in his Crosby Street studio. Basquiat showed up an hour late, mumbling that he had been at the Metropolitan Museum admiring a thirteenth-century crucifix by Cimabue. The Cimabue painting had been damaged during the 1966 flood in Florence, Italy, but had been recently restored and was on temporary loan at the Met. Janssen remembered the meeting: "We spent two or three hours together talking about different things, including the Cimabue painting, which I'd also seen. We had an extraordinary conversation, because he wasn't high. He was sober and brilliantly intelligent. He was very taken with Cimabue's depiction of the dying Christ and explained that he did something similar when he painted a Black man on a refrigerator door."

Janssen had further interactions with Basquiat, but the artist was always high. "I only saw him smoke pot. I never saw him use coke or heroin. He was not someone I liked when he was high, because he didn't want to talk about anything except money. He would never talk about his art or what others were making." However, the visit to Basquiat's studio left a profound impression on Janssen: "I had a revelation about how intelligent he was and how educated he was about the history of painting. I discovered then that he was as great as his paintings."

Janssen followed Basquiat's career closely. He bought five paintings in 1982, five more in 1983, and then two in 1984. The last work he bought, in 1985, cost him $20,000. He then stopped collecting Basquiat, not because he ran out of wall space but because he felt the artist had lost his edge and was creating pale imitations of his earlier work.[10]

Around the time Janssen stopped adding to his Basquiat collection, the Museum of Contemporary Art (MOCA), in Los Angeles, approached him about potentially donating works to the new museum. Founded in 1979, MOCA was the first museum in the city devoted to contemporary art. Local philanthropists, including Marcia Weisman, had banded together to create it. Weisman knew Janssen and came to his home for lunch to see his collection and discuss the possibility of donations. After Janssen showed her around, Weisman dismissed his collection, saying, "Unfortunately, you don't have anything of interest to us. You don't have a Roy Lichtenstein, you don't have an Andy Warhol, nor a Mark Rothko." Taken aback, Janssen told her he had great works by Jean Dubuffet, Jean-Michel Basquiat, and other great artists. Yet he remembered Weisman flippantly telling him, "No, I'm not interested in anything that you have." The lunchtime meeting was quickly drawn to a close.

ELI BROAD HAD IMPECCABLE TIMING in both business and art collecting. The Bronx-born, public school–educated Broad graduated from Michigan State University with a degree in accounting in 1954. After working as a CPA for a few years, he collaborated with a friend to create a company focused on building tract homes in Detroit. Their timing was propitious as the auto industry was starting to boom. First-time home buyers flocked to their well-designed, low-cost offerings. They soon expanded nationally, especially into California, where Broad moved the company. By 1969, the Kaufman and Broad Building Corporation (since renamed KB Home) had become the first home-building company listed on the New York Stock Exchange. Less than fifteen years after graduating from college, Broad was a multimillionaire.

Itching for more, Broad began working on his second fortune when, in the early 1970s, he bought an underperforming Baltimore-based life insurance company. He transformed it into a retirement savings giant focused on the burgeoning needs of millions of baby boomers. The rebranded company, called SunAmerica, grew rapidly and went public in 1989. That year, Broad joined the *Forbes* magazine list of the four hundred richest Americans with an estimated net worth of $310 million.

Broad and his wife, Edye, had started collecting art in the mid-1970s. They first bought works by Impressionist and Modernist artists, like Vincent van Gogh and Henri Matisse—selections that reflected impeccable yet unadventurous taste. But as they studied great collectors from the past, they came to believe that the very best art collections were formed when the art was made, rather than works being purchased long after the artists had died. In the late 1970s the couple shifted to collecting contemporary art.

With passion and great wealth to back it up, the Broads were pursued by every contemporary art dealer in the world. They were regularly offered the best of everything, and when they fell in love with an artist, they bought their work in depth. They first acquired Basquiat at the end of 1982, buying three paintings, including one with a grimacing face that many critics deem one of the artist's most important works. By the end of 1985, they owned fourteen works. If hung together, they would make up a nearly ninety-foot-long frieze.[11]

The Broads opened their eponymously named museum in Los Angeles in 2015 to showcase their substantial collection, which at the time comprised around two thousand works. They donated thirteen Basquiat works to the museum, many of which are regularly on view.

BY THE END OF 1982, Basquiat's artistic style was firmly established, with numerous influential collectors recognizing his talent. Understanding how he accomplished this requires acknowledging his intellectual prowess, which enabled him to create the richly layered artworks of his early years and navigate the complex personalities and dynamics of the contemporary art world. Importantly, all of this took place before his friendship with Andy Warhol. While their relationship would help boost Basquiat's profile, his artistic identity was already fully formed before their paths crossed.

AKIRA IKEDA
GALLERY

CHAPTER 4

FAME (1983–1985)

IN EARLY 1985, BASQUIAT APPEARED ON THE COVER OF *THE NEW YORK TIMES MAGAZINE*, reaching millions of readers nationwide. The cover featured a barefoot Basquiat dressed in a black Armani suit, seated in front of one of his large paintings. The accompanying story, titled "New Art, New Money: The Marketing of an American Artist," explored his remarkable rise to fame in a contemporary art market then on fire.

Basquiat's family and friends gathered for a celebratory dinner at his father's Brooklyn brownstone. Seated around the table that night were Gerard Basquiat and his partner, Nora Fitzpatrick, Jean-Michel and his then girlfriend, Paige Powell, and a few other family members. Also present was Andy Warhol, who had become a close confidant and mentor to Jean-Michel. Their paths had intertwined, forging a connection that would endure in their lifetimes and beyond.

Basquiat in Tokyo during an exhibition of his work at the Akira Ikeda Gallery, November 1985.

WHEN EARLY COLLECTORS BEGAN purchasing works by Basquiat in 1981, the US economy was mired in a recession. A combination of high unemployment, soaring inflation, and exorbitant interest rates had eroded consumer and investor confidence. But in early 1983, the US economy rebounded as new monetary and fiscal policies took hold, heralding a decade of remarkable prosperity. The economy grew at a furious pace, surpassing what had occurred over the previous ten years. The unemployment rate, which had peaked at 10.8 percent at the end of 1982, declined sharply, along with the number of people living in poverty.

Optimistic about the future and reveling in their newfound financial freedom, consumers eagerly embraced a culture of indulgence. Television shows, movies, and magazines glorified luxury goods and extravagant lifestyles. It was during this decade that S. I. Newhouse Jr., the chairman of Condé Nast, transformed the company into a magazine powerhouse with stylish publications such as *Vogue*, *Vanity Fair*, and *Gourmet*. Additionally, the merger between Louis Vuitton, the fashionable luggage company, and Moët Hennessy, the champagne and cognac behemoth, gave rise to the luxury goods titan known today as LVMH.

With so much money available for luxury goods, the 1980s was a fantastic time to be an artist. Collecting contemporary art became an exciting and glamorous endeavor, attracting larger audiences than ever before. In contrast to early Basquiat collectors, who tended to rely on their own discernment and judgment, new buyers often sought the guidance of art advisors to rapidly build their collections. Among the most sought-after advisors of the time was Estelle Schwartz. Anthony Grant, a prominent figure in Sotheby's contemporary art department during that period, remembers her influence: "She was the one who would tell people what to buy. She would tell them, 'This is what you should be looking at right now.' They would hang on to her every word.

She probably placed the lion's share of Basquiat works to collectors in the New York area."[1]

One type of art, dubbed Neo-Expressionism, was especially popular with art advisors. The Neo-Expressionist movement marked a dramatic revival of figurative painting. It arose in response to the dominance of conceptual and minimalist art throughout much of the previous decade, which many collectors and critics deemed sterile or overly intellectual. Neo-Expressionism delved into a wide variety of themes, such as existential angst, personal identity, and sociopolitical issues. The movement was not homogeneous, and its artists employed a diverse array of subject matters and stylistic approaches. However, the work tended to be bold and dramatic, with expressive, sometimes violent brushwork, and emotive, often distorted figures.

A small group of American, Italian, and German artists associated with the movement captured most of the spotlight. Julian Schnabel and David Salle were the leading American figures, while the Italian luminaries—Sandro Chia, Francesco Clemente, and Enzo Cucchi—were often referred to as the Three C's. Prominent German artists included Georg Baselitz, Jörg Immendorff, and Anselm Kiefer. Sophisticated marketing by the galleries representing these artists ensured that their works were featured in prestigious group shows, biennials, and exhibitions devoted to the avant-garde. As enthusiasm for this movement grew, collectors scrambled to join in. Works by the leading Neo-Expressionists began appearing together on the walls of collectors across the country and around the world. Bruno Bischofberger, the Zurich-based gallerist, represented many Neo-Expressionists, including the top American and Italian artists. When Basquiat began to be represented by his gallery in the autumn of 1982, he joined the global gang of artists whose creations were taking the market by storm.

Basquiat and his fellow Neo-Expressionist painters shared many artistic traits, but two qualities set him apart. He was the sole Black artist in the group, which generated a strong interest among many buyers to see his work. And he was the only artist who consistently painted himself into the picture. While the other leading American, Italian, and German Neo-Expressionists drew inspiration from myths and other fictive content, Basquiat often depicted himself and the world he inhabited.

It is also essential to recognize that Basquiat was part of a broader wave of talented Black artists active in the 1980s. Figures such as Frank Bowling, Ed Clark, Robert Colescott, Charles Gaines, Sam Gilliam, David Hammons, Kerry James Marshall, Howardena Pindell, Martin Puryear, Faith Ringgold, Betye Saar, Alison Saar, Stanley Whitney, and Jack Whitten were all producing significant work during this period. While these artists are now widely collected and represented in major museum collections, Basquiat stood out at the time as one of the few represented by top galleries and consistently featured in the art press.

Celebrity happens when who you are and what the world wants converge. Into the booming appetite for highly expressive art stepped the highly expressive Basquiat—a tall, handsome, bisexual, self-taught young Black man who was ambitious, well read, and unapologetically provocative. Sexy and cool, he challenged and charmed those around him, making him an ideal figure for the 1980s art boom and a natural fit for Bischofberger's gallery.

BRUNO BISCHOFBERGER POSSESSED a rare combination of skills. He had a razor-sharp intellect, an extensive knowledge of art history, and, perhaps most important, exceptional commercial instincts. These qualities enabled him to extend his influence over the contemporary art world. Although he did not have a gallery in New York, Bischofberger had what mattered the most: strong relationships with deep-pocketed collectors from around the world. They respected his eye for talent and his ability to create an air of exclusivity around the artists he represented.

As the youngest of four siblings in a family of professionals, Bischofberger had charted his own distinct path. His father was a doctor, his mother a dentist, and his siblings all pursued careers in medicine or dentistry. In contrast, Bischofberger developed a passion for Swiss folk art, particularly the peasant paintings created by farmers in the Appenzell region and painted and carved furniture from the fifteenth to nineteenth centuries. His fascination was sparked during visits to his father's family, where he was exposed to these objects. At fourteen, he began cycling to nearby villages, seeking tips from locals on items he could buy with money his father had staked him. By seventeen, he had amassed a significant collection and established relationships with museum curators who were starting to research and organize exhibitions on this type of work. While in college, Bischofberger further honed his eye by studying art history, with minors in classical archaeology and European ethnology.

With a passion for collecting, Bischofberger opened his own art gallery in 1963 after completing his education. At the time, Zurich had only three other galleries, a stark contrast to the bustling art scene there today. Reflecting on his motivation, Bischofberger said "I became an art dealer because I wanted to deal with artworks that would enable me to collect and live with art. I always felt more like a collector than a dealer."[2]

While Bischofberger was deeply fascinated with historical works, he quickly developed an eye for emerging trends in contemporary art. In the early 1960s, Pop Art was the movement making waves. Bischofberger called Paris gallerist Ileana Sonnabend to propose a Pop Art show with her assistance. Sonnabend, a key tastemaker introducing artists like Andy Warhol and Roy Lichtenstein to European audiences, agreed. The resulting exhibition, entirely sourced from Sonnabend, opened in June 1965.[3] Attended by Sonnabend and her husband, Michael, as well as Roy Lichtenstein and his girlfriend, the show featured early large works by Warhol and Lichtenstein, priced between $500 and $1,000.

Despite Bischofberger's enthusiasm, his Swiss clientele was unimpressed: Nothing sold. "They thought Pop Art was for vulgar nouveaux riches and showy playboys," Bischofberger recalled. Undeterred and recognizing the movement's significance, he traveled to New York the following year to meet the artists featured in his show, including Andy Warhol. This trip marked the beginning of his commitment to exhibiting many of these artists alongside a few contemporary European talents.

Convinced of Warhol's importance, Bischofberger made his first major investment in the artist's work in 1968. Using borrowed funds, he purchased eleven early paintings directly from Warhol during one of his frequent trips to New York.[4] He also proposed having the "right of first refusal" on any new works Warhol created. Delighted by Bischofberger's enthusiasm and willingness to pay, Warhol agreed to the arrangement—a handshake deal that lasted until Warhol's death nineteen years later. Their collaboration extended beyond art sales, as the two co-founded *Interview* magazine with Peter Brant, another devoted Warhol admirer.[5]

Bischofberger frequently purchased Warhol's new work, sometimes acquiring entire series. Yet aside from Warhol, he rarely directly represented the artists he exhibited, instead relying on his relationships with their primary galleries to source works. By the late 1970s, he shifted his approach: "I was always on the lookout for the next generation of artists because I was determined to get in early so that I could represent them directly," he explained, and he began representing emerging talents such as Julian Schnabel, David Salle, and the Italian Three C's.[6]

Bischofberger first encountered Basquiat's work during a tour of the *New York/New Wave* exhibition that Diego Cortez gave him in the spring of 1981. "It was a pretty messy show, with all these different rooms filled with art," Bischofberger noted. "At the end was a large room with a huge wall that was filled with his works. When we were heading back to Manhattan, Diego asked me what I thought about Basquiat. I told him it looked interesting, and that it made me think a bit of other artists like Cy Twombly and maybe Jean Dubuffet." Intrigued, Bischofberger decided to keep an eye on the young artist.

Later that year, while Basquiat was working in the basement studio at Annina Nosei's gallery, Cortez convinced Bischofberger to visit his apartment on West Thirty-Sixth Street to view works by Basquiat that he had for sale. By then, Bischofberger had heard more about Basquiat's talent from some of the Neo-Expressionist artists he represented. Impressed by what he saw, Bischofberger bought around fifteen paintings and twenty-five drawings, which he shipped to Europe. In March of the following year, he attended Basquiat's solo show at Nosei's gallery, only to find it completely sold out by the time he arrived.

Bischofberger exhibited the works he had acquired from Cortez at his Zurich gallery in September 1982. Basquiat traveled to Zurich for the exhibition, accompanied by his new studio assistant. Around this time, Basquiat told Annina Nosei that he would be leaving her gallery to be represented by Bischofberger. Like Bischofberger's arrangement with Warhol, their agreement was sealed with a handshake. Additionally, Bischofberger agreed to resolve a nettlesome financial issue that had been troubling Basquiat. Cortez had not paid Basquiat the money he was owed from the sale of works to Bischofberger, just as he had previously shortchanged Basquiat on the sale to Gene Schwartz. Bischofberger paid Basquiat the share he was due and then handled the dispute with Cortez directly.

Bischofberger actively promoted Basquiat's work, organizing six exhibitions at his Zurich gallery during the artist's lifetime. He also arranged shows in cities like Tokyo and Paris, and even in the Ivory Coast, in collaboration with local galleries and museums. Furthermore, to ensure Basquiat had representation in New York, Bischofberger partnered with the Mary Boone Gallery from mid-1983 to 1986, which included exhibitions in 1984 and 1985.

Bruno Bischofberger (right), who represented Basquiat after he left the Annina Nosei Gallery, with Brook Bartlett and Basquiat at the Cresta Clubhouse in St. Moritz, Switzerland, January 30, 1983.

Despite their twenty-year age difference, Basquiat and Bischofberger developed a close bond and found comfort in each other's company. "He taught me about jazz music," Bischofberger recalled, "introducing me to Billie Holiday, Charlie Parker, and Max Roach. I helped him learn about wine, architecture, and classical music." Basquiat became close to Bischofberger's family, staying with them in St. Moritz multiple times, including Christmas in 1983. They also traveled together to visit other artists represented by Bischofberger, giving Basquiat the opportunity to connect with them in their homes and studios. Among these visits, Bischofberger's introduction of Basquiat to Warhol would prove to be especially important.

ARTISTS HAVE THEIR HEROES, and for Basquiat, Andy Warhol was the ultimate figure of fascination. Thirty-two years his senior, Warhol captivated the young artist. Basquiat first encountered Warhol in 1979 when he impulsively interrupted Warhol's lunch at a SoHo restaurant to sell him a handmade postcard. On another occasion, Glenn O'Brien featured a drawing by Basquiat in his March 1981 column for *Interview* magazine. Before the article was published, he took Basquiat to the Factory to introduce him to Warhol, but the matchup did not occur.[7] It was Bruno Bischofberger who finally made the introduction, bringing Basquiat to meet his hero in early October 1982 at Warhol's studio.

When they met, Warhol's iconic paintings of Marilyn Monroe, Campbell's soup cans, and Mao Zedong from the 1960s and early 1970s were in museums and top collections around the world. Yet interest in Warhol's new work had waned as he had delved into more provocative and sexual subject matter. One of his major creative projects in 1974 and 1975 was a series called *Ladies and Gentlemen*, comprising nearly three hundred paintings based on photographs of trans women and drag queens taken in his studio. From 1976 to 1978, his *Torsos and Sex Parts* paintings were based on photographs of men standing naked or engaging in various sex acts. The works in this series included images of flaccid and erect penises, anal intercourse, and an occasional female torso. Toward the end of this series, Warhol began creating works known as his *Piss*, *Oxidation*, and *Cum* paintings. The *Piss* paintings involved urinating, pouring, or dripping urine onto a prepared canvas, while the *Oxidation* paintings used metallic paints on the canvas to allow the urine to oxidize and create abstract shapes in shades of green. The *Cum* paintings were similar to the *Piss* paintings but utilized ejaculate collected from individuals at the Factory.

With little demand for these works, Warhol relied on commissioned portraits of celebrities, athletes, and collectors to fill the financial gap. It was Bruno Bischofberger who initially suggested the idea of commissioned portraits to Warhol. Typically measuring forty inches square, the portraits were based on Polaroid photographs taken by

Andy Warhol and Basquiat at Warhol's studio during a visit arranged by Bruno Bischofberger, October 4, 1982.

Warhol during lunches held at the Factory with his subjects. Warhol would choose the best photograph, sometimes in collaboration with the sitter, and have it enlarged so it could be silk-screened onto a canvas painted with a vibrant base color. Warhol produced hundreds of these portraits, with sitters such as Imelda Marcos and O. J. Simpson paying $25,000 to be immortalized by the artist. Warhol's active social life and frequent visits to Studio 54 and other popular nightspots helped generate a steady stream of portrait requests that kept the Factory busy.[8]

Bischofberger had another idea that Warhol embraced. He would meet the artists Bischofberger was promoting. The ground rules were simple: They would get to know each other over lunch and then use the experience to create and exchange portraits. The hope was that these trades would spark friendship and, more important, create a pathway for mutually beneficial self-promotion.

Basquiat went home after their October lunch and quickly painted a double portrait of the two of them. He had it delivered to

Warhol later that day.[9] While this made for a fun and interesting moment, it did not immediately foster a close bond between the two artists. Paige Powell, a business associate and Warhol confidante, remembers what happened: "I saw him in Andy's studio with Bruno. But Andy was kind of afraid of Jean-Michel. He was cautious about people ever since Valerie Solanas shot and almost killed him in 1968. Andy was also worried about anybody who looked kind of druggy."[10] It was only when Powell started dating Basquiat the following spring that Warhol's suspicions about Basquiat began to melt away.

Paige Powell had joined *Interview* magazine as an advertising associate shortly after she moved to New York City in 1980. She had a talent for securing new advertisers and finding clever ways to expand

Basquiat and his girlfriend, Paige Powell, vacationing in Hana, Hawaii, February 1984.

existing relationships.[11] Powell and Warhol became close friends and spent a great deal of time together, even, at one point, discussing adopting a baby together.[12]

Powell first met Basquiat a few months after his lunch with Warhol when, as a side gig to her *Interview* job, she was looking for artists to include in a group show she was organizing. Her boyfriend at the time, Jay Shriver, one of Warhol's studio assistants, arranged for her to meet Basquiat at his Crosby Street studio. After hearing Powell's pitch, Basquiat agreed to participate in her show. Over the next few months, the group show morphed into a solo exhibition of new work by Basquiat. The show opened in April 1983, and shortly thereafter, Powell and Basquiat began dating, a relationship that would last for two years.

Powell got to know Basquiat's family during this time and occasionally traveled with them. When she met Gerard Basquiat, she saw him as the embodiment of an immigrant success story. In addition to a Brooklyn brownstone, Gerard had a nearby shop selling home goods and a rental property on Manhattan's Upper West Side. "He had a quiet grand manner about him," she recalled. "He was very formal in both his demeanor and how he dressed."

Jean-Michel Basquiat often confided in Powell about his strained relationship with his father, whom he felt had been very controlling and tough during his upbringing. "Many of Basquiat's Downtown friends were under the impression that he had this cruel father," Powell explained. "But part of the problem was that Jean-Michel was extremely experimental, while his father was a very straight, conservative man. Gerard recognized his son's artistic talent but wanted him to do something other than being an artist." Despite this tension, Paige observed that "Jean-Michel had great respect for his father and sought his approval. Their interactions were a mix of laughter and conversation, but at times, they would provoke each other." On a trip to Hawaii with Gerard, Jean-Michel, and Gerard's girlfriend, Nora Fitzpatrick, Powell recalled how father and son fiercely competed over everything, from tennis scores to dinner choices. Powell also met Jean-Michel's mother, Matilde: "He absolutely adored her. Although he accepted Nora as Gerard's partner, he preferred to keep his distance from her."

As Basquiat's relationship with Powell blossomed, so too did his friendship with Warhol. The two artists were soon gallivanting around Manhattan, visiting nightclubs, eating in chic Downtown restaurants, and working out together. Traces of their relationship appear frequently within Warhol's diaries. Starting in 1976, Warhol began dictating the events of the preceding day to his assistant. These entries, detailing moments both high and low, delivered in a flat and affectless tone, fill thousands of pages. Excerpts from these diaries

Basquiat and Andy Warhol at the Factory, 1984.

were unveiled to the public after Warhol's death in the form of an eight-hundred-page bestselling book, *The Andy Warhol Diaries*. Some early mentions of Basquiat appear within longer entries:

> *Wednesday, May 18, 1983:*... Paige is upset–Jean Michel Basquiat is really on heroin–and she was crying, telling me to do something, but what can you do? He['s] got a hole in his nose and he couldn't do coke anymore, and he wanted to still be on something, I guess. I guess he wants to be the youngest artist to go. Paige gave him a big show uptown last month and she's the reason he's been around the office–they're "involved."
>
> . . . .
>
> *Monday, August 15, 1983:* Cabbed to meet Jean Michel Basquiat at the workout with Lidija, he was doing it with us. . . . He's in love with Paige Powell.
>
> . . . .
>
> *Monday, August 22, 1983:* Went to meet Jean Michel at the office and I took pictures of him in a jockstrap.[13]

Around the time Warhol began keeping his daily diary, he also started carrying a Minox 35EL camera to document his life visually. The Andy Warhol Foundation later donated the negatives and contact sheets of these photographs to the Cantor Arts Center at Stanford University. Among them are numerous images of Basquiat eating in restaurants, socializing at parties, and spending time with Andy at the Factory. These photos exude a striking intimacy. Within the archives are also pictures of a fully nude Basquiat. Far from secretive or taken without his consent, these photos were captured at the Factory or in hotels, often with others present. Basquiat appeared comfortable with the male gaze and with the dynamic of a clothed fifty-something photographing a naked twenty-something.

Warhol's friendship with Basquiat soon extended into a landlord-tenant relationship when Basquiat began renting a building

Warhol owned in the East Village. The two-story space at 57 Great Jones Street, a former horse stable, served as Basquiat's studio on the ground floor, with his living quarters above. Basquiat signed a five-year lease with an annual rent of $48,000, with Bruno Bischofberger acting as guarantor. At the time, this was a big number for an East Village carriage house. True to his commercially savvy nature, Warhol was not extending any special favors or discounts to his young friend.

With Warhol's growing influence in Basquiat's life, Paige Powell arranged a lunch between Gerard Basquiat and Warhol at *Interview* magazine's new offices. Jean-Michel did not join them. Warhol had recently relocated his offices, studio, and *Interview* into a five-story building on East Thirty-Third Street, near Madison Avenue. Warhol, who loved real estate, bought the decommissioned Con Edison substation in 1981 and then spent the next few years renovating it to become his new Factory.[14]

Gerard Basquiat and Warhol hit it off. "Gerard really appreciated meeting Andy," remembered Powell, "and seeing that he owned this huge Midtown office space. I think this was when Gerard realized the financial success Andy had achieved as an artist." This was also likely the moment when Gerard was able to see beyond his son's past troubles and grasp the potential associated with the artistic path he was pursuing so ardently.

Warhol and Gerard were reunited when Gerard hosted a small dinner party at his Brooklyn home in February 1985 to celebrate his son's appearance on the cover of *The New York Times Magazine*. "It was a small, beautiful party," Powell recalled. "Andy, Jean-Michel, and I were there, along with Gerard, Nora, his sister Jeanine, and a few other people. Jean-Michel was really happy to be surrounded by the people who loved him. His family was so proud of him. It was a beautiful evening."

Gerard Basquiat, Jean-Michel, and Jeanine at Gerard's brownstone, celebrating his son's appearance on the cover of The New York Times Magazine, *February 1985.*

Matilde Basquiat also became acquainted with Warhol. According to his diary, Warhol first met her at a party Jean-Michel held at the Great Jones loft to celebrate her fiftieth birthday. She later accompanied Jean-Michel to Warhol's studio while they were working on a series of paintings eventually known as the *Collaboration* paintings. Matilde even sat for her own Warhol portrait, as did Gerard and one of Jean-Michel's sisters.

Warhol's close relationship with Basquiat helped him understand the challenges and complexities of Basquiat's life, particularly his struggles with addiction and fluctuating moods.

> *Tuesday, August 7, 1984:* Keith [Haring] wanted to go to Rounds, the gay place at 53rd and Second, and I didn't, so I said I'd never been there because I hadn't in five years, and so we walk in the door and

Jean-Michel and his mother, Matilde, at the belated birthday party he hosted for her in his Great Jones studio, September 1984.

the first thing the waiter says is *(laughs)*, "Mr. Warhol! It's so nice to see you again!" Jean Michel wouldn't go to Rounds. He called this morning and told me that in the old days when he didn't have any money he would hustle and get $10 and he didn't want to remember that.

. . . .

Sunday, October 7, 1984: Jean Michel is so difficult, you never know what kind of mood he'll be in, what he'll be on. He gets really paranoid and says, "You're just using me," and then he'll get guilty for getting paranoid and he'll do everything so nice to try to make up for it.

. . . .

Tuesday, May 14, 1985: . . . Jean Michel was in a dark mood. . . . I didn't lecture him about the heroin he takes because I didn't want to have a fight.[15]

Basquiat with attendees at the opening of Primitivism in 20th Century Art: Affinity of the Tribal and the Modern, *at the Dallas Museum of Art, June 1985.*

While Warhol could observe and comment on Basquiat's struggles with addiction from a distance, Paige Powell experienced them up close. After two exhausting years of witnessing the recurring cycle of attempts to get clean followed by relapses, Powell finally reached her breaking point. A few months after Gerard's celebratory dinner, she ended her relationship with Jean-Michel. Determined to take action, Powell arranged to meet Gerard in person to tell him in no uncertain terms about Jean-Michel's drug habits. It was not an act-of-revenge meeting, because she still needed to maintain a professional rapport with Jean-Michel during his visits to Warhol's office. "I'm not involved anymore in any way with Jean-Michel," Powell reminded Gerard, "so it is important for you to understand his drug habits because he needs your help. You need to talk to him about it." Gerard agreed but insisted that Powell tell Jean-Michel about their conversation. "He kept saying, 'You have to tell him that I know. You need to tell him that you told me everything.'" Powell resisted Gerard's pleas, believing that she had done her duty. The purpose of the meeting, after all, was to pass the responsibility baton to Gerard. But Gerard pestered her with phone calls over the next few days until she finally relented.

Powell went to see Jean-Michel at the Great Jones loft. Upstairs in the bedroom area, she told him about her conversation with Gerard and her hopes that he would get help for his drug issues. While hearing this, he became enraged. "He took a glass vase," she recalled, "and started to throw it at me. As I was running down the stairs, it shattered on the wall near me. Some glass shards hit the top of my head and I started bleeding." Disoriented and shaken, she fled out the front door. "It was so unexpected. I didn't know what to do." She hailed a cab and headed uptown, eventually darting into a movie theater to compose herself.

Later that night, Powell spoke with Warhol, who told her that Jean-Michel had called him right after the incident to say how awful he felt. After relaying this, the ever-cool and detached Warhol offered his advice: "Never, ever get involved in family affairs." For Powell, despite feeling chastised by Warhol, the incident brought a sense of relief. "While Andy was sort of reprimanding me, I knew that things with Jean-Michel were now finally over."

CHAPTER 5

ENDGAME (1986-1988)

SUSTAINING A CAREER AS A PROMINENT MUSICIAN, PLAYWRIGHT, OR ARTIST IS A CHALLENGING TASK.

After five years of relentless creativity, producing nearly eight hundred paintings, Basquiat had developed a recognizable style that collectors and curators could easily spot. Yet he faced a daunting challenge: What does one do after creating something so bold and distinctive? Would he venture into new territory or recycle the images that brought him fame?

Beginning around 1986, Basquiat's manic creativity took a noticeable downturn. He produced fewer works, with more misses than hits. Many were pale reminders of his earlier successes. Perry Rubenstein, who had overcome his own struggles with addiction and was now a private art dealer in New York, recalled how "his paintings from 1986 to

Keith Haring and Basquiat, December 1987.

1988, with a few notable exceptions, were just awful. I'd go to his studio on Great Jones Street and be sad for him. He'd become a junkie and was selling unfinished paintings to anyone who would give him cash."

Basquiat's self-confidence had been badly shaken by harsh reviews he and Andy Warhol had received for the exhibition of their *Collaboration* paintings, which had opened in September 1985. The two artists made more than one hundred paintings together, investing significant time and creative effort in the project. Working at the Factory, Warhol would typically initiate a piece by painting a newspaper headline, corporate logo, or mundane advertisement on a large canvas. Basquiat would then respond with aggressive applications of paint, often breaking apart or distorting Warhol's original image, and occasionally incorporating faces, masks, or figures into the composition.[1]

Bruno Bischofberger purchased many pieces from the series. Together, the two artists and their dealer decided to exhibit a selection of them at the Tony Shafrazi Gallery in SoHo. The show featured sixteen paintings that Bischofberger had consigned to the gallery for sale. Unfortunately, the exhibition was a flop. The juxtaposition of Warhol's cool and detached style with Basquiat's more emotive approach resulted in many beastly mash-ups.

The art beat reporter for *The New York Times*, Vivien Raynor, offered a scathing assessment of the collaboration, remarking that it "looks like one of Warhol's manipulations, which increasingly seem based on the Mencken theory about nobody going broke underestimating the public's intelligence. Basquiat, meanwhile, comes across as the all too willing accessory."[2] The most damning comment in the review, however, was aimed straight at Basquiat: "Last year, I wrote of Jean-Michel Basquiat that he had a chance of becoming a very good painter providing he didn't succumb to the forces that would make him an art world mascot. This year, it appears that those forces have prevailed."

The harsh criticism Basquiat received in this and other reviews marked a sharp departure from the more positive notices he had grown accustomed to. It was a terrible blow, particularly as he had shared with many in his circle that he hoped collaborating with the far more famous Warhol would enhance his standing in the art world. Basquiat soon began spending more time alone.

The sudden death of Warhol, following emergency gallbladder surgery, dealt another crushing blow to Basquiat's already fragile psyche. Warhol had been one of the few adults in his life whom he trusted to a degree and relied on. His passing, in February 1987, further untethered Basquiat from reality.

Basquiat's ongoing struggles with addiction compounded his inability to navigate these significant setbacks. From an early age, he had turned to drugs while dealing with the lasting effects of childhood traumas and the harsh realities of life on the streets. When he achieved early fame, he traded the hardships of homelessness for the relentless pressures of being a highly sought-after artist, deepening his dependency. These challenges left him without the tools he needed to revive and rejuvenate himself.

HOPING TO ESCAPE HIS DEMONS in New York, Basquiat traveled constantly. In early 1988, he arrived in Paris for an exhibition at the Yvon Lambert Gallery. What was initially intended as a brief visit turned into a multi-week stay in a city he loved. During his time there, he had a photo session with a young photographer, which would prove to be a telling moment.

Basquiat arrived at the gallery with a box of chocolate éclairs, two cans of Coke, and a paperback book.[3] After apologizing for being tardy, he mentioned to the photographer, Jérôme Schlomoff, that he had not had lunch yet. They were soon sitting in a room adjacent to where the camera and lights were set up, eating the pastries and getting acquainted. Schlomoff had been gaining recognition in the Paris gallery scene for his portraits of artists. The previous year, for example, he had photographed Keith Haring. After seeing Haring's portrait, Basquiat had agreed to have a session with Schlomoff while in Paris.

After their snack, Schlomoff and Basquiat made their way back to the photo shoot area. While leading the way, Schlomoff suddenly realized that he had lost sight of Basquiat. Looking around, he noticed that Basquiat had returned to retrieve the book he had brought along—*The Subterraneans*, by Jack Kerouac, a leading light of the Beat Generation. When Basquiat caught up with Schlomoff, he pointed at the book and said he would like to be photographed with it. Although Schlomoff typically did not photograph people with objects, he agreed, wanting to preserve the convivial atmosphere that had developed over the éclairs. However, he asked Basquiat why it was so important. Basquiat then revealed the significance behind his request, telling him, "It's my Bible. I'm constantly reading this book. When I'm finished with it, I start reading it again. I sometimes open it randomly and just read from that point on. It's a very important book for me." The physical object, with well-thumbed pages, the cover cracked and scratched, had clearly been read countless times.

The novel chronicles a tumultuous love affair between an alcoholic white man in his thirties and a younger woman of mixed Native American and African American heritage. The story is set in the vibrant jazz scene of San Francisco in the early 1950s. The characters and their friends are fragile and self-absorbed. Like Kerouac's more famous work, *On the Road*, Basquiat's favorite book was written in a stream-of-consciousness style, with unstructured and unpunctuated descriptions of emotions and experiences. Understanding the nonlinear narrative, conveyed through fragmented conversations and memories spanning time, requires intense concentration.

Basquiat went on to share with Schlomoff his disillusionment with the art world, including galleries, collectors, and the press, saying that the pressure had become overwhelming. "I want to stop painting and become a writer," he confided. However, his New York friends had been skeptical when he had shared these plans, insisting that he was a natural-born painter, not a writer, and doubting his ability to author a book. Undeterred, Basquiat looked Schlomoff in the eye and declared that he would teach himself: "I will learn to write just like I learned to draw and paint." He also revealed that he hoped to move to Los Angeles, in search of a quieter life, where he could concentrate exclusively on writing.

As they walked to the temporary photo studio, Schlomoff agreed to take two portraits, the first one without the book. While Basquiat settled in front of the camera, they continued chatting, and the conversation moved on to Andy Warhol. But after a few moments, Basquiat quietly asked if they could stop speaking about him, saying, "It's just too painful for me to remember our time together."

To lighten the mood, Schlomoff suggested that Basquiat do something with his hands. Basquiat soon had one hand shielding an eye, which drew attention not only to the arresting gaze in his other eye but also to the jewelry he was wearing. Around his neck hung a bolo tie, typically associated with Texas or the American Southwest. But instead of a turquoise centerpiece, it featured a sculpted face of a Black boxer with a boxing glove poised to strike him. Sensing the metaphorical significance and feeling the magic in the air, Schlomoff took the shot.

For the next portrait, Basquiat held the Kerouac book below his chin, concealing his necklace from view. However, the expression in this pose was sterner and more determined than in the previous one. In his own enigmatic way, Basquiat was sharing what he intended to do in the next stage of his career.

After the photo session, Schlomoff returned to his studio to develop the film. A few days later, he delivered the portraits to the gallery so they could be given to Basquiat. Several weeks later, he received word that Basquiat was thrilled with how he had been portrayed in the photographs. These portraits became some of the last taken of Basquiat before his untimely death six months later.

Jean-Michel Basquiat, February 1988.
Credit © Jérôme Schlomoff, 1988

Jean-Michel Basquiat, February 1988.

Credit © Jérôme Schlomoff, 1988

BASQUIAT WAS DISAPPOINTED and frustrated with his standing in the art world. One issue that particularly gnawed at him was that his paintings sold for far less than works by other prominent Neo-Expressionist artists. Among his contemporaries, the American Neo-Expressionist Julian Schnabel stood out. Nine years senior to Basquiat, Schnabel loved working on unconventional surfaces, such as wooden boards adorned with shards of broken pottery, upon which he painted a range of subjects, from abstract imagery to portraits of his friends. Schnabel's best broken-pottery paintings were selling for around $800,000, while Basquiat's best works fetched only $30,000. Another leading American Neo-Expressionist, David Salle, saw his best artworks sell for around $250,000. The Italian Neo-Expressionists—Sandro Chia, Francesco Clemente, and Enzo Cucchi—were also commanding astonishingly high prices.[4]

Basquiat was frustrated that his own works were selling for a mere fraction—approximately 10 percent—of the prices achieved by his Neo-Expressionist peers. Moreover, as news of Basquiat's troubled state spread within the art world, some collectors who owned his pieces began to worry. If Basquiat was an artist in decline, maybe it was best to sell his works now rather than holding on to them for the long haul. This unease was evident in the number of Basquiat's artworks appearing at auction, particularly from 1986 onward. In comparison to artists like Julian Schnabel and David Salle, three times as many of Basquiat's artworks were being put up for sale.

Basquiat was keenly aware of his market position, frequently discussing it with figures like Bruno Bischofberger, Mary Boone, and Perry Rubenstein. While he was still a very expensive artist relative to most young practitioners at the time, the pricing disparities and surge in auction sales fueled his belief that the art world was conspiring against him. His grievances about pricing contributed to his decision to sever ties with the Mary Boone Gallery in New York. Seeking new representation, Basquiat leaned on Bischofberger to help secure an Uptown gallery. Galerie Lelong, a respected establishment on West Fifty-Seventh Street, agreed to show his work. Basquiat signed an agreement with Bischofberger and the gallery, entitling him to a monthly stipend in advance of sales from exhibitions. However, Basquiat supplied the gallery with only two pieces.

Vrej Baghoomian represented Basquiat in 1988 before he died.

Ignoring the agreement, Basquiat instead chose to work with the Vrej Baghoomian Gallery. Baghoomian was a rough, money guy, who had recently opened his gallery just north of SoHo. He had learned the art trade as a bookkeeper at the gallery run by Tony Shafrazi, who was his cousin. He also had a background providing cash to hard-up galleries and artists, using their art as collateral. After shows in top galleries around the world, Basquiat was now being represented by a minor player. It was a steep fall in status and a sign of just how lost he had become. Baghoomian enticed Basquiat to work with him by offering substantial up-front payments, rather than monthly installments, which allowed Basquiat to continue his extravagant spending and sustain his costly drug habits without inhibition.[5]

Basquiat struggled to create works for his debut exhibition at the Baghoomian gallery.[6] His close friend Glenn O'Brien recalled the selection for the show, writing, "It was painted in a few days after weeks of him being unable to paint and threatening to cancel. He felt like he had to put up or shut up and give in to what he thought was being whispered behind his back."[7] Despite the challenges, Basquiat managed to pull off quite a feat, as the show included some of the best pieces he had produced in the previous two years.

Following the opening night preview, Baghoomian hosted a dinner at a nearby restaurant for Basquiat's friends and family, as well as top prospects who might buy something from the show. Gerard Basquiat attended the event, as did David Bowes, one of Jean-Michel's early friends.

Bowes and Basquiat did not have a chance to talk during the opening or at dinner, as they were seated apart from each other at a long table. Once dessert and coffee were served, Bowes excused himself and went to the bathroom. Basquiat noticed that he had left the room and followed him so they could have a private conversation.

"He was feeling very vulnerable and looked very fragile," remembered Bowes. "I'd also been heavily involved with drugs and knew how terrible it can make you feel. I spent time trying to encourage him by telling him how brilliant the show was and how despite how he felt then, he's going to be able to pull himself together." It was an important moment for the two of them. "I had been as much into drugs as he was," Bowes acknowledged. "We used to do all sorts of things together. But at the time, he knew that I was clean. I wanted to give him the confidence that he too could get himself straightened out."

As they conversed, the bathroom door slammed open. Gerard stood in the doorway as if he was expecting to uncover some illicit activity. "It was a really strange way to meet him," Bowes recalled, "and from what I understand of his character, it was a perfect way. Jean and I just stood there, mid-sentence, mouths half open. Gerard looked at me and gruffly said, 'What? I can't talk to my son if I want to?' And I said of course he could." Jean-Michel then introduced David to Gerard.

Bowes returned to the dining room, leaving Jean-Michel with his father. "When I think about that moment, it breaks my heart,"

Bowes said. "We were talking about something important, about Jean-Michel getting straightened out. There wasn't another occasion after that night for me to speak with him. Whoever was with him on the day he died, they were not his friends. They left him there to die."

Among the notable works in the Baghoomian show was *Riding with Death*. Inspired by a drawing by Leonardo da Vinci, Basquiat depicted a life-sized, emaciated Black man struggling to ride the skeletal remains of a horse against an otherwise unadorned background.[8] It was a stark and haunting image that would prove disturbingly prophetic.

After the show closed, Basquiat traveled to Hawaii in yet another attempt to detox and rejuvenate himself. When away, he often sent letters to his mother, updating her on his activities and plans. From Hawaii, he wrote saying he would return to New York in August before embarking on a roots trip to Africa with friends.[9]

Stories of severe drug addictions rarely have happy endings. An unending night soon enveloped Jean-Michel. On August 12, 1988, the twenty-seven-year-old artist died of a heroin overdose at his Great Jones loft, following a night of partying after his return from Hawaii. For his friends and colleagues in the art world, his death was tragic but not entirely unexpected. Keith Haring, a close friend, told a reporter shortly after his death that "the last few years his friends were really scared for him. He was really playing with death, pushing it to the extreme. But there was no point in telling him. He knew what he was doing. He knew what the risks were. He had friends that died. His friends could only hope that it wasn't going to happen. But it was not a surprise to anyone when he died."[10]

A closed-casket funeral for family members and close friends was held on August 17 at the Frank E. Campbell Funeral Chapel on Manhattan's Upper East Side. Basquiat was then buried at Green-Wood Cemetery in Brooklyn. On November 5, a memorial service was held at Saint Peter's Church in Manhattan.

Jean-Michel Basquiat's gravesite in Green-Wood Cemetery.

Parents hope they never have to bury their children. Gerard and Matilde were left to endure the immense grief of losing their son. Like many parents who lose a child to addiction, feelings of guilt, anger, and regret likely haunted them for months, if not for the rest of their lives.

AFTER BASQUIAT'S DEATH, critics endeavored to look beyond his notoriety and evaluate his artistic legacy. The two most passionate and unflinching portraits of the artist landed in opposite corners.

Greg Tate, who had joined *The Village Voice* as a staff writer the year prior to Basquiat's death, initially focused on covering the Black music scene. However, he soon branched out to cover all aspects of Black culture. One of his earliest cover stories was a eulogy titled "Flyboy in the Buttermilk: The Crisis of the Black Artist in White America"; the title on the newspaper's front page was accompanied by a Basquiat painting of a menacing skull.[11]

In Tate's eyes, Basquiat was an exceptional talent worthy of admiration. He loved the cacophony of words and images the artist used, as well as the poetic connections that could sometimes be found between them. He noted Basquiat's myriad influences, from Black folk art and cartoons to American consumer culture. But what resonated deeply with Tate was that Basquiat's art was unmistakably and fervently centered around the Black male experience in America, encompassing both mundane and heroic aspects, as well as ugly chapters in the nation's racist history. For Tate, "if you're Black and historically informed there's no way you can look at Basquiat's work and not get beat up by his obsession with the Black male body's history as property, pulverized meat, and popular entertainment." Basquiat's choice of subject matter held intensely personal significance for Tate.

The verve with which Basquiat pursued being a star also mightily impressed Tate. He wrote, "No area of modern intellectual life has been more resistant to recognizing and authorizing people of color

Greg Tate wrote a particularly heartfelt obituary for Basquiat that appeared in The Village Voice.

than the world of the 'serious' visual arts. To this day it remains a bastion of white supremacy." Tate believed that Basquiat's genius extended beyond his artistic prowess to encompass his keen skills at playing the game of politics and patronage in the art world, all the while steadfastly preserving his identity. In doing so, Basquiat became a bona fide celebrity in the art world and perhaps "the most financially successful Black visual artist in history."[12]

On the opposing side was Robert Hughes, the chief art critic for *Time* magazine and a regular contributor to *The New York Review of Books*, *The New Republic*, and other publications. Millions of people became acquainted with modern art through his influential eight-part documentary series for the BBC and PBS, titled *The Shock of the New*, which extolled the virtues of modern art from the Impressionists onward. The accompanying book became an international bestseller.[13]

Hughes's assessment of Basquiat came in a *New Republic* article titled "Requiem for a Featherweight: The Sad Story of an Artist's Success."[14] Hughes was familiar with Basquiat's work, having encountered it in the *New York/New Wave* show. He had a favorable opinion of it, yet he viewed the then-twenty-year-old Basquiat as an unformed talent who, to advance his career, needed to acquire genuine drawing abilities. Drawing on his reading of modern art history, Hughes argued the best twentieth-century artists possessed hard-earned drawing and painting skills, including leading Abstract Expressionists like Willem de Kooning and Philip Guston. It was this foundational knowledge that enabled them to rebel and create groundbreaking art that shocked the establishment. For Hughes, it was difficult to regard Basquiat as a serious painter of the Black male experience if he could not sketch a nude figure or make a reasonable landscape painting.

Hughes also questioned the foundation of Basquiat's commercial success. He criticized what he perceived as a "cluster of toxic vulgarities," attributing the artist's popularity, in part, to the utilization of a racist marketing trope. According to Hughes, Basquiat's supporters propagated "the racist idea of the black as naif or as rhythmic innocent, and to the idea of the black artist as 'instinctual,' outside 'mainstream' culture, and therefore not to be judged by it: a wild pet for the recently cultivated white." Despite Basquiat's early promise, Hughes believed he never developed into a painter of substantial quality. He thought the artist was "a small, untrained talent caught in the buzz saw of artworld promotion, absurdly overrated by dealers, collectors, and, no doubt to their future embarrassment, by critics."

AT THE TIME OF HIS DEATH, the prevailing view about Basquiat tended to align more with Hughes than with Tate. With his fifteen minutes of fame over, Basquiat risked being remembered as a fascinating footnote in the glamorous and decadent art world of the 1980s, rather than as a lasting cultural star.

STOP

CHAPTER 6

POSTHUMOUS MAELSTROM (1988–1989)

NEWS OF BASQUIAT'S DEATH SPREAD QUICKLY. After hearing about it from a friend, Paige Powell immediately called Gerard Basquiat, whom she found devastated and stunned. While she was trying to console him, Gerard pleaded for her assistance, saying, "I need your help, I need your help. People have been going in and out of his place all day, taking artwork and removing other stuff from his house. I need your help." Powell urged him to get a locksmith over to secure the Great Jones loft, and Gerard then asked her to help him find a lawyer familiar with the art world who could assist him.

Powell was soon sharing Gerard's revelations about the looting of Jean-Michel's loft and his pressing need for legal representation

The entrance to Green-Wood Cemetery in Brooklyn where Basquiat is buried.

with her friends Francesco Clemente and his wife, Alba. Francesco happened to know of a lawyer, Michael Stout, who worked with Salvador Dalí and the photographer Robert Mapplethorpe. Perhaps he could be of assistance? After discussing the matter with Stout, Powell introduced him to Gerard, who promptly decided to retain him.

Managing the affairs of a deceased person can be an emotionally wrenching and complex legal process for those left behind. Basquiat's young age, chaotic life, and unique mix of inheritable assets made the task especially challenging. While Basquiat's family and friends grappled with their grief, Stout and his team began the arduous task of discovering what Basquiat owned and owed.

Stout quickly secured the Great Jones loft, which appeared as though it had been ravaged by a storm. While his team set about organizing the physical chaos within the apartment, Stout focused on identifying Basquiat's financial assets and liabilities. He discovered a checking account at a nearby Citibank branch with a balance of $32,957.[1] Although Basquiat preferred cash, only $2,121 was found in his loft, likely due to much of it being stolen during the frenzy after his death. Stout also found that Basquiat was due to receive a few additional payments from Bruno Bischofberger and another gallery for *Collaboration* paintings that Basquiat had sold them earlier in the year.[2] But aside from these assets, Basquiat had no investment accounts, real estate holdings, or notable valuables such as cars, jewelry, or furniture.

What he did own was art. While some of it was stored in the Great Jones loft, Stout and his team made an important discovery amid the scattered papers and documents: unpaid invoices from two art-storage facilities. After a few phone calls, they made their way to these facilities with the checks needed to bring the accounts up to date and the required documentation to demonstrate their authority to inspect Basquiat's property. No one knew what to expect when the storage units were opened.[3]

Behind the doors was a treasure trove of artworks that Basquiat had stashed away. When the items from the storage facilities and the Great Jones loft were finally cataloged, the numbers were staggering. Basquiat had kept more than one thousand pieces of his own artwork, consisting of 171 paintings and 917 drawings.[4] To put that in perspective, he made around one thousand paintings and two thousand drawings during his brief career. Basquiat's Estate now owned nearly 20 percent of his paintings and approximately half of his drawings. These artworks would give his father great power to control and influence his son's legacy. With time, they would also generate unimaginable wealth for Basquiat's two sisters.

The treasure trove extended beyond Basquiat's own work. He had twenty special pieces by Andy Warhol, received as gifts from his mentor or obtained through art exchanges. Additionally, there were two enormous *Collaboration* paintings, along with works by a handful of other artists.[5]

Basquiat exhibited canny forethought in sequestering a substantial portion of his artistic output, including early work.[6] In his other affairs, however, planning for the future was not on his mind. He passed away without leaving a will or any indications of his wishes. Fortunately, New York State law defines what must happen in these situations to prevent prolonged disputes among surviving family members. In the absence of a will, if an individual without a spouse or children passes away and has surviving parents, their estate is automatically divided equally between them.

Gerard and Matilde, who remained estranged, would share equally in Jean-Michel's Estate once the legal settlement process was completed through the New York State court system. Every estate requires an executor, someone responsible for marshaling assets, settling debts, and distributing what is left to beneficiaries in a timely manner. Matilde agreed to have Gerard appointed as the executor.[7]

Jean-Michel left his father with one more significant task: He had never filed income tax returns during his lifetime, despite earning a substantial living as an artist. While he might have believed he could evade the issue, the Estate could not ignore it, as the Internal Revenue Service would likely audit the unusual Basquiat Estate tax return. Failure to address the matter could have severe consequences for the assets Gerard and Matilde were set to inherit. Gerard now faced the daunting challenge of reconstructing Jean-Michel's earnings. He would then need to pay all outstanding income taxes, including penalties. Furthermore, substantial estate taxes were due within nine months of Jean-Michel's death. Taken together, the Estate faced looming tax payments that could amount to hundreds of thousands or even millions of dollars. However, there was only $32,957 in readily available cash to sustain the Estate. Gerard, still grieving the loss of his son, faced an imminent liquidity crisis. It was the art-world equivalent of being house rich, yet dangerously cash poor.

GERARD NEEDED TO SELL ASSETS to address his liquidity crisis, but which ones? Rather than touching the extensive collection of works by his son, he instead elected to offer works by other artists in a sale at Christie's. This marked the beginning of his decades-long effort to retain as many pieces as possible by Jean-Michel, allowing him to maintain greater control over his son's legacy. Among the pieces he decided to sell were the works by Andy Warhol, except for two paintings he wanted to keep private due to their controversial subject matter, as well as portraits Warhol had made of Gerard, Matilde, and one of Jean-Michel's sisters.[8]

One Warhol work that troubled Gerard depicted Jean-Michel with dreadlocks; he is looking directly at the viewer, but his face is covered with greenish blotches. What makes this painting so provocative? It is one of Warhol's *Oxidation* paintings. The greenish blotches resulted from urine being poured on a canvas that had been primed with metallic paint and a silk-screened image of Basquiat's face. Basquiat received this painting as part of the portrait-exchange deal organized by Bruno Bischofberger in 1982. Yet AIDS was ravaging the New York creative community around the time of Basquiat's death. Rumors passed that Basquiat might have succumbed to the disease, given his dreadful physical condition at the time. Gerard likely wanted to keep private anything that could possibly imply his son's association with this stigmatized illness.

The other work of concern was a life-sized double portrait of a nearly nude Basquiat wearing only a modest jockstrap. Warhol took the photo used in this painting early in his relationship with Basquiat. He later created a few jockstrap paintings and gave one to Jean-Michel. Gerard was probably concerned that the homoerotic nature of the portrait, if marketed and promoted in a public auction, would lend credence to the persistent speculation that Warhol and Basquiat had had an intimate relationship at some point. Gerard chose to keep this towering painting, which stood nearly seven and a half feet tall, in storage.[9]

The proceeds from the sale of the artworks were intended to assist Gerard in addressing his pressing liquidity issues. Yet his plans were thrown into disarray the day before the scheduled auction in February 1989. Unexpectedly, a lawyer contacted Christie's, claiming that his client was the true and rightful owner of all the works consigned for sale. The lawyer would later reveal that his client was Kelle Inman, Basquiat's last girlfriend. Inman had been out clubbing with Basquiat the night before his fatal drug overdose and had discovered his lifeless body the following morning.

The day of the auction was filled with drama. When Christie's requested credible evidence supporting Inman's brazen claim of ownership, her lawyer failed to provide it. Christie's then informed him that the sale would proceed as planned that afternoon. In response,

Inman's attorney filed a request for a restraining order to halt the sale. Moments before the auction was set to begin, the court denied Inman's application. However, the judge ruled in her favor on one crucial point: The Estate was not permitted to receive any proceeds from the sale until the ownership dispute had been fully litigated.[10]

Despite the successful sale, particularly of the Warhol pieces, Gerard was unable to access the almost $400,000 generated from it.[11] These funds would have greatly alleviated his financial difficulties. It would take months of costly legal battles before the court threw out Inman's spurious claim that she had a verbal contract with Jean-Michel entitling her to many of the works from the Estate. Unfortunately, her lawsuit was only the beginning of a series of legal disputes that would plague the Estate.

IN HIS QUEST TO RAISE FUNDS, Gerard turned his attention to finding a gallery that could selectively sell artworks from the Estate. Although several of Basquiat's previous dealers, including Bruno Bischofberger, vied for the opportunity, Gerard decided to forge a new path and selected the Robert Miller Gallery.

Located in a prime Midtown location where blue-chip galleries congregated, the Robert Miller Gallery represented an impressive roster of well-known artists, including Louise Bourgeois, Joan Mitchell, and Diane Arbus. Robert Miller was a noted obsessive focused on making sure everything was done at the highest level. The gallery space was pristine, with impeccably maintained white pickled floors that were meticulously sanded, stained, and polished every summer when the gallery was closed. Artworks were expertly lit and displayed. The gallery had a large staff to attend to clients and handle the needs of the artists they represented.

Beyond the gallery, Miller and his wife enjoyed a splendid two-story apartment on East End Avenue, which they used for hosting gallery-related social events. The grand residence was filled with beautiful furnishings and wonderful art. Following exhibition openings, they would host lavish buffet dinner parties frequented by celebrity clients such as Calvin Klein, John McEnroe, and Richard Gere.

John Cheim, a senior director at the gallery, vividly remembers the moment when Miller received an unexpected call from Gerard, who wanted to discuss gallery representation.[12] Whispering to Cheim, Miller shared the news: "It's Gerard Basquiat, asking if we're interested in showing Jean-Michel's work." Familiar with the artist and his work, Cheim quickly jumped up and down and emphatically whispered, "Yes, yes, yes." Gerard emphasized that he wanted a complete break from the whole Downtown milieu. "He did not want Jean-Michel's legacy to be associated with Keith Haring, graffiti art, or what he perceived to be Downtown decadence," Cheim recalled. "He wanted a bit of Uptown elegance to help separate his son from his past excesses." In May 1989, the gallery sent out thousands of notices to clients and the press, announcing its representation of the Basquiat Estate.

Upon learning the news, a furious Vrej Baghoomian, who had represented Basquiat before he died, filed a $40 million lawsuit against Gerard and the Robert Miller Gallery. He claimed exclusive rights to sell all the Basquiat works owned by the Estate, citing a verbal agreement he had with Jean-Michel before his passing. Furthermore, Baghoomian demanded a 50 percent commission on these sales. In response, the Estate denied Baghoomian's claims and filed a countersuit. Among other accusations, the Estate alleged that Baghoomian had fraudulently taken at least twenty paintings by Basquiat that rightfully belonged to the Estate. This was an existential moment for Gerard. If he lost, he would lose control of the Estate. For Baghoomian, it would be a career-making money gusher.

Baghoomian soon upped the ante when he sought a court order to restrain the Robert Miller Gallery from selling any artworks owned by the Estate while the case was being litigated. The court granted his request, which tied Gerard's hands. Baghoomian then went even further, requesting that the court remove Gerard as the executor of the Estate, accusing him of obstructing Baghoomian's property rights. Although the court rejected this request, it demonstrated the extreme measures Baghoomian was willing to take in the hopes of either winning his lawsuit or badgering Gerard into a settlement.

The sale restrictions imposed by the court applied to the Estate and the Robert Miller Gallery, but not to Baghoomian himself. He proceeded with a posthumous exhibition of Basquiat's work in October 1989, accompanied by a lavish catalog featuring essays and full-page illustrations of the artworks. He was determined to prevail as Basquiat's dealer.

By the end of 1989, the Estate was in desperate need of cash to cover its expenses. Gerard was forced to petition the court to borrow $500,000 against the Estate's assets, to ensure that there would be funds to meet the ongoing financial obligations, including the substantial legal fees the Estate was incurring to fight the Baghoomian lawsuits.[13] Additionally, Gerard took a leave of absence from his accounting job to focus on the Estate's challenges, telling a reporter, "People took advantage of Jean Michel. He was very young and had a loose lifestyle, and the minute he died all these people came up with groundless claims. Aside from the tremendous expense, the litigation is an emotional burden and very time-consuming."[14]

ESTATE TAX RETURNS OFTEN REVEAL hidden truths, and the document Gerard submitted to the IRS on May 11, 1989, is no exception. It provides fascinating insights into Jean-Michel Basquiat's lifestyle and the wealth his parents inherited.

Basquiat had a penchant for extravagant spending, channeling nearly all his earnings into supporting his lavish lifestyle. He traveled constantly, staying in the best hotels and resorts. For extended periods, he maintained a room at the Ritz-Carlton in New York as a sanctuary from his Great Jones loft. Known for his generosity, he often gave friends cash or gifts. His drug habits also consumed a significant portion of his finances.

But just how much money was he spending each year? Gerard's advisors had the task of piecing together Basquiat's earnings as part of the estate tax return. They reached out to his galleries to obtain sales records and meticulously reconstructed his business expenses, including costs for assistants and studio space.[15] Based on this analysis, the Estate had to pay nearly half a million dollars in delinquent federal, state, and local income taxes, covering the period from 1985 until Basquiat's death in 1988.[16] Although his exact earnings were not reported in the estate tax return, it is possible to reverse engineer them using prevailing tax rates at the time.

Rough calculations suggest that Basquiat was making around $250,000 annually, which is equivalent to $600,000 in today's dollars.[17] Since he did not save money in investment accounts, purchase real estate, or pay taxes, all his earnings were devoted to supporting his extravagant lifestyle.

Given the significant art collection inherited by Gerard and Matilde, determining its exact worth was a challenging task. Unlike publicly traded stocks with transparent prices, artwork values are more subjective. To establish the fair market value for estate tax purposes, Christie's was engaged to appraise all the art in the Estate.[18]

Christie's examined each painting, drawing, and notebook, assigning a monetary value to each piece. These estimates aimed to reflect the likely selling price of the artworks shortly before Basquiat's death. Christie's valued all the Basquiat artworks in the Estate at $3.2 million, which is the equivalent to approximately $7.5 million in today's dollars. This valuation underscored how Gerard and Matilde were now the joint owners of a valuable artistic legacy that, with time, would grow tremendously in value.

The bulk of this value resided in the 171 paintings they inherited. Prior to Jean-Michel's passing, strong Basquiat paintings had fetched prices ranging from $20,000 to $30,000 at auction. Works from the next tier down in quality sold in the range of $10,000 to $20,000, while smaller and less compelling works went for under $10,000. Using these quality indicators, the Estate had twenty-nine works in the top category, eighty-seven in the second tier, with fifty-five in the lower category. These figures show that Basquiat preserved many of his important works, rather than solely keeping unsellable or unfinished items from the final years of his life.

No one likes paying estate taxes, also known disparagingly as "death taxes." To mitigate the tax burden, Gerard chose to aggressively discount the value of the art using what is called a "blockage discount" strategy. When an artist passes away, their estate can use an arcane yet very important valuation tool related to supply and demand. The concept can be understood through a hypothetical example: If luxury brand Hermès attempted to sell ten thousand Birkin handbags per month instead of the usual controlled offering of one thousand bags, the market price would plummet due to oversupply.[19]

The same principles apply to artworks. If the Basquiat Estate flooded the market with all the paintings and drawings simultaneously, prices would crash due to the surplus of available pieces. Applying this logic, the individual valuations provided by Christie's overstated the value of the objects, as the appraisers assumed a "normal" market scenario. Executors of artists' estates often claim a blockage discount to estimate the reduction in value if they were compelled to sell the objects all at once.

While Christie's appraised the Basquiat artworks at $3.2 million, it also supported a 70 percent blockage discount factor in a side letter. Gerard reported the $3.2 million figure to the IRS but then reduced it by $2.3 million to account for this discount factor. This adjustment trimmed the Estate's tax bill by approximately $1 million. Being an experienced and astute businessman, Gerard likely figured, "Nothing ventured, nothing gained." It was now up to the IRS to evaluate the reasonableness of his claim.

BASQUIAT JOINED A LEGENDARY GROUP of young creatives whose lives were tragically cut short due to their struggles with addiction. Prominent names include John Belushi (who died when he was thirty-three years old), Kurt Cobain (twenty-seven), Janis Joplin (twenty-seven), Jimi Hendrix (twenty-seven), Jim Morrison (twenty-seven), Amy Winehouse (twenty-seven), and Basquiat's frequent subject, Charlie Parker (thirty-four).

Following Basquiat's death, demand for his artwork skyrocketed as more people than ever before sought to own a piece of his legacy. Speculative capital also entered the market, with investors hoping to profit by buying his works and selling them for a higher price a short while later. This surge in demand caused prices to soar, with his paintings and drawings trading at around ten times their pre-death values. For instance, a painting called *Air Power*, which depicted a standing figure on a colorful background, had sold at Christie's for $29,700 in 1987, just a year before Basquiat's passing. Yet approximately a year after Basquiat died, the same painting sold for $319,000.

The euphoria for work by Basquiat meant that the pieces owned by his parents, which Christie's had valued at $3.2 million, were now worth in the vicinity of $30 million. The IRS was now likely to view Gerard's blockage discount claims with more skepticism. Furthermore, Vrej Baghoomian grew more determined in his lawsuits, as a favorable judgment could yield him $15 million, representing his 50 percent sales commission based on the current value of the Estate's property. These complex and vexing issues would continue to loom over Gerard for years to come.

CHAPTER 7

MORE FAMOUS THAN RESPECTED (1990–1996)

WHEN INTEREST IN BASQUIAT'S WORK SOARED AFTER HE DIED, Vincent van Gogh, everybody's favorite artist-as-tortured-genius, was experiencing his own marketplace moment. He had created two portraits of Paul Gachet, the doctor who had treated him for depression in the months leading up to his death. One portrait was in the Musée d'Orsay, in Paris, while the other, considered the stronger of the two, came up for sale at Christie's on May 15, 1990.

Ryoei Saito, the CEO of a Japanese paper-manufacturing conglomerate and a passionate collector, purchased it for $82.5 million,

Maya Angelou around the time of Basquiat's death, 1988. In 1993, a children's book combining her poetry with Basquiat's painting was published.

making it the most expensive painting ever sold at auction. Soon after, Saito told his friends that he wanted to be cremated with his new treasure when he died, so that his children could avoid paying estate taxes on it. Fortunately, when he passed away, a few years later, his family ignored his wishes, deeming them part of his mordant sense of humor.[1]

Shortly after this record-breaking sale, the world economy swooned, dragging the markets for Van Gogh and Basquiat down with it. After years of impressive growth, the US economy tumbled into recession. Given the art market's heavy dependence on American buyers, this alone would have prompted a market correction. But the decline was further intensified by the popping of property and stock market bubbles in Japan. Throughout much of the late 1980s, Japanese buyers, including Saito, had been hoovering up art using cheap capital borrowed against their inflated domestic assets. This abruptly ended when falling stock and land prices in Japan forced them to retrench.

The early 1990s were a dismal time for the art market. Auction prices plummeted for many well-known artists, and works by young artists went unsold. Galleries downsized or went bankrupt as their best clients exited the field of play. This was particularly true for buyers who had entered the market in the 1980s with the belief that art was a sexy new asset class for making quick profits. As they realized their collections were now worth less than what they had paid for them, many withdrew from the market and never returned. The carnage was unprecedented. In 1991, art market sales tumbled by nearly 65 percent relative to the previous year. The recovery would be slow and painful.[2]

For many artists, the market never fully recovered from this rout. The work of Pierre-Auguste Renoir, known for his depictions of voluptuous women, well-dressed children, and beautiful landscapes, was highly valued by Japanese speculators, who drove his prices to dizzying heights. As his prices soared, many serious collectors of

Impressionism succumbed to the hype. Instead of approaching the rapid price surge with caution, they viewed it as validation to spend even more to acquire Renoir's works.

The false allure of rising Renoir prices tripped up Hermann and Else Schnabel, collectors based in Hamburg, Germany. In May 1988, they spent $8.8 million to acquire a Renoir painting of his girlfriend nursing their young son. The Schnabel family held on to the artwork for the next thirty-two years. But when they sold the painting at Christie's in December 2020, it fetched only $2.4 million, nearly 73 percent less than its original purchase price. While the couple and their heirs may have enjoyed living with it, an expensive artist falling out of favor can be a harsh reality of another order.

The market for Basquiat experienced similar effects. *Air Power*, a painting from 1984, exemplifies the sharp repricing that affected his market. During the posthumous surge in his prices, it sold for $319,000 at Christie's in November 1989. Yet six years later, during the art market's downturn, it went for just $120,144, a decline of approximately 60 percent. Lower-quality works by Basquiat faced even harsher treatment, selling for around 20 percent of their pre-crash prices.

While interest in art declined during this period, Basquiat's downturn was exacerbated by concerns about his legacy. Many collectors viewed him pejoratively as a market-driven artist. Instead of following the more traditional trajectory of early recognition at an important gallery, strong institutional support, and then gradual price increase, Basquiat's path seemed reversed. He gained fame partly through his association with Andy Warhol and then, tragically, through his death, which led to a surge in prices. Yet many collectors were confused about his real significance. One collector, active at the time, felt there was a "commercial taint to Basquiat's marketplace that was a turnoff to many of us. It seemed to be more about money than art. All the hype about him made it hard to see why he should be respected as an artist."

A further complication was that most institutions were similarly skeptical and kept their distance. Reflecting on those days, a director of a major institution confided, "Many museums didn't want to support Basquiat's work because they were concerned about becoming part of a hype machine that could fizzle out over time." Furthermore, "I don't think being Black helped his case, either. His drug use was certainly a negative. Museums at the time were also not interested in showing or collecting what many considered to be street art."

Diminished collector interest in Basquiat's work, combined with limited institutional support, resulted in significantly lower sales. In 1989, a boom year, auction sales totaled $9.9 million. Yet in 1991, they amounted to less than $800,000.[3] "One of the reasons we didn't push his work into sales," remembered Anthony Grant, the head of the Post-War and Contemporary department at Sotheby's at the time, "was that there were no real buyers out there except for Jose Mugrabi, Peter Brant, and Enrico Navarra. They became very, very committed to Basquiat's work when others wanted little to do with it."

WHEN AN ARTIST'S WORK PLUMMETS in value, interest rarely returns to previous levels. You cannot unburn the toast. Those who invested in their work feel disappointed and move on to other artists. Galleries dedicate fewer shows to them, auction houses avoid featuring them in their sales, and the critics who once praised them try to change the subject. Once begun, it is hard to reverse a downward spiral in the art world.

In Basquiat's case, however, Mugrabi, Brant, and Navarra chose to defy this well-established pattern and instead doubled down. Over the course of the 1990s, they bought hundreds of works by him, preventing his prices from plummeting further. They also played a critical role in promoting his work, which led to increased awareness and respect for it. All three possessed big personalities and large appetites for risk-taking, along with enthusiastic belief in the artist. In times of trouble, they were the essential catalysts that shot Basquiat to prominence. Without their influence, his journey to becoming one of the most significant artists of the twentieth century would have been delayed, if it occurred at all.

Jose Mugrabi, who would come to own the largest collection of works by Basquiat in the world, grew up in Jerusalem in the 1940s. The eldest of seven children, he worked in the family's grocery store. While Israel has since become an economic powerhouse, during that time, it was a struggling country where making a living was challenging for many. When he was sixteen, he left for Bogotá, Colombia, to work for an uncle who owned a textile business. Naturally inquisitive and possessing a keen business sense, in his early twenties he ventured out on his own as a cloth merchant, buying and selling fabric. During the next two decades, he met and married the love of his life, had two sons, and built a substantial business.

By the early 1980s, Colombia had descended into a narco-state where gun violence and for-hire kidnappings were commonplace. Tired of living with the constant physical threat, in 1982 Jose moved his family to the United States. After a brief period in Miami, they settled in New York City, where they still reside today.

Art did not play a role in Jose's life before he moved to New York. "I never lived with art and knew nothing about it," he told me.[4] "My knowledge of it was below zero." But with wealth and empty walls to fill, he began buying art through an art advisory unit established by Citibank in its private banking division. "I relied on Jeffrey Deitch, the manager of the group," Mugrabi recalled, "to suggest what I should buy." His first purchase was a Renoir landscape painting for $121,000 in 1982. He went on to acquire more works by traditional European artists, including Auguste Rodin, Alfred Sisley, and Honoré Daumier. "I bought simply what I liked," he said, "based purely on emotion."

Jose Mugrabi and his wife, Mary.

Five years after buying his first painting, Mugrabi had an epiphany that altered the trajectory of his art collecting and his life. He veered away from his more conservative tastes and began buying works by Andy Warhol and other contemporary artists in bulk. His Warhol epiphany occurred during his first visit to an art fair in Basel, Switzerland, in June 1987. While strolling through the fair with a friend, he was captivated by four colorful paintings displayed side by side. His friend told him they were by Andy Warhol, who had died earlier that year. Mugrabi immediately bought all four pieces for around $150,000; they were part of a series Warhol had created using an image of Leonardo da Vinci's *Last Supper* mural.

At the fair, Mugrabi met Bruno Bischofberger, who, learning of his Warhol acquisition, invited him to come to his Zurich gallery when the fair was over. Mugrabi made the trip and ended up buying nearly fifty works by Warhol, including several featuring Marilyn Monroe. "I reacted very emotionally to the works," he recalled. "Bruno was also a very good talker who helped me understand that Warhol, who was painting American culture, was the most important artist of his generation."

Within a year of buying these works, Mugrabi organized an exhibition featuring many of them at a gallery on Madison Avenue. A Japanese buyer approached him and offered to purchase the entire show for a substantial premium relative to what Jose spent. Once the deal was finalized, Mugrabi felt he was on to something very important about buying, exhibiting, and selling valuable artworks. He soon devoted most of his time to buying art, especially works by Andy Warhol. A few months later, he paid a record-breaking price of $3.96 million at Sotheby's for a Warhol painting featuring twenty images of Marilyn Monroe on a vivid orange background.[5] It had everything one could possibly want in a great Warhol painting: scale, color, and repetitions of Monroe's iconic face. Today, the painting would likely fetch over $100 million.

Mugrabi also fell in love with Basquiat. He bought a few works before the artist died. But his obsession with Basquiat truly intensified when he acquired twenty paintings from Bruno Bischofberger in November 1989: "I felt the power. I felt something very emotional about his work. Jean-Michel is completely different from Impressionism, which is about beauty. If you buy a Renoir, you look at the pretty figure or landscape." But for Mugrabi, Basquiat "was just painted emotion. All his urges, ideas, and fears are right there for you to see. He was kind of like Van Gogh."

Three months after buying his first batch of Basquiat works, Mugrabi returned for more. In January 1990, he purchased an additional seventeen pieces from Bischofberger. Mugrabi now owned more than forty works by the artist. At the time, only Gerard and Matilde Basquiat, along with Bruno Bischofberger, owned more.

The art market's downturn, which began in earnest in 1991, dealt a severe blow to Mugrabi. Many of the artworks he had been fervently buying dropped substantially in value. This harsh reckoning was made worse when his art-buying business partner, Sammy Ofer, an Israeli shipping magnate, accused him of being rash and reckless. Starting in the late 1980s, the two of them had teamed up to buy works by artists such as Andy Warhol, Jackson Pollock, and Pablo Picasso. The second set of Basquiat paintings Mugrabi had bought from Bruno were jointly owned by the two of them. Their disagreement eventually led to a protracted arbitration proceeding in London, resulting in the forced sale of numerous artworks and the dissolution of their friendship.

"It was a disaster," Mugrabi lamented. "We were selling Basquiat paintings that we once bought for $200,000 for $40,000 or less." Nevertheless, he remained a steadfast believer in the long-term potential of owning Basquiat's work. When the jointly owned pieces were sold, he repurchased most of them using his own funds. These were in addition to even more Basquiat works he was buying at the time.

While an ardent Basquiat enthusiast, Mugrabi was also mindful of market conditions. He wanted quality at reasonable prices. In the early 1990s, Gerard Basquiat visited his home to discuss selling him works from the Estate. Accompanying Gerard was Jeffrey Deitch, who had left his position at Citibank to establish his own art advisory business. However, no deals were made, as the Estate still valued the works at pre–market crash prices. "It was an odd meeting," Mugrabi recalled. "They showed me some works, but their prices were five times the market. There were a lot of other great pieces available at the time with much better pricing, so it didn't make sense to buy things from them."

Over the course of the 1990s, Mugrabi honed his business model as a collector and private art dealer, operating on a scale few have achieved. He bought Warhol, Basquiat, and a few other artists in great depth because he believed they were undervalued, with significant long-term potential. Yet he did not have a gallery or a large staff; nor did he represent these artists. He operated out of an unassuming office in midtown Manhattan, alongside his two sons, David and Alberto, and his longtime assistant, Esty Neuman. Artworks were stored in two facilities, one in Switzerland, and the other outside New York City.

From time to time, Mugrabi would trade in and out of the markets for the artists he owned to generate income. For example, he might consign a work to an auction house or arrange for a group of pieces to be displayed in a gallery exhibition. Simultaneously, he purchased additional works, perhaps from a seller in need of quick cash. Through these actions, Mugrabi became the primary source of liquidity in the Warhol and Basquiat markets. This position provided him with keen insights into who owned which works and their willingness to sell now or in the future. He also learned about what people were looking to acquire and their price sensitivity.

To enhance awareness and interest in Basquiat, Mugrabi also created packaged exhibitions featuring works from his collection, which he loaned to small and midsized museums. For instance, in 1999 the KunstHausWien, in Vienna, hosted an exhibition of Basquiat works from the Mugrabi collection. "I do a lot based on my emotions, but there is also a system," he explained. "I must like the artist a great deal. I also need at least one hundred paintings in storage. Because to push and to create all this, you need a machine, you need an inventory."

Mugrabi relentlessly promoted Basquiat using this business model. His involvement in the market has been extraordinary—as of the end of October 2024, he either currently owns or has owned 453 pieces by Basquiat, representing approximately 30 percent of the available Basquiat market.[6]

While Mugrabi was confident in buying in bulk, Peter Brant, another significant Basquiat collector, employed a different strategy. "I was buying with emotion," Mugrabi recalled. "But Peter Brant, who was the *maestro grande*, was buying with his head. He selected each work with a microscope, always looking for the best."

Peter Brant grew up in a cultured, affluent family in Queens, New York. His parents immigrated to the United States from Bulgaria before the outbreak of World War II. His father co-founded a pulp and paper business, which soon provided the family with great luxuries. "I became interested in art because my father collected late-eighteenth-century French paintings and some English pieces," remembered Brant.[7] While Peter was growing up, father and son took regular skiing trips to Switzerland.

During one trip while he was in high school, Brant met Bruno Bischofberger, who had recently opened his gallery in Zurich. The two quickly became friends, bonding over a shared interest in art. At the time, Brant's tastes tilted toward Old Masters and Impressionism, yet Bischofberger opened his mind up to contemporary art: "It was Bruno who told me that the greatest artists of our day were living in New York and that I should forget about Impressionism and buy what is new." Brant heeded Bischofberger's advice, and this set him on a path to becoming one of the most passionate and successful contemporary art collectors of the past fifty years.

When Brant was twenty years old, Bischofberger introduced him to Leo Castelli, the great gallerist, who represented many important contemporary artists. In 1968, after Brant had bought multiple works from Castelli, including several paintings by Andy Warhol, he introduced Brant to Warhol. "I was one of his clients that liked Andy's work the most," Brant recalled, "so Leo thought I should know him." This introduction marked the beginning of a twenty-year friendship that involved Brant investing in Warhol's *Interview* magazine (alongside Bruno Bischofberger), providing financing for three of Warhol's films, and amassing an exceptional collection of Warhol's work. The collection even includes a portrait of Peter Brant's father, Murray Brant, which Peter commissioned in 1975.

By the early 1980s, Brant was involved in running his family's paper business and was living in Greenwich, Connecticut, with his wife and children. In addition to Warhol, he acquired major pieces by artists like Jasper Johns, Claes Oldenburg, and Carl Andre. "Peter is a real connoisseur with a very, very, very high taste level," remembered one auction house specialist who knew him well. "In addition to knowing a great deal about modern and contemporary art, here's a man who understands English silver, eighteenth-century wallpaper, Art Deco furniture, and many other categories. He is obsessive, perhaps the most obsessive collector I know."

Brant first encountered Basquiat's art in a London gallery during a trip in 1983. However, it took another year before Brant began buying his work. Over the course of several dinners with Andy Warhol and the young artist, Brant developed a deeper appreciation for Basquiat. Brant recalled, "Andy adored Jean-Michel, and . . . he was never one to really talk about other artists, other than always saying nice things about all artists. But he was really passionate about Jean-Michel's work, and this was before they started doing their *Collaboration* paintings."

The first Basquiat painting Brant bought was from Bruno Bischofberger, followed by additional purchases from various other sources. "I was buying what I thought were the best works," he said. By the time Basquiat died, Brant owned close to ten major pieces. Loving Basquiat's work and believing that he was one of the most important artists of the twentieth century, he continued buying after the artist died. For example, when Annina Nosei had a memorial exhibition of Basquiat's work in November 1988, Brant bought *Per Capita*, an almost seven-by-thirteen-foot painting.

Peter Brant and his wife, Stephanie Seymour.

During the art market's downturn, Brant did not waver, and continued buying Basquiat's work. "From 1990 to about 1995," he recalled, "I bought maybe six or seven Basquiat works a year. It was a terrific time to buy because so many people with great works were looking to sell and move on."[8]

Unlike Jose Mugrabi, Brant did not purchase artworks with the intention of selling them. "That's not me," he said. "What I do is collect an artist's work in depth. As I need the funding to continue to buy, to support this disease that I have, that only poverty will cure, I've sold certain things. Every time I've sold a Basquiat painting, I always felt like crying. I take it as a defeat, not as a victory."

Collectors with the means and desire to buy expensive contemporary art knew of Brant's connoisseur's eye and exacting standards. Brant's belief in Basquiat's artistic prowess served to validate the artist's significance for many potential buyers. When visitors saw great Basquiat works displayed in Brant's sprawling Greenwich, Connecticut, home or large SoHo apartment during parties and events, what they may have once ignored became something to covet. With time, these interactions would help cultivate the next cluster of Basquiat collectors.

Enrico Navarra's path to becoming a champion of Basquiat's work was indeed unconventional. Born in Paris in 1953 shortly after his parents immigrated from Naples, Italy, he was raised chiefly by his father, a tailor, because his mother passed away when he was just three years old. School was not Navarra's thing, despite his keen intelligence. He dropped out of high school and left home when he was sixteen. He banged around for a while, making money as a card player. He was also willing to do any job for the right amount of money, which led him, from time to time, to engage in thuggish behavior. Since he was a strapping six-footer with a commanding presence, most people would want to avoid being in a fight with him.

Around the age of twenty, Navarra transitioned into the legitimate commercial world and became a traveling salesman. His early sales experiences involved selling cash-counting machines and rugs. A few years later, after managing a club at a ski resort, he ventured into brokering fine art prints by artists like Marc Chagall and Salvador Dalí. Discovering an opportunity, he bought unsold prints at deep discounts from French publishing houses and then resold them to galleries and bookshops in Paris, New York, and Tokyo at marked-up prices. He was good at it, which eventually led to a friendship with Ida Chagall, Marc Chagall's daughter and the executor of his Estate. Through this relationship, he progressed from selling prints to selling higher-value paintings and drawings. With Ida Chagall's encouragement, Navarra established his namesake gallery in 1987 in a fashionable part of Paris, across the street from the Bristol Hotel.

Navarra was generous and impulsive. "He'd meet someone and, feeling a connection with them, would say, 'Let's organize a show,'" said Géraldine Pfeffer-Lévy, who worked closely with Enrico Navarra for many years.[9] "Everything was possible with Enrico. The sky was the limit. He was a tremendous amount of fun to work with, because we ended up doing things around the world, like taking a Chagall exhibition to Moscow and China with special catalogs for both shows." Navarra's charisma and his flair for bringing people together at dinners and events he hosted in his homes and gallery enabled him to build an enviable network of relationships with collectors, dealers, and museum professionals from around the world.

Navarra frequently traveled to New York to see what was in demand and to source works for his gallery exhibitions. Although he never met Basquiat, he was aware of his work and went to many of the same clubs Basquiat frequented. He was only seven years older than Basquiat, and they both reveled in the city's nightlife. Before Basquiat died, Navarra bought three of his works, intending to feature them in a future group show.[10]

Following Basquiat's death, one of Navarra's mentors, Jean-Louis Prat, encouraged him to embrace Basquiat as a great artist and organize an exhibition devoted to him. Prat, known for his role as the director of the Maeght Foundation, which housed a remarkable col-

Enrico Navarra.

lection of twentieth-century masterpieces by artists such as Alberto Giacometti, Joan Miró, and Alexander Calder, possessed a discerning eye for art.[11]

Inspired by his mentor, Navarra bought an additional fourteen Basquiat works and organized an exhibition that debuted in late 1989. As was his custom, he produced a beautiful illustrated catalog for the show. He loved making coffee-table-worthy books for his exhibitions, since they served as powerful reminders to potential buyers of an artist's significance. Rather than selling the books, Navarra gave them away as part of his client-development strategy, preferring this approach over investing in booths at art fairs in the hopes of meeting new prospects.

After the show closed, Enrico got an unexpected call from Gerard Basquiat, whom he did not know. Their common language was French, which Gerard knew from growing up in Haiti. Gerard told

Navarra that he needed to pay the Estate licensing fees for having used artwork images in his exhibition catalog. This was new territory for Navarra, as he was used to working with the Chagall Estate and with living artists where this issue had not arisen before. Alert to building new relationships, Navarra suggested that they meet during his next trip to New York to resolve the matter.

Speaking with his lawyers, Navarra learned that the Basquiat Estate owned the rights to images for every Basquiat artwork, even pieces the Estate did not own. Copyright laws, which govern the use of these images, give the owner exclusive control over whether and how these images can be used. While there were a few exceptions to these rules, such as allowing the press to freely use images in articles, the Basquiat Estate had the power to grant or deny permission and set fees for their use by a commercial enterprise like the Galerie Enrico Navarra.

Navarra came to his meeting with Gerard with a clever idea. Instead of paying for the images he had already used, Navarra proposed creating a much larger book that would encompass approximately two hundred paintings. Navarra would pay a small portion of the licensing fees up front, with the remaining balance due when the book was published. At the time, there were no books that comprehensively showcased Basquiat's work. While galleries had created numerous exhibition catalogs during his lifetime, these were hard to find and focused solely on the works featured in those specific exhibitions. Enrico's ambitious idea resonated with Gerard, who agreed to his proposal. Neither of them understood at the time the profound impact this book would have on the Basquiat market.

Enrico and his team began collecting images and information for the book, which involved reaching out to all the galleries that showed Basquiat's work. With forty-six solo exhibitions and numerous group shows during his lifetime, it was an enormous undertaking.[12] During Enrico's trips to New York, he would share drafts of the book with Jose Mugrabi and Peter Brant, seeking their input. Géraldine Pfeffer-Lévy, who accompanied Enrico on many of these trips, remembered that "each time we'd go to New York, he'd show Jose and Peter the layout of the book and say, 'Look at this masterpiece, look at this one, look at this great piece.' They'd sit there for hours together poring over drafts of the book."

Meanwhile, Gerard established the Authentication Committee of the Estate of Jean-Michel Basquiat. Designed to assess whether artworks were in fact made by his son, the committee was composed of gallerists and curators familiar with Basquiat's work, including Diego Cortez, Annina Nosei, and John Cheim. The committee played a vital role in identifying and filtering out the fake Basquiat artworks that had started to infiltrate the market. Enrico relied on Gerard and the committee's expertise to determine which works would be included in the book.[13]

While the book was being created, Enrico began buying Basquiat in depth. But with limited financial resources compared to Jose Mugrabi and Peter Brant, he relied on partnerships and debt to acquire them. "I traveled a lot with Enrico when he was buying all the Basquiats," remembered Sebastien Moreu, who worked with him.[14] "Enrico always wanted to involve other dealers and professional collectors in the market. He bought a lot, but he also encouraged other dealers to take, perhaps, a thirty percent share of a painting. He didn't want to keep all the cake for himself." When Enrico was unable to buy something, perhaps because he was short of cash, he would try to convince someone else to buy it. "Enrico believed it was important to build a network of people who believed in the artist and who would remain involved in it for the long haul," Moreu said. "He felt that the work would have to be bought and sold frequently if Basquiat's market was to become stronger."

One person who joined forces with Enrico was Lio Malca, a distant relative of Jose Mugrabi's. After Basquiat's market tumbled in the early 1990s, Malca bought a few pieces. "I remember sitting in Enrico's gallery shortly after I met him," recalled Malca.[15] "I was so happy to find somebody else who believed in the artist and who was putting his balls in the game." Navarra told Malca about his discussions with two galleries in Tokyo that had works by Basquiat they wanted to sell. "We need to buy them," Navarra told Malca, explaining that he was purchasing paintings by sending an up-front deposit, with the balance due later. Liking the idea, Malca joined in. "The pieces we bought were maybe $50,000; the most expensive was probably $120,000. We were sending $10,000 or $20,000 as deposits. There were so many pieces on the market that sellers were happy to accept our payment terms."

Needing more funds to support their acquisitions, Navarra and Malca soon learned of an art-financing company in New York that lent money to people who could use fine art as collateral. After meeting with the company, they had the fuel they were looking for. "We were really good at buying works for great prices," Malca said. "Suppose we bought a painting for $100,000. The art-finance company would do their own appraisal and come back valuing the piece at maybe $140,000. They'd give fifty percent of it as a loan, so we'd get $70,000 and use it to buy more pieces. Boom, bam, boom, bam, boom." While the loans were expensive, costing sometimes 15 percent a year, they gave Navarra and Malca the financial resources they needed.

After working on the book project for nearly five years, in 1996 Navarra released something extraordinary. Rather than the two-hundred-page catalog he had first proposed, he had created a lavishly illustrated, slipcase-covered, two-volume publication that showcased more than 850 works in its final form. Weighing in at twelve pounds, the brawny catalog included around 80 percent of the artist's paintings.[16] It was a beautiful, seductive object that helped create desire for Basquiat in the minds of many collectors.

As was his practice, Navarra gave the book away rather than selling it. The launch party for it coincided with the opening of Navarra's second Basquiat exhibition, in November 1996. It included many of the great works he had bought over the previous five years, including *Untitled (Fallen Angel)*, *Baby Boom*, and *Untitled (The Devil).* Gerard and Nora Fitzpatrick, came to the exhibition, as did about two thousand people during the run of the show.

Getting the catalog into the hands of the right people around the world became Navarra's next obsession. He sent multiple copies to dealers, collectors, and auction house specialists, so that they could keep one for themselves and give the others to those who could help expand interest in Basquiat. Sotheby's and Christie's started giving the publication away at dinners they hosted for top clients. It was also distributed at high-quality events taking place at art fairs like Art Basel and exhibitions like the Venice Biennale.

The first edition of the book included around 550 works. Over the next six months, the catalog was enlarged, adding close to two hundred additional works. The third edition, released in November 1996, added more than one hundred works. In 2013, the gallery released a supplement to the third edition containing seventy-three additional works, along with annotated notes and corrections to some of the object information used in previous editions. In addition to the English-language catalogs, Navarra also printed editions in French and Italian. Across all editions and languages, the Galerie Enrico Navarra estimates that twenty-five thousand copies of the book were printed and given away. A near catalogue raisonné of this sophistication had never before been created not to be sold.

Every Basquiat collector, as well as those who hoped to be one, soon had a copy of the catalog. They used it to pinpoint works they loved, perhaps with the hope of acquiring one. Or when offered a work, they could now easily compare it with other pieces. Prior to the catalog's publication, there had been a significant gap in the art world's understanding of the quantity and quality of Basquiat's paintings. This lack of knowledge created hesitancy among potential buyers, as they struggled to gauge the scarcity and volume of his work.

The elegant Navarra catalog solved this problem, and that soon helped put a spring back into the step of the Basquiat marketplace.[17]

BEING EXHIBITED AND COLLECTED by top museums is an important marker of success. The Whitney Museum of American Art, a respected institution then located on Manhattan's Upper East Side, began work on a Basquiat retrospective in the early 1990s. The show had the potential to elevate Basquiat's status from that of a mere "famous for being famous" figure to a respected artist recognized for his creative achievements.

Richard Marshall, a Whitney curator, spearheaded the show, but securing approval to proceed was no easy task. John Cheim, a director at the Robert Miller Gallery, who collaborated with Marshall on the show, said, "He encountered considerable resistance from the museum due to persistent doubts about Basquiat's significance." The Whitney had a complicated relationship with the artist. Although one of his paintings was included in the 1983 Whitney Biennial, the museum hesitated the following year to accept *Hollywood Africans*, one of Basquiat's notable works, into its collection. Doug Cramer, a Los Angeles–based TV producer and museum trustee known for shows like *The Love Boat* and *Dynasty*, offered to donate the painting. However, museums often decline art donations when they question an artist's enduring relevance. Marshall, confiding in Cheim, expressed frustration over the struggle that had ensued before the painting was eventually accepted. "Cramer was on the board and gave the museum a lot of money, yet there was so much resistance to accepting it," Cheim learned from Marshall. "It became, 'Okay, we'll let him give us that stupid Basquiat painting.'"

Gerard Basquiat harbored his own grievances with museums. "He was angry and contemptuous of people in the art world who did not take Jean-Michel seriously until he died," Cheim recalled. Museums ranked high on his list of targets. "When Herb and Lenore Schorr"—important early Basquiat collectors—"offered major paintings to museums after Jean-Michel's death, they were unceremoniously rejected. It was a stinging rebuke that Gerard never forgot."

Despite these challenges, Richard Marshall was able to prevail. His retrospective debuted in October 1992 with three prominent sponsors: Madonna, an early Basquiat girlfriend; MTV, which had risen to prominence since its launch in August 1981; and AT&T, which sought to diversify its foundation's visual arts program and engage with a broader audience.[18] The large show featured nearly 125 works, with the majority created between 1981 and 1983.

In a surprising turn of events, the Metropolitan Museum of Art decided to showcase two Basquiat works concurrently with the Whitney retrospective. Lowery Stokes Sims, a curator at the Met specializing in twentieth-century art and one of institution's few curators of color, borrowed two mural-sized paintings from the Estate. These works had once adorned the walls of the Palladium, an East Village nightclub.[19] The Palladium, established in 1985 by Steve Rubell and Ian Schrager, the masterminds behind the Studio 54 discotheque, had commissioned Basquiat, Keith Haring, and other artists to embellish the vast club space.[20]

One of the two works displayed at the Met was a forty-foot-long canvas featuring a vibrant red background with the heads and bodies of Black men. It had previously been in the Mike Todd Room, an opulent VIP bar filled with mirrors and candelabras. The Met Museum, known for its august halls, acquired a touch of disco flair when the two murals found their place in galleries dedicated to modern and contemporary art.[21] In a gesture of gratitude to Sims, Gerard donated two Basquiat drawings to the Met, marking the first and—to the best of my knowledge—only time Gerard made such a contribution to a museum.

The Whitney retrospective garnered generally positive reviews. Roberta Smith, a newly appointed art beat reporter for *The New York*

Times, began her review with a veiled criticism, stating, "Jean-Michel Basquiat's art may deserve a more thoughtful retrospective than the one that opens today at the Whitney Museum of American Art. But this aggressive, jam-packed survey . . . will give everyone plenty to think about."

Smith then succinctly captured the crux of the matter: "While alive he was variously viewed as a genius, an opportunist, an untrained primitive or idiot savant, and because of his blackness was once called the exotic and exploited mascot of a mostly white downtown art world. After his death, many saw Basquiat as a victim of his own success; his rapid ascent and early demise in the 80's became emblematic of everything that was wrong and dangerous in that overheated decade, with its seeming overnight successes and waiting lists for unproduced works and rocketing art prices." But in the final analysis, she believed that Basquiat's work was worthy of our attention, because "there is something gripping, real, and original about his art."[22]

The Whitney exhibition marked a significant milestone in the transformation of Basquiat's reputation. Yet other important institutions in major cities, such as Los Angeles, Washington, Chicago, Atlanta, and San Francisco, as well as museums in Europe, declined to host the show.[23] The lack of significant follow-on venues exemplified the prevailing ambivalence among museum directors and curators regarding Basquiat's significance. The Whitney exhibition also failed to exert any noticeable influence on his prices, which continued to decline after the show concluded in New York in early 1993.

AS THE ART WORLD MEANDERED through the Whitney retrospective, a slightly more rebellious effort took shape, aimed at bringing Basquiat into the homes of individuals who would not typically set foot in an art museum. The ingenious tool of subversion came in the form of a children's book. Its impetus was rooted in the bellicose proclamations of a conservative US senator known for his uncompromising disposition.

In 1989, Jesse Helms, a Republican senator from North Carolina, launched a campaign denouncing the National Endowment for the Arts for promoting art he deemed offensive. His vehement critiques of artists like Robert Mapplethorpe, Andres Serrano, and Karen Finley swiftly dominated headlines and ignited a fierce public debate about artistic freedom and the government's role in supporting the arts. Feeling pressured by the debate, the Corcoran Gallery of Art, in Washington, DC, made the controversial decision to cancel a Robert Mapplethorpe retrospective just three weeks before its scheduled opening. Controversy followed the show when it proceeded, as scheduled, to Cincinnati, Ohio, where the museum and its director were criminally indicted for displaying allegedly obscene works. While the museum eventually prevailed, the subsequent obscenity trial in September 1990 emerged as a pivotal moment in America's culture wars.

Appalled by these events, Sara Jane Boyers, a music industry lawyer, art collector, and mother of two based in Los Angeles, sought a course of action. "One morning, I woke up and thought, I want to create a children's book. I believed that through this medium, I could not only introduce children and their families to the marvels of contemporary art and artists but also subtly and politically influence them to appreciate and embrace the arts," she explained.[24] Boyers identified Basquiat as the artist to highlight in her book. "I was very familiar with his work and felt he was a perfect fit because his paintings were so expressive and layered with potential meanings."

Boyers then set her mind on finding a poem that could work in dialogue with Basquiat's art to spark meaningful conversations when the book was read to children. She came upon, in *And Still I Rise*, a collection of Maya Angelou's poetry, "Life Doesn't Frighten Me," a concise yet evocative poem. At the time, Maya Angelou was widely recognized, with a wealth of books, awards, and screenplays to her credit. In contrast, Basquiat's recognition had yet to extend significantly beyond the confines of the contemporary art world.

Armed with her concept, Boyers set about bringing the book to life. Using photocopies of Basquiat's works sourced from auction catalogs and art magazines, she fashioned a mock-up of it. During a visit to New York, she pitched the idea to the Robert Miller Gallery. "They liked the mock-up," she recalled, "and then put me in touch with Gerard Basquiat. At the end of my meeting with him, he agreed to let me use the images." Next, she acquired the rights to the Angelou poem.[25] With all the key pieces in place, Boyers and her agent then began marketing the book to various publishers, eventually securing a publishing deal.

When the book was released, in the fall of 1993, it was an immediate hit. *Publishers Weekly* noted:

> Boyers . . . deserves a standing ovation for her performance in pairing Angelou's poem with abstract paintings by the late Basquiat. "Dragons breathing flame / On my counterpane / That doesn't frighten me at all. / I go boo / Make them shoo / I make fun / Way they run / I won't cry / So they fly"—had it been teamed with representational or whimsical illustrations, the verse might well have lost its dignity; instead, the proximity of Basquiat's edgy, streetwise pictures adds even greater power and authenticity to Angelou's refrain, "Life doesn't frighten me at all."

And *School Library Journal* wrote,

> The art provides a jolting counterpoint to the optimistic words, reflecting a dark, intense vision. Violent splashes of color bleed and drip one into another, and white letters are scratched into black backgrounds. Stark figures with grotesque features face off against one another. Symbols such as arrows, birds, crowns, and letters emphasize the artist's anger and sense of irony. The choice of the paintings, taken as they were from an extant body of work, give levels of meanings to a poem already strong with images of its own. A powerful exploration of emotion and its expression through the careful blend of works and art.

"The book sold like mad the first year and continued to sell well year after year," said Boyers. A significant factor contributing to its success was the newfound fame of Maya Angelou. While Boyers was working on the book, Angelou was invited to compose and recite a poem at Bill Clinton's first inauguration, on January 20, 1993. Her captivating delivery brought her to the attention of the millions worldwide who watched the event. By the time Boyer's book was released, later that year, Angelou had become a well-known celebrity with broad appeal.

Initially launched as a children's book, *Life Doesn't Frighten Me* quickly transcended its intended audience and crossed over into other categories. "People began giving it to friends diagnosed with cancer or feeling depressed, to help them through their challenges," Boyers related. Since its debut, several hundred thousand copies of the book have been sold, and it remains in print to this day.

A notable feature of the book was its cover illustration: a Basquiat painting featuring a *Tyrannosaurus rex* topped with a crown.[26] This clever marketing tactic tapped into children's fascination with dinosaurs. Curators, however, have never had the same admiration for this painting, titled *Pez Dispenser*. It was not included in the Whitney retrospective and has been absent from many of Basquiat's subsequent retrospectives. Nevertheless, thanks in part to Boyers's book, it has become a beloved artwork among legions of Basquiat fans worldwide. Their fandom has made it one of the most widely reproduced works, regularly licensed by companies for use on T-shirts, shoes, and other merchandise. Boyers's efforts make for a wonderful tale of how a poem and a children's book cover helped propel an image into the public consciousness.

BY THE MIDDLE OF THE 1990s, after a tremendous amount of hard work, Gerard Basquiat finally secured complete control of his son's Estate. Vrej Baghoomian's attempt to snatch it away from him had ended in defeat when, in late 1991, the judge presiding over Baghoomian's lawsuit had dismissed his claims as being without merit. Shortly thereafter, he skipped town, leaving behind his artists, employees, and creditors.

Gerard's victory over Baghoomian was made even sweeter when, in May 1992, he won a copyright-infringement lawsuit against him for the unauthorized use of artwork images in the lavish catalog he had created for his posthumous Basquiat show. Unlike Enrico Navarra, who was able to charm his way out of a similar problem, Baghoomian was out of luck: Gerard was in no mood to give his nemesis a pass. The court ordered Baghoomian, who remained missing, to pay the Estate $209,000 in penalties—equal to approximately $450,000 in current dollars.[27]

Baghoomian resurfaced in New York a few years later to open another gallery, but he soon found himself embroiled in a dispute with a Paris gallery regarding the sale of three potentially fake Basquiat works. The taint surrounding Baghoomian grew larger still when his cousin Tony Shafrazi filed a lawsuit accusing him of selling him a fake Basquiat and refusing to refund his money.[28] While Baghoomian professed his innocence against these and other allegations, an air of disreputability clung to him. He shuttered his gallery and departed both New York and the art world.

Fighting Baghoomian was not Gerard's only significant battle in the early 1990s. Three years after filing his son's estate tax return, he received an unwelcome certified letter from the IRS. In the original tax filing, Gerard had claimed a 70 percent discount—previously mentioned as the "blockage discount factor"—on the value of all the Basquiat paintings and drawings owned by the Estate. This significantly reduced the Estate's value for tax purposes and lowered the tax bill. However, the IRS informed Gerard in the letter that it was disallowing blockage discounts of any kind, among other adjustments. The agency presented Gerard with two options: Pay an additional $1 million in taxes within ninety days or file a petition with the US Tax Court to challenge the IRS's new assessment. Gerard opted for the latter.

Shortly before the case was slated to go to trial, the parties agreed to a settlement. Rather than completely disallowing a blockage discount, the IRS permitted the Estate to reduce the value of the paintings and drawings by 40 percent. The Estate was now required to pay only $81,685 in additional taxes, a significant reduction from the initial $1 million demand. It was a huge victory. Gerard's tenacity had paid off.

Yet victories like this are not free. Buried in the settlement agreement were the legal fees the Estate incurred defending itself against the IRS, Vrej Baghoomian, and other litigants, which totaled $769,321, or about $1.5 million in today's dollars. It was a substantial sum and a reminder that pursuing justice in such matters is neither cheap nor fast.

By the middle of the 1990s, after spending close to seven years managing his son's Estate, Gerard, trained as an accountant, was now well schooled in the inner workings of the art world. The more he learned, the more resolute he became in wanting to keep as much of Jean-Michel's work as possible. "He really didn't want to sell very much," remembered John Cheim. "He would sell one painting here and there to support the Estate, maybe some drawings. He wasn't greedy at all. He didn't want to make a gazillion dollars. He just wanted his lifestyle and to support his son's legacy and sell enough to keep that going." Knowing that Peter Brant, Jose Mugrabi, and Enrico Navarra were active buyers who believed in Basquiat's long-term potential likely reinforced in Gerard his conviction to retain his son's work for the long haul.

With little urgency or inclination to sell, particularly now that the financial burdens of the Vrej Baghoomian and IRS lawsuits were behind him, Gerard decided to leave the Robert Miller Gallery and operate independently. If he needed to sell something, he could consign it to whichever gallery or auction house offered the best terms at the time. If someone at a gallery or museum wanted to organize a show of his son's work, they could negotiate directly with him to license images of the artworks for their catalog. He was also able to keep his pulse on the market through the operations of the Basquiat Authentication Committee. After a tremendous amount of hard work, Gerard was now firmly in control of his son's legacy.

CHAPTER 8

CREATIVE EMBRACE (1996–2000)

BASQUIAT WAS A COOL DENIZEN OF THE DOWNTOWN SCENE, BUT THE collectors who bought his work during his lifetime were surprisingly square. Business leaders, doctors, and lawyers adorned their walls with the art of this hip young Black man. Yet, as stories of Basquiat's creative but tragically short life circulated in the 1990s, his personal narrative became an important attraction point for new buyers. His irreverent attitudes, counterculture behaviors, and unwavering refusal to conform resonated with boundary-pushing creatives—especially rock stars. These celebrated tastemakers, who were far more

Debbie Harry and Basquiat dancing at the opening party for William Burroughs's exhibition of his paintings at the Tony Shafrazi Gallery, December 1987.

famous than the well-heeled but relatively anonymous collectors who had initially purchased his work, shone a spotlight on Basquiat's achievements, which contributed to his growing fame.

The first, and perhaps most significant, union between Basquiat and rock and roll occurred when U2, the Irish rock band, bought a significant Basquiat painting in the early 1990s. The mastermind behind the purchase was Adam Clayton, the bass guitarist, who had co-founded the band with fellow teenagers Bono (lead vocals and rhythm guitar), Edge (lead guitar and keyboards), and Larry Mullen (drums) in 1976. Their rise to stardom was swift: Within four years, they had released their debut album, *Boy* (1980). By their fifth album, *The Joshua Tree* (1987), they had become stadium-filling superstars, captivating audiences with anthems like "I Still Haven't Found What I'm Looking For." At the turn of the decade, U2 was one of the most iconic bands in the world.

Reflecting on that period, Adam Clayton described how a rare pause in U2's relentless schedule allowed him to step outside the band's insular world and explore new creative horizons.

> I'd been in this amazing U2 bubble for ten years. It was just head down: work, work, work. But I didn't know anything about anything. I was like, just a guy who got into a band when I was seventeen or eighteen. We worked through to *The Joshua Tree* with album tour after album tour. We then rolled into an album called *Achtung Baby* that we'd soon take out on tour. Yet I saw in the calendar that there was a six-month period when I could do whatever I wanted to do. I wanted to go somewhere where I'd be stimulated and excited. I decided to move to New York City.[1]

With the freedom to choose any destination in the world, Clayton opted for New York over Tokyo, Rio, or Berlin, where the Wall had recently come down. "I was obsessed with New York," he said, "because all the great music that we had been influenced by came out of the city: the CBGBs kind of punk scene, Patti Smith, Television, Blondie, the Talking Heads, Iggy Pop, Richard Hell and the Voidoids. All of that happened in New York." Despite his numerous visits to New York for performances, Clayton never quite felt at ease or truly connected to the city. The band would drop in for a few days, do some shows, and then blow through a whirlwind of crazy people, zany places, and late nights. While this was fun, the city beyond the clubs was foreign to him. "I decided I'm going to stare down this unease," he recalled. "I'm going to move to New York and try to understand the place. I'm not going to let that crazy energy unhinge me." He was soon getting up early, walking around the town, and seeing the city in a different light. His time in New York would prove to be the beginning of a journey to understand, embrace, and surround himself with contemporary art, something that continues to occupy him to this day.

Guiding Clayton through his exploration of New York's art scene was Catherine Owens, an Irish artist friend who lived in the city. Owens, later responsible for much of the design work for U2's spectacular stadium shows, introduced Clayton to galleries and artists' studios. "It was an exciting time," Clayton recalled, "because the graffiti artists were having an impact. They were my age at the time, in their late twenties and early thirties. I realized these were my people, in terms of their expressions and what they were trying to say."

Owens brought Clayton to see works by Basquiat. "Her selling point," Clayton said, "was that he was our age and the Jimi Hendrix of painting. He went to clubs all the time and painted in Comme des Garçons suits. His work also had an incredible energy that you didn't see in artists who developed later in their lives." Although Clayton had some prior knowledge of Basquiat, he did not know much about his work or his personal narrative. "We were in Area and other clubs when we were in town for our shows, so Jean-Michel was likely there," Clayton acknowledged. "But we weren't particularly focused then on contemporary art. We were instead interested in this new musical form of hip-hop, Fab 5 Freddy, graffiti artists, and Keith Haring. We didn't brush up against Jean-Michel in quite that way."

Clayton and Owens were soon spending time at the Robert Miller Gallery, looking at works by Basquiat and other artists handled by the gallery. As Clayton saw more and more pieces by Basquiat, he grew convinced of how special he was. "With Jean-Michel's work, there was always the music, there was always the street, there was always the journey out of Africa and into America as slaves and this confusion, trying to find, to kind of determine, an identity. Maybe as a foreigner, I could see more clearly the dilemma in America between the races."

While he loved art, and had the financial resources to acquire it, Clayton was not an impulse buyer. He took his time, carefully examining and discussing Basquiat's works, not only at the Robert Miller Gallery but also at the Tony Shafrazi Gallery. During this process, he learned what to look for in great pieces: a crown; something from early in Basquiat's career; a head or masklike motif; and some kind of language or words. And then, of course, colors and brushstrokes that conveyed a kinetic energy.

When Robert Miller presented Clayton with *Untitled (Pecho/Oreja)*, he immediately knew he'd found what he'd been looking for. A masklike face, with piercing eyes and an X-ray–inspired jawline, stares out at the viewer. Scrawled text, scattered marks, and a three-point crown surround the figure. Everything has been rendered quickly, with uninhibited spontaneity, as you would expect from an early work made when the artist was only twenty-two years old. There is no calm in this commanding six-foot-square piece—just syncopated improvisation that would appeal to a musician like Clayton.

Buying the painting was not a slam dunk. The art world can be a confusing, off-putting place where value is hard to determine. Clayton struggled with it: "Coming from the creative world myself, I would look at a work and think, 'How is this worth the numbers that are being attributed to it?' I absolutely loved Basquiat's imagery, the punk rockiness and challenge of it. But I was a little taken aback by the numbers for someone who was still a relatively unknown artist." Instead of splurging alone, Clayton decided to see if his bandmates would go in on the work with him.

Adam Clayton, the U2 bassist.

"It was really quite odd," remembered Clayton. "Everyone knew I was in New York living a different kind of life and immersing myself in the art world. I think there were fax machines back then, so I probably sent them some images. I remember saying on the call, 'I know this is going to sound mad, but I really think this artist is going to be very significant. He's going to grow in stature. I've selected a painting and I think it would be a great thing for all of us to own it. I don't think we will regret it.' I think the band kind of looked at each other, and went, 'Well, what do we know? We don't know anything about this, but we trust our guy. And if our guy is saying this is something we should be a part of, then yeah, we're in.' It was very courageous of Larry, Edge, and Bono."

Clayton explained, "It was just that first blush of what it was like for us to be in the world. We were all wondering what sort of world we were in at that stage. We'd been so caught up for ten years in the day-to-day demands of being a rock-and-roll band and touring the world." Their decision to acquire the Basquiat painting was driven by instinct, not academic knowledge. "When somebody put a Basquiat under my nose back then and said, 'Andy Warhol and this guy are going to own this century,' that was not something that was immediately obvious to

U2 in Tangier, Morocco, around the time they bought the Basquiat painting, 1991.

me or to the rest of the band. They responded emotionally to the work as being young, punk, and pure energy. And God, maybe it'll do well, maybe not. But at least it's not a piece of seventeenth-century religious art. They saw it for what it was."

The painting was shipped to Dublin, where it was given pride of place in the band's recording studio. But this was not just a space where they worked on songs from time to time. It was their headquarters. "It was where we spent the greater part of our week and the greater part of our lives," Clayton said. Given their fame, record label executives, business leaders, and creatives in the fields of music, fashion, and art made their way to visit the band in the studio. The Basquiat painting hung in a large dining space where meetings took place. It was the heart of the studio, where people naturally gravitated. The work was visible to everyone who came there. "We realized," Clayton remarked, "the people visiting us would be the type to really understand and take interest in the work."

For the Basquiat Estate and the Robert Miller Gallery, this was priceless placement. It heightened awareness of Basquiat among the thousands of people who visited the studio over time, many of whom had the means to acquire a work themselves. The band's stamp of approval helped validate Basquiat's significance for them. But this happened only because a showstopping painting was hanging in the studio. It was not an insipid, minor piece by the artist. "I'm sure the commercial side of Robert Miller's brain was aware of all of this," Clayton noted. "But he also probably felt it's a great union of visual artists and music artists. He would have liked the romance of it."

The painting proved to be a terrific long-term investment for the band. When they bought it, in the early 1990s, they paid for it via a newly introduced Irish pension-plan scheme. The program let people sock away money for the long haul in a tax-advantaged account, like a 401(k) plan in the United States. The Irish system permitted investments in art, in addition to the usual panoply of stocks and bonds. However, due to changes in the pension rules, the band was no longer allowed to keep the painting in this account, which led them to sell it at Sotheby's in July 2008. "It was a funny thing," Clayton observed, "that the vehicle that allowed us to buy the painting in the first place was also the vehicle that created a situation where we had to let it go." After spirited bidding, the painting sold for $10.1 million.

Other rock stars with an appreciation for art and design followed in U2's early footsteps. David Bowie began collecting art in earnest in the early 1990s, drawn to works spanning centuries, from a sixteenth-century Old Master painting by Tintoretto to pieces by contemporary South African artists. In 1995, Bowie acquired two

Basquiat paintings, initially purchasing a modestly sized work for $93,426 at auction. But like many Basquiat collectors before him, he soon felt that one was not enough. Just five months later, he bought *Air Power*, a more commanding piece, for $120,144—60 percent less than its previous auction price shortly after Basquiat's death. Bowie's purchase came at a time when Basquiat prices were nearing their lowest point, making him a very prescient, albeit probably inadvertent, art investor.

Lars Ulrich, the Danish drummer and founding member of the heavy metal band Metallica, also fell in love with Basquiat. The band achieved international stardom in 1991 when their fifth album went number one around the world. The band's tremendous commercial success enabled Ulrich to pursue a passion: assembling a collection of great works by twentieth-century artists. The first group of artists he collected in depth was associated with the CoBrA avant-garde movement. These artists were known for their colorful and expressive works inspired by children's art and myths. He also collected work by Jean Dubuffet, a French artist known for his rebellious approach

Metallica's Lars Ulrich, who collected Basquiat's work in depth, September 1996.

to art-making that often involved using sand, butterfly wings, and balled-up foil.

Ulrich researched these artists in depth to pinpoint their best works. Through this knowledge and a willingness to pay up for great historical pieces, he assembled a substantial collection by the mid-1990s. He then began casting about for contemporary artists whose work would hold up well by comparison. He quickly zeroed in on Basquiat.

Shortly after Enrico Navarra's Basquiat catalog was released, Ulrich obtained a copy and used it to study Basquiat's art and identify the pieces he wanted to pursue. By the end of the decade, he had bought four major pieces, including *Untitled (Boxer)* from Jose Mugrabi and *Profit I* from Bruno Bischofberger. These works resonated deeply with Ulrich, as they shared similarities with the punk, theatrical, and performative nature of his heavy metal music performances.[2]

During the 1990s, Basquiat's appeal extended beyond the realms of music and attracted the attention of prominent figures in the fashion and film industries as well. Gianni Versace, the well-known fashion designer, purchased a Basquiat painting and four *Collaboration* works in 1996, when his fashion business was thriving and on the verge of going public through an IPO.

The actor Johnny Depp also joined the ranks of Basquiat collectors. In an essay included in Enrico Navarra's catalog, Depp proclaimed that people seeing Basquiat's work either loved it passionately or despised it with a vengeance, leaving no middle ground. Depp appreciated these reactions because, he said, that sort of polarization was "a very difficult result to achieve in any art form."[3] Depp went on to describe how his personal reaction to Basquiat's work was also polarized: "There are some of his works that kill me and some that do absolutely nothing for me. But once you are touched by him, you are burned into either a kind of emotional stillness, or you may find yourself on the verge of doubling over into a painful belly laugh." That fine line between poignancy and humor was essential to Depp because "as much honesty and history and life experience that he spewed into his drawings, paintings, objects, writings, whatever . . . he had a killer sense of humor. Even in some of his most poignant works, his devilish sense of the absurd came through like gangbusters, completely unfiltered. As did his heartfelt disappointments in the human race and his hopes for it."

In the 1990s, Basquiat became one of the most sought-after artists among accomplished creatives. Their validation reinforced the idea that Basquiat was a special and important voice, potentially one of the most significant of his time. Even though Madonna did not own any works by Basquiat, her association with him became a compelling aspect of the narrative surrounding the artist. As Madonna's fame grew, her relationship with Basquiat became an ever more potent talking point used by art dealers and promoters, including Jose Mugrabi, Enrico Navarra, and Lio Malca, to generate interest in Basquiat's work.

Yet beyond the circles of collectors and art-world cognoscenti, Basquiat remained relatively unknown. It would take a movie and a deeply researched and yet explicit, some would say at times salacious, biography to introduce his personal story and artwork to a broader audience.

IN THE 1990s, a night at the movies might have been the most universally enjoyed form of entertainment—with a significantly larger audience than museum exhibitions drew. A staggering 1.3 billion movie tickets were sold in the United States alone in 1996. The top-grossing film that year was *Independence Day*, which attracted nearly seventy million viewers. Even the one hundredth most popular movie managed to sell around four million tickets.[4] In contrast, blockbuster museum exhibitions struggled to attract even half a million visitors, and that happened only when they involved well-known artists like Claude

Monet or Vincent van Gogh. Exhibitions featuring contemporary artists were lucky to get fifty thousand visitors.

The public's awareness of Basquiat began to soar when his story was brought to the screen in 1996. The movie was largely financed by Peter Brant, the avid Basquiat collector. Despite its low budget and art-house nature, the film, titled simply *Basquiat*, managed to assemble an exceptional A-list cast, surpassing expectations for a production with a mere $3.3 million budget. As one character in the movie exclaims, "No one wants to be part of a generation that ignores another Van Gogh." For the cast, being involved in the movie was a way to pay tribute to a fellow creative.

The first-time director, who also invested his own money in the production, was Julian Schnabel, the American Neo-Expressionist artist. Peter Brant, who collected Schnabel's work extensively along with that of Basquiat and a few other contemporary artists, developed a close friendship with Schnabel. During their summer get-togethers at Schnabel's Montauk home, they would binge-watch movies. "I was so impressed with Julian's knowledge of scripts and the techniques of moviemaking that I started to encourage him to make a movie," Peter told me. In the early 1990s, they decided to focus on Basquiat as the subject for a film. "Normally it would be too soon to do something about an artist who had passed away so recently," Peter acknowledged, "but his life story and the work he created was just so great. Julian grabbed on to it."

Schnabel excelled at casting the movie. His reputation and extensive network of connections in the art and entertainment worlds played a crucial role in getting many top actors to take a risk on a first-time director working with a modestly budgeted movie about a painter. "I think he got their confidence," remembered Peter, "because he was a great artist himself, and they figured he would know how to deliver an interesting movie about a painter of the same generation."

Jeffrey Wright in the lead role of Basquiat, *which debuted in 1996.*

Starring as Basquiat was Jeffrey Wright, who had recently won a Tony Award for his role in *Angels in America*. David Bowie played Warhol, wearing wigs and glasses borrowed from the Andy Warhol Foundation. Dennis Hopper played Bruno Bischofberger, and Christopher Walken took on the role of an obnoxious interviewer asking Basquiat rude questions about being a Black artist. Courtney Love was a sexy Downtown scenester, and Tatum O'Neal played a wealthy collector buying a painting from Annina Nosei. Other important roles were handled by Benicio Del Toro, Willem Dafoe, and Parker Posey. Schnabel, who co-wrote the script in addition to being its director, included a thinly fictionalized version of himself, portrayed by Gary Oldman.

With such an outstanding cast and Schnabel's involvement, prerelease publicity for the film was easy to generate. During the filming in New York, *The New Yorker* published a long dispatch from the set, detailing how the actors approached their roles and worked with the first-time director. Around this time, David Bowie bought his two Basquiat paintings, adding them to his growing art collection. Apart from his love for Basquiat's work, Bowie probably felt the artist's market was about to undergo significant change due to the movie.

When the movie was released, in the summer of 1996, it packed a wallop. It received strong reviews in many top newspapers, including *The New York Times*, *The Washington Post*, the *Los Angeles Times*,

Poster used to promote Basquiat.

and the *Chicago Tribune*. Roger Ebert, the influential Chicago newspaper film critic who had a hit national television show with Gene Siskel, gave it a thumbs-up. Moreover, it was featured at the Venice Film Festival, where it was nominated for best picture.

It is intriguing to consider how Basquiat might have reacted to Schnabel's portrayal of him. Most people interviewed for this book who knew Basquiat during his lifetime, when sharing their thoughts about the movie, believed that Jeffrey Wright captured Basquiat perfectly in his performance. "Jeffrey Wright was fantastic, and he was able to do so because he did extensive research for his role," said David Bowes. However, some of those closest to Basquiat, were more critical of the script, particularly in how Schnabel inserted himself into the narrative and then aggrandized the role he had played in Basquiat's life. As Bowes recalled, "Jean-Michel didn't really like or respect Julian."

For general audiences who were unaware of these intricacies, the movie provided a welcome glimpse into the wild Downtown New York art scene and Basquiat's journey through it. The film attracted almost seven hundred thousand viewers during its theatrical run in the United States, with even more when it was released internationally. With it, Basquiat achieved a level of stardom that was previously unimaginable for a visual artist. It was a breakthrough moment that propelled him far beyond the confines of the art world. Following the movie's release, Basquiat's prices began to rise again, marking the beginning of a long-lasting bull market for his artwork.

Despite its commercial success, Gerard Basquiat hated the movie. "He was always against it," remembered Brant. "He didn't want us to do it, even though we were friends. Any mention of drugs or anything like that, he would not approve of it." Gerard discouraged those in his circle from assisting with the production and refused to grant Schnabel permission to use images of Basquiat's artwork in the film. The ever-determined Schnabel came up with a clever work-around: He simply created all the faux-Basquiat works seen in the movie.

Two years after the movie was released, Basquiat's fame expanded further with the publication of a biography with a provocative title. *Basquiat: A Quick Killing in Art*, by Phoebe Hoban, presented a narrative of sex, drugs, and fame leading inexorably to Basquiat's death. *The New York Times* reviewer observed that "Hoban leaves little to the imagination in her unsettling biography of the painter."[5] Filled with long quotes from her interviewees, "the resulting vignettes read like pulp fiction," said the reviewer, noting that this helped make the unauthorized biography "compulsively readable."

Yet for Gerard, reading page after page filled with sordid details about his son's drug- and sex-filled lifestyle was painful. Unlike the stylized docudrama of the *Basquiat* movie, Hoban's book, as the *Times* reviewer noted, left little to the imagination indeed. Gerard's pain soon turned into the apparent need for revenge. A few months after the book came out, just moments before Hoban was set to begin an evening lecture at a university, she was served. Someone walked up to her and, after confirming her identity, handed her documents that named her in a lawsuit. Her publisher was served the next day.

Interestingly, Gerard was not suing them for defamation or invasion of privacy. Those types of cases would have been difficult to win, due to Hoban's First Amendment rights and the thoroughness of her research. He had instead chosen to sue for copyright infringement, a tactic he had previously employed against Vrej Baghoomian. While Hoban's book did not include reproductions of Basquiat's artwork, it did feature twenty-five photographs of Basquiat and individuals in his life. Seven of these images included snippets of Basquiat's artwork in the background or alongside the photographed individual. It was the presence of these fragments that became the basis for Gerard's lawsuit.[6]

In commercial endeavors such as books or movies, it is important to obtain permission from the copyright owner before using even seemingly innocuous image fragments. If obtaining permission is costly or challenging, the offending image can be blurred out. This is why obscured artworks are often seen in magazine articles and TV shows. If Hoban and her publisher had had a more amicable relationship with Gerard, perhaps he would not have taken legal action. However, he detested the book.

For their relatively innocuous transgressions, Hoban and her publisher were now potentially liable for substantial penalties. US copyright laws set statutory minimums for each instance of copyright infringement. Gerard claimed in his lawsuit that because seven artworks were used illegally, he was entitled to a minimum of $700,000 of damages; there were also other demands. The attorneys representing Hoban and her publisher responded to Gerard's complaint by denying that the "book embodies reproductions of the Works and that such alleged reproductions constitute infringement of copyright in the Works." Nevertheless, several months later, they reached an out-of-court settlement, the specifics of which were not disclosed to the public. Given Gerard's tenacious pursuit of the lawsuit and the legal backing he probably found for it in copyright case law, the Estate likely obtained a substantial settlement in exchange for dropping the legal action.[7]

BASQUIAT ENJOYED incorporating easily recognized symbols into his paintings and drawings, with notable examples including the crown motif and the ™ trademark icon. However, it was the copyright symbol © that he employed most frequently. He first utilized it during his high school years when he and his friend Al Diaz created the SAMO graffiti tag. By incorporating the copyright symbol into their work, they were playfully asserting their legal rights to their creative endeavors. Yet building owners viewed the situation differently, believing the artists' work to be acts of defacement that violated their property rights. Most of the images were swiftly erased within days of being created.

While Basquiat delighted in employing the copyright symbol, it was his father who truly grasped its power. As the Estate held the copyright to every Basquiat artwork, Gerard had exclusive authority to determine who could use images of that art. Those who failed to get his approval—Vrej Baghoomian, Phoebe Hoban, and a skateboard manufacturer, among others—faced costly legal challenges. The untold, and perhaps more important, story, though, is how Gerard used copyrights to influence and even censor the content and portrayal of his son's life and artistic influences. Museum curators and galleries, eager to organize exhibitions featuring Basquiat's works, had to obtain Gerard's approval before using artwork images in their catalogs. If they were denied, their hopes of mounting an exhibition would be dashed. Gerard's censorious requirements also restricted what many felt permitted to say about Basquiat's fraught family life, bisexuality, and struggles with addiction. Consequently, much of the literature produced over the past three decades has tended to overlook or trivialize numerous critical influences that shaped Basquiat's artwork.

One curator who worked with Gerard spoke of how he expressed his editorial demands.[8] To support the exhibition, Gerard had a condition: He needed to read the catalog essays well in advance of publication, to ensure that what was being said was truthful—a seemingly benign request. However, as the curator got to know Gerard better, it became evident which topics would provoke his ire. "He wanted to continue to be a father to his son, even though Jean-Michel was now dead," the curator told me. "He didn't want his son to take drugs. Moreover, for a man from his generation, it was very problematic that Jean-Michel was bisexual. The things he didn't want Jean-Michel to do in his lifetime were the things he didn't want mentioned or highlighted in the catalog." When these topics were raised, Gerard would aggressively push back and challenge the curator for evidence, saying, "Were you in the bathroom or bedroom with him?" In need of Gerard's support, the curator, like many others, felt compelled to downplay Basquiat's struggles with addiction and meticulously avoid any mention of his sexuality.

Gerard's ire also extended to lines of inquiry about Jean-Michel's traumatic family life. Requests to interview Matilde or her family were routinely dismissed by Gerard, which enabled him to be the only storyteller available for information and insights about Basquiat's formative years. Not wanting to rock the boat, curators found it best to advance a romanticized view of Jean-Michel's difficult childhood. The result of these constraints is a sanitized narrative of his life, stripped of the depth and history necessary for a meaningful analysis of his art.

Like many creatives before him, including Janis Joplin, Kurt Cobain, and Charlie Parker, heroin was an extraordinarily dangerous yet important way for Basquiat to boost his creativity. Victor Bockris, known for his extensive writings on influential cultural figures such as Keith Richards, Patti Smith, and the Velvet Underground, described how drugs affected Basquiat's creativity. Bockris began his career in 1977 working at Andy Warhol's *Interview* magazine. His circle of friends included Debbie Harry, the lead singer of Blondie, and William Burroughs, the noted Beat Generation author. It was through his connection with Harry, who had a close relationship with Basquiat, that Bockris was introduced to him in 1981. Learning of Basquiat's affinity for the Beat Generation, Bockris then introduced him to Burroughs. The four of them were soon spending time together.

"You need to have a very intelligent view of drugs," Bockris said.[9] "When you take the right amount of heroin, it gives you a lot of energy. If you take too much, you get listless. It's a remarkably good drug to work on because it completely unplugs your worry cord. Many artists are high-strung, ultra-nervous individuals living on tightropes from which they cannot afford to look down. Heroin cures those ills by pulling that cord right out of its socket." The energy and relief it provides "makes you eager to live, happy to be alive, blessed and vigorous.

You feel very excited about what you're doing and just want to get on with your work." Of course, the drug can be a terrible trap. "I would never encourage anyone to take it," Bockris added, "because it just takes your soul, it takes your life, it destroys everything. It catches up with you very badly, but it's often a three-year honeymoon before the ugly addiction issues kick in."

Bockris believes that Basquiat was a controlled drug taker in his early years because he was always in good shape. "He wasn't slovenly, like so many people get on drugs. He hadn't lost a sense of time or a sense of mission yet." During this period, Basquiat was extraordinarily productive, making many of his best works. Bockris suggests that "one must view his drug taking as being something that played quite a vital

Basquiat and William Burroughs, December 1986.

role in his rise to fame. It gave him the ability to work for long periods of time and to be creative without worry or fear."

By Bockris's accounting, Basquiat's heroin honeymoon ended in 1985. At the end of the honeymoon phase, addicts need ever larger amounts of the drug to achieve their previous highs. But no matter how much they take, the experience they crave proves elusive. It is one of the great traps associated with using heroin. William Burroughs, who wrote about his own heroin addiction, told Bockris about visiting Basquiat at his Great Jones studio. He arrived to find the dining table piled high with empty heroin bags. When Burroughs told Basquiat that it was ridiculous to be using so much of the drug, Basquiat happily replied that he could handle more of it than anyone else.

As Basquiat's drug use accelerated, his productivity declined. So, too, did the quality of his work. Unlike his earlier pieces, which are filled with crossed-out words and heavily painted surfaces, the late works often have a rudimentary and incomplete feel. Curators prone to puffery will sometimes refer to these late works as being highly experimental and playful. They may be, but more realistically, many are probably the result of a now-listless artist high on too much heroin looking for a quick and easy way to make paintings for upcoming exhibitions. Basquiat's addictions were simply too central to his short life to downplay the impact they had on his art making.

Gerard's control over the official family narrative also prevented writers who needed his support from exploring Basquiat's sexuality. Freed from this constraint, curators might find hints or allusions to Basquiat's sexuality within his work. One notable aspect of Basquiat's output is the conspicuous absence of women within it. One scholar who meticulously examined the thousands of paintings and drawings he created identified only nine instances of full-length female figures. Instead, Basquiat predominantly showcased images of Black men, often portraying them naked with raised arms.[10]

Curators typically interpret these figures as a visual manifestation of resistance against racial injustice, symbolizing empowerment, defiance, and a challenge to societal structures perpetuating racism. While this interpretation provides an important perspective, additional viewpoints exist. For instance, a gay collector familiar with Basquiat's bisexuality shared with me his belief that Basquiat's anger extended to both the racism *and* the homophobia he experienced during the 1970s and 1980s. From this collector's perspective, heteronormative interpreters of Basquiat's work have been too quick to approach him solely through a race-based lens.

Jasper Johns provides an interesting case of how interpretations of an artist's work have evolved over the past two decades and what it may mean for Basquiat. The ninety-four-year-old artist has never openly discussed his sexuality or his relationship with fellow artist Robert Rauschenberg. Likewise, Johns has not explicitly addressed the issue of homosexuality in his artwork. Yet many art critics and scholars now interpret certain elements within it as reflective of his sexual identity. Jonathan Katz, an associate professor at the University of Pennsylvania, is a seminal figure in the realm of queer art history, with one of his focus areas being the work of Jasper Johns. "Johns is a highly intelligent and perceptive thinker about questions of identity and representation," Katz shared.[11] "Johns enjoys exploring how meaning is constructed, how it is socially molded, and how significance is bestowed upon things. In the 1950s, when he was maturing as an artist, it was a time of great homophobic violence, arguably the worst era to be queer in America. If you risked being branded as perverted, or otherwise criminalized by virtue of your sexuality, then the question of how meaning clings to social constructs became a matter of great interest to him."

Like many artists, Johns delights in being elusive regarding the interpretation of his work. When questioned about it, he often speaks in riddles or deflects the inquiry back onto the questioner. Yet time and again, scholars have discovered traces of his sexuality within his work, including references to his painful breakup with Robert Rauschenberg, inspirations drawn from gay poets such as Frank O'Hara and Hart Crane, and the incorporation of physical objects, like balls and a plaster cast of a penis.[12]

In the late 1950s, Johns embarked on his now iconic flag series, in which he depicted the American flag through a series of paintings, drawings, and prints. At first glance, these works appear to be straightforward representations of the flag. But on closer examination, the juxtaposition of a widely recognized symbol crafted with unexpected materials and techniques, such as collage and encaustic, in various colors and sizes, helps to muddle its traditional symbolism. "There's nothing real about a flag," Katz said. "A flag is a social and cultural construct, endowed with significance by us. Each variation in the flag series constitutes a kind of philosophical inquiry. If I paint the flag entirely in white, to what extent does its meaning remain unchanged? If I place two flags next to each other, does it alter the meaning?"

One of the few instances Katz found of Johns directly addressing homosexuality is in a drawing he created in 1969 titled *Two Flags*. Katz explained, "It's one of his classic flag drawings where he beautifully renders two flags hanging vertically next to each other—a motif he returned to frequently in his work. On the back of this drawing, Johns wrote in his distinctive handwriting 'drawing of two fags.' It's notable that he created this piece in the year of the Stonewall riots, which helped ignite the modern LGBTQ civil rights movement." Basquiat's Black bodies, like Johns's flags, may spring from similar impulses.

Basquiat's childhood was also marked by significant trauma, including a life-threatening car accident, periods of intense parental discord, and the loss of his mother to recurring bouts of mental illness. According to curators who worked with Gerard, he steadfastly refused to discuss his son's childhood or adolescent sufferings, which led many writers to present a streamlined and romanticized view of Basquiat's upbringing. As a result, essays in Estate-supported publications overlook the connection between youthful suffering and the imagery Basquiat used in his artwork. The gripping sadness that permeates so much of his best work—in the scowling faces, the disembodied figures, the nihilistic phrases—is rarely associated with his youthful misery.

Basquiat's complex cultural identity is similarly oversimplified. When curators discuss Basquiat's cultural heritage, they tend to underplay his notable Puerto Rican identity while overstating his tenuous associations with Haiti. Basquiat's early childhood was spent in a multigenerational Puerto Rican household with his maternal grandparents, aunts, uncles, and cousins. During his high school years, he lived in Puerto Rico for two years and returned there at least once for an extended vacation. He spoke Spanish and often included Spanish words in his paintings and drawings. By comparison, a Haitian identity is hard to find in his works. Basquiat once told a *New York Times* interviewer that he had never been to Haiti and that there had been no Haitian art whatsoever in his home while he was growing up. Moreover, he did not speak Haitian Creole, the French-based language of Haiti. Yet curators, when citing Basquiat's cultural background, often mention Gerard's Haitian heritage first, followed by his mother's Puerto Rican background, and tend to give them equal weight. Since Gerard controlled the Estate's licensing rights, it is not surprising that those who needed his support would foreground his heritage over Matilde's vastly more important Puerto Rican influence.

Gerard's editorial stipulations, particularly regarding sensitive topics like addiction, sexuality, and early traumas, have significantly influenced much of the serious art historical criticism that has been written about Basquiat over the past three decades. Paradoxically, for an artist whose work is so profoundly tied to his personal identity, much of the existing literature has neglected critical aspects of his character and life experiences. (The Basquiat Estate refused permission to include images of his artwork in this book because these and other issues are openly addressed.)[13]

THE METHODS EMPLOYED by the art market to identify its contemporary art stars underwent a transformation in the 1990s, and this affected the reception and valuation of artists like Basquiat. To understand this shift, it is useful to momentarily step back and briefly examine what previous generations deemed interesting and important contemporary art.

During the eighteenth and nineteenth centuries, new art was often viewed through the lens of nationalism, where a nation's greatness and its people were believed to be mirrored in its art. But the devastation of World War I reinforced a shift in perspective among collectors and critics. They rejected the concept of nationalism and instead sought artistic expressions that transcended national boundaries. Style emerged as the new criterion for categorizing contemporary art. These forms of creative expression were frequently encapsulated into pithy, one-word "isms," such as Cubism, Surrealism, and Abstract Expressionism. Artists associated with these new isms flourished and became sought after by art buyers in search of innovation. Eventually, each style yielded to a subsequent avant-garde ism that pushed beyond the boundaries set by its predecessors.

Starting in the mid-1980s, there was a shift in which an artist's identity and how it was expressed through their work began to take precedence over style as the defining categorization. Curators and academics began to examine art through the lens of the artist's race, gender, and sexuality, and how their work engaged with issues such as repression, discrimination, and inequality.

One of the earliest examinations of Basquiat's Black identity and its influence on his work came in a catalog essay for his 1985 exhibition at the Mary Boone Gallery. The piece was written by Robert Farris Thompson, a professor of art history and African American studies at Yale University. Thompson had previously written a book called *Flash of the Spirit: African and Afro-American Art and Philosophy,* which delved into how African civilizations, including Yoruba, Kongo, and Mande, influenced the creative traditions of Black people in the United States, Haiti, and other Atlantic basin nations.

Basquiat, having read the book, invited Thompson to his Great Jones studio. They quickly became friends, which led Basquiat to give Thompson a painting to memorialize his visit.[14] Alert to making connections and leveraging them to advance his career, Basquiat asked Thompson to write the catalog essay for his upcoming Mary Boone exhibition. In this essay, Thompson expressed his belief that Basquiat was the first contemporary artist to blend an appreciation of Western art history with the visual legacy of the Afro-Atlantic world. He saw Basquiat's work as a manifestation of "a tough-minded and multilingual creole discourse on form and meaning appropriate to New York today, not only as center of world art but also as a unique gathering place of Black Puerto Ricans, Haitians, Dominicans, Jamaicans, Colombians, and Brazilians, defining a not so secret African city." Thompson's essay, while insightful, had a limited impact, as it was published in a gallery catalog with a narrow readership.[15]

The concept of identity as a subject worthy of artistic exploration transcended the confines of academia and burst into the public discourse, largely due to two exhibitions hosted at the Whitney Museum in the 1990s. In 1993, the Whitney's important biennial survey of contemporary art showcased a majority of artists whose work explicitly tackled issues of race, gender, and sexuality. For example, Pat Ward Williams showed a billboard-sized photograph featuring five young Black men seated on a bench, overlaid with a spray-painted graffiti scrawl that boldly declared, "WHAT YOU LOOKN AT." Another artist, Daniel Martinez, designed admission tags for visitors to wear after purchasing tickets, with one tag stating, "I CAN'T IMAGINE EVER WANTING TO BE WHITE" in stark black uppercase letters. Throughout the exhibition, text panels and wall labels described how the artworks related to topics such as the AIDS crisis, income inequality, and America's history of racism.

The lead curator for the show, Elisabeth Sussman, was resolute in making an unequivocal statement about what constituted interesting art of the early 1990s. The show, however, was lacerated in the press, even by the standards of previous Whitney Biennials, which the press loves to treat as a soccer ball. Yet Sussman's timing was impeccable, as her show marked the moment when the contemporary art world began its decades-long shift toward viewing identity as the paramount source of meaningful artistic content.

Thelma Golden, who has been instrumental in promoting Black artists.

A second exhibition at the Whitney, one that opened about a year after the biennial, further highlighted the growing importance of identity-based art. Thelma Golden, a young Black curator, organized an exhibition titled *Black Male: Representations of Masculinity in Contemporary American Art*. The show challenged stereotypic depictions of Black men through the works of twenty-nine artists, including Basquiat. It delved into themes of beauty, racism, and gendered roles by utilizing the Black male body as subject matter. Despite being fiercely critiqued at the time, the 1994 *Black Male* exhibition is now seen as a prescient indicator of the art world's shifting center of gravity. Following the show, Golden went on to curate numerous influential exhibitions, mentor some of the most important artistic voices of the era, and, in 2005, become the director of the Studio Museum in Harlem.

Over the second half of the 1990s, an artist's identity and how it shaped and influenced their work became a critical lens through which galleries and curators selected contemporary artists they deemed significant and deserving of recognition. In this context, Basquiat experienced a renewed relevance, which helped set him apart from his Neo-Expressionist peers from the 1980s. His work was now discussed within an intellectual framework that emphasized how he had shed light on the history and experiences of Black people, especially the experience of young Black men.

Contemporary art collectors alert to these attitudinal shifts began to regard Basquiat as *the* Black artist to own. His appeal was further heightened by the fact that he was a traditional artist who created bold and colorful paintings and drawings. Much of the identity-inspired work produced during this period was somber and involved large-scale photography, video, or installation art that was difficult to incorporate into a home setting. In contrast, Basquiat's art was a visual feast, leaping off the walls and offering enjoyment without the need for wall labels to help a viewer grasp their significance.

THE ART MARKET REBOUNDED in 1996, after being in the doldrums for five years. A robust and sustained economic recovery made collectors feel comfortable loosening their purse strings once again. The uptick in demand affected many collecting categories, from antiquities to modern art. Yet a status revolution was underway. Interest in post-war and contemporary art was outstripping other categories, particularly for top artists like Andy Warhol and Willem de Kooning, whose prices began to rival, and at times surpass, those commanded by revered names of previous generations, such as Claude Monet.

The shift in tastes was exemplified by an acquisition made by the Museum of Modern Art (MoMA). In October 1996, the museum purchased Andy Warhol's *Campbell's Soup Cans*, a seminal artwork comprised of thirty-two panels depicting the iconic soup cans, for a staggering $15 million. A month later, yet another record-breaking sale recalibrated expectations for what significant contemporary artworks would cost. A masterwork by Willem de Kooning, the celebrated Abstract Expressionist known for a series of paintings depicting women, soared past its pre-sale estimate of $8 to $10 million to sell for $15.6 million. The Christie's auctioneer proclaimed afterward, "Happy days are here again. The evening was a triumph. This is the first time in living memory that a contemporary painting sold for more than any Impressionist or Modern work."[16]

Further fueling the market fervor was the sale of a collection owned by Victor and Sally Ganz, who began buying art in the early 1940s with a particular emphasis on Picasso. By the mid-1960s, they owned eleven major paintings by him. Despite their substantial wealth from the costume jewelry business Victor ran, Picasso's works became prohibitively expensive. They shifted instead to collecting contemporary art, with a focus on four artists: Jasper Johns, Robert Rauschenberg, Frank Stella, and Eva Hesse.

Two decades later, their beautiful duplex apartment on the Upper East Side of Manhattan was filled with great works by these artists, along with their staggering Picasso collection. When Victor died in 1987, the collection passed to his wife. When Sally died ten years later, her children had to sell most of the collection to raise funds to pay inheritance taxes.

Christie's marketed the sale of the Ganz collection to wealthy buyers worldwide as a special moment when they could compete to own great pieces by important artists that had been assembled by astute collectors. The lavishly illustrated catalog accompanying the sale featured an unprecedented surprise: the prices the Ganzes had paid for each artwork, along with when and where they had acquired them. Such transparency regarding acquisition costs had never been included in a high-end auction catalog before. It was a crass yet effective way to remind potential bidders of the extraordinary returns that could sometimes be reaped by owners of exceptional artworks. Over the course of the two-week auction preview period, twenty-five thousand individuals flocked to Christie's, likely exceeding the number of visitors to the Whitney and Guggenheim museums during the same period. More than two thousand people attended the November 1997 evening auction, an unprecedented figure for such an event.

The Christie's sale was a resounding success, as numerous auction records were shattered, not only for Picasso but also for the contemporary artists the Ganzes loved. One striking example was a piece by Eva Hesse, an important American sculptor, that was composed of nine fishnet bags, each stuffed with crumpled balls of plastic, suspended together on a wall by strings and nails. It is an unforgettable piece that evokes dangling breasts or testicles. The Ganzes bought *Unfinished, Untitled or Not Yet* for $3,375 in July 1972; it sold for $2.2 million, which was a new world record for the artist.[17]

The robust art market caught the attention of investors who salivated with thoughts of owning a profitable auction franchise like Christie's. Around the time of the Ganz sale, SBC Warburg Dillon Read, an investment-banking firm, approached Christie's about taking the publicly traded London Stock Exchange company private via a leveraged buyout. After months of negotiating, the Warburg deal fell apart. Yet shortly thereafter, François Pinault, one of France's richest businessmen and an avid collector of modern and contemporary art, announced his acquisition of the company in a deal that valued Christie's at $1.2 billion.[18]

The sixty-two-year-old Pinault commanded a business empire that included well-known French brands such as the upscale Printemps department store chain and the famous Château Latour wine estate. He also owned various US-based enterprises, ranging from the

Vail Ski Resort in Colorado to Samsonite luggage and two shoe companies. While Old Masters, Impressionist, and furniture sales had been Christie's bread-and-butter business, Pinault was determined to push the tradition-bound company toward contemporary art.

In the wake of the deal's announcement, one of Pinault's first actions was to reach out to Philippe Ségalot, the global head of the newly formed Contemporary Art Department at Christie's. Ségalot and his team were responsible for selling contemporary art stars, representing artists who rose to prominence in the 1960s, 1970s, and 1980s. Prior to joining the auction house, Ségalot had been a Paris-based art advisor who worked closely with Pinault on building his contemporary art collection. The deal reunited the two of them.

"We changed everything," said Ségalot.[19] "We could be very creative in the way we put together auctions and then put all our energy into promoting them. We were the future of Christie's because we were addressing the next generation of collectors. We made the department and the sales much cooler than other parts of Christie's." For example, instead of the conventional Sunday brunch for clients before a sale, they hosted grand Saturday night parties with great music and food. Artists were also invited to install their work and contribute to auction catalogs, further enriching the experience. Ségalot enjoyed Pinault's unwavering support. "He was," Ségalot recalled, "always the one to say, 'I trust you, I'm behind you.' He knew contemporary art extremely well and was such a daring guy in his professional life. He understood risk-taking."

Ségalot's first major New York evening sale took place on November 12, 1998. The fifty-lot auction included two Basquiat paintings. The larger and more significant of the two pieces portrayed a life-sized Black man with dreadlocks gripping an arrow in his left hand. One of Basquiat's best paintings, *Untitled (Self-Portrait)* from 1982 had a pre-sale estimate of $400,000 to $600,000.[20]

The night of the sale, the lobby of Christie's Park Avenue headquarters was packed with people checking in for the ticketed event. Guests intending to bid received a package containing a bidding paddle along with tickets indicating their seat assignments. Ushers guided them into the main auction room, where they settled into their designated spots. Jose Mugrabi, Peter Brant, and Enrico Navarra were all in attendance that night.

The lobby was also filled with influential gallerists, art advisors, and other art-market participants, who were invited to watch the proceedings and, perhaps, be viewed as someone prepared to bid. Until someone raised their paddle—most bidders kept theirs tucked away—it was hard to know who among the attendees were there to buy something and who simply relished observing the spectacle of exorbitant sums being spent on art.

While the bidders, consignors, and important market participants found their designated seats in the main auction room, another area began to fill up—a windowless room serving as a sort of "Siberia" within the hierarchy of the art world. Here, individuals lower down in the art-world pecking order could observe the auction proceedings on a TV monitor. Although it was possible to place a bid from this room, through a junior auction employee stationed next to the monitor, no serious bidder would ever consider sitting in this space.

Peter Brant prized the major Basquiat painting for sale that night and had gone to the auction with the intent of buying it. But after bidding it up to $650,000, which with fees equated to an all-in price of around $720,000, he dropped out. Three bidders persevered, vying for the artwork. "It just started going higher and higher, well past $1 million," Brant remembered. "It was crazy because I had recently purchased *Boy and Dog in a Johnnypump,* which is one of Basquiat's absolute best paintings, for $1 million from Bruno Bischofberger."

As the bidding intensified, one of the remaining bidders was seated at the front of the main auction room, another communicated via telephone with a Christie's specialist, and the third, surprisingly, was sitting in auction Siberia. When bidding reached the $2 million mark, the participant in the main auction room, who had never purchased a major Basquiat painting before, withdrew from the contest.

The two remaining participants slugged it out, which took some time as bids from the anteroom had to be relayed to the auctioneer in the main room. The phone bidder was ultimately victorious, securing the work for an extraordinary $3.3 million. This astonishing price was more than three times what Brant had recently paid for his masterwork and about six times the previous auction record for a Basquiat painting. The next day, *The New York Times* hailed the sale with an article titled "Graffiti Artist Makes Good: A Basquiat Sells for a Record $3.3 Million."

In a market driven by perception, Basquiat was now on fire. The $3.3 million figure became the new benchmark that owners of major works by Basquiat would expect to see before contemplating the sale of a major piece. Owners of lesser-quality Basquiat works also ratcheted up their asking prices.

Yet doubts about the legitimacy of the anteroom underbidder soon surfaced. Following the sale, Peter Brant and his network nosed around. "After auctions, we do our research," he told me. "We figure out who participated and who didn't. We just couldn't find out anything about this strange fellow who was sitting in the adjacent room and bidding wildly. It was all very odd." Within a few days, Christie's determined that the underbidder was a phony. A troubled thirty-something, he had falsely claimed to have his father's permission to participate in the sale. Not only had he bid on *Untitled (Self-Portrait)*, but he had also secured winning bids on several other lots. Christie's was ultimately compelled to cancel these sales, which made for disappointed consignors.

Christie's had a different dilemma with the Basquiat painting, as the successful buyer had been driven up to $3.3 million by an illegitimate underbidder. Resolving this issue was made more pressing by who the buyer was: Philip Niarchos, an important Christie's client and the eldest son of a Greek shipping billionaire who was also a noted art collector.

To resolve the matter, Christie's CEO flew to see Niarchos to explain what had happened. When presented with the option of cancelling the sale, he turned it down. Instead, Niarchos negotiated a lower price more aligned with the level at which Christie's could confirm that a genuine underbidder had dropped out. Lars Ulrich, Metallica's drummer, had been the third bidder in the race, the one sitting in the main auction room. As he assuredly had the means to afford the artwork, the point at which he withdrew became the basis for negotiations. While the final price paid by Niarchos remains confidential, it was likely in the vicinity of $2.4 million, rather than the $3.3 million reported in *The New York Times*. Although significantly lower, it still represented a new world record for Basquiat by a substantial margin.

Philip Niarchos with his father, Stavros Niarchos, circa 1970.

Although the sale took place nearly thirty years ago, the false underbidder was willing to share his recollections of that evening. "It was a long time ago, but I remember that night vividly," he said. He mentioned being friends with Warhol and Basquiat, perhaps as a way to justify his actions. However, he expressed no remorse: "It was a crazy night. There was no premeditated malice on my part, and whoever ended up with the pieces made a lot of money over time. Christie's general counsel absolved me of any and all fault."

With this record sale, Basquiat joined the extraordinarily exclusive club of contemporary artists whose works had broken the $1 million barrier. Multiple factors contributed to his ascent, but the pivotal catalysts were the efforts by Jose Mugrabi, Peter Brant, and Enrico Navarra to promote his work. While they, along with others, celebrated Basquiat's newfound status, no one could have possibly imagined that this was just the beginning of the art market's deification of Basquiat.

CHAPTER 9

CRITICAL APOTHEOSIS (2001–2010)

BROOKLYN ENTHUSIASTICALLY EMBRACED BASQUIAT WHEN THE BROOKLYN MUSEUM OPENED ITS RETROSPECTIVE OF HIS WORK in 2005, featuring more than one hundred works spread across two floors. The exhibition served as a tribute to one of the borough's most famous figures.

This retrospective marked the first comprehensive showcase of Basquiat's work in New York since the Whitney Museum's exhibition. While there had been a few gallery shows and the occasional sighting of his pieces at Sotheby's or Christie's, most Basquiat enthusiasts could experience his art only online or through dedicated books.

Paige Powell and Gerard Basquiat at the Los Angeles opening of the Basquiat retrospective, which debuted at the Brooklyn Museum, 2005.

Arnold Lehman, the director of the Brooklyn Museum at the time, was determined to make Basquiat's work accessible and interesting to everyone. The museum invested in an ambitious community-engagement program, which included lectures, musical performances, and children's events. "We had a very dynamic public programming effort," recollected Lehman.[1] "You name it, we did it. And it went on for the entire course of the exhibition, including free evening events." These efforts paid off. "Attendance at the show was staggering, breaking museum records," he told me. "The diversity of the audience was also notable, which was very rewarding, as we'd made a commitment to be more actively engaged with communities of color in Brooklyn."

One couple particularly motivated to see the show was Jay-Z and Beyoncé. "Someone from his office called and asked if I could give them a tour," Lehman said. "My assistant set it up to occur right before the show opened to the public. We spent a really long time in the exhibition. They asked great questions, particularly Jay-Z. We looked at every picture in the show. There was zero rush." As you might imagine, Lehman took scores of people through the exhibition. "But the people that I had the best time with," he noted, "were Jay-Z and Beyoncé. I think they really connected with Jean-Michel's ambition and creativity."

The show had a profound impact on Jay-Z leading him to incorporate references to Basquiat in his lyrics. In "Grammy Family Freestyle," a song about his struggles with success, Jay-Z exclaimed, "Inspired by Basquiat, my chariot's on fire," while in "Ain't I" he extolled his talents as a streetwise performer by stating, "I got Warhols on my halls' walls, I got Basquiats in the lobby of my spot." His references to Basquiat, however, went beyond mere name-dropping in the vein of rap stars doing shout-outs about cognac, luxury cars, and jewelry. Basquiat held a deeper meaning for Jay-Z, as he explained in his biography:

> One critic said about Basquiat that the boys in his paintings didn't grow up to be men, they grew up to corpses, skeletons, and ghosts. Maybe that's the curse of being young, black, and gifted in America–

> and if you add sudden success to that, it only makes it more likely that you'll succumb, like Basquiat did in a loft not far from the one I live in now, a loft filled with his art. But I don't think so. I don't accept that falling is inevitable—I think there's a way to avoid it, a way to win, to get success and its spoils, and get away with it without losing your soul or your life or both. I'm trying to rewrite the old script, but Basquiat's painting sits on my wall like a warning.[2]

Jay-Z's influence spread to other rap stars as well. Kanye West, Swizz Beatz, Nas, and others began referencing Basquiat in their songs. By the end of the decade, Basquiat had become a revered figure in the hip-hop community. The shout-outs from these musicians, along with the articles they generated and the discussions on talk radio, created millions of new Basquiat fans around the world, people eager to learn more about his life and work.

Jay-Z and Beyoncé were not the only special guests at the Brooklyn Museum. Matilde Basquiat, Jean-Michel's mother, also attended the exhibition. She was invited to the private opening and asked her youngest brother, Reuben Andrades Sr., to go with her. Reuben recalled, "I used to spend a lot of time with her because I lived a few blocks away, with my family. She wanted to see the show but insisted that I accompany her, so I took her there." For Matilde, it was a return to a familiar place—a museum she had visited often with Jean-Michel during his childhood, where she had encouraged his creativity and imagination.

Matilde and Reuben strolled through the exhibition unaccompanied. "She was proud of him, you know, proud of what he accomplished," Reuben said. After taking in the show, they returned home, only to discover later that a grand-opening event had taken place that night, complete with speeches and a dinner with Jean-Michel's sisters in attendance. Yet Gerard and Matilde's daughters had not invited them to these aspects of the celebration, a painful reminder of the deep division that persisted within the family.

THREE YEARS AFTER the Brooklyn Museum show, Matilde passed away at the age of seventy-four, after a bout with cancer. A funeral was held a few days later, and the program for it featured a lovely picture of Matilde on the cover. Her favorite photograph was accompanied by a caption in her own handwriting: "I like this picture, it shows my happiness."

During the service, Reuben Andrades Jr., Matilde's oldest nephew, spoke about his memories of her. Reminiscing about that time, Reuben told me, "Matilde was a good person, and I spent a lot of time with her. She faced challenges with a mental illness, but it didn't define her all the time. Matilde was the type of person who meant what she said and did exactly what she said she would do. She was a serious person, just like her father, who was my grandfather. She had the same dignity as him. When my grandfather spoke, everyone listened." Reuben also recalled the close bond between Jean-Michel and his mother: "He was very attached to her and loved her deeply." Matilde's daughters, Lisane Basquiat and Jeanine Heriveaux, attended the memorial service but elected not to speak at it. Gerard, unsurprisingly, did not attend.[3]

Following the memorial service, several surprises came to light. Despite their estrangement since their separation in 1967, Gerard and Matilde had never officially divorced. Additionally, no will was found for Matilde, which is unusual, given that individuals diagnosed with a terminal illness or their immediate family members typically ensure that a will is in place to reflect their final wishes. This is especially noteworthy considering the significant financial stakes involved in Matilde's case.[4]

In any event, as in the situation when Jean-Michel Basquiat died without a will, New York State law dictated the prescribed order of inheritance. Under these laws, 50 percent of her Estate automatically

The cover of the program distributed at Matilde Basquiat's funeral, November 2008.

went to Gerard tax-free. The remaining 50 percent was to be divided equally between Matilde's two daughters. However, their portion would be subject to estate taxes, which were expected to be substantial, due to the value of the art Matilde jointly owned with Gerard. With Matilde's 50 percent share in her son's Estate, the new distribution resulted in Gerard owning 75 percent of the Estate, while each sister owned 12.5 percent.

As the surviving spouse, Gerard was appointed the executor of Matilde's Estate. Aside from her 50 percent share in the Jean-Michel Basquiat Estate, Matilde did not possess much else—just some cash in a checking account and a one-quarter interest in the 36 Covert Street home, which she owned jointly with her three siblings. While Gerard and the IRS would tussle for many years about the value of the art, they ultimately agreed that what he and Matilde owned was worth $147 million at the time of her passing.[5] This was a sharp increase from its valuation at $3.2 million when Jean-Michel passed away in 1988.[6]

Despite her immense wealth, Matilde had led a modest life. She rarely ventured beyond her Brooklyn neighborhood, refrained from indulging in personal purchases, and avoided making improvements to her home. But this did not exempt her Estate from being liable for taxes on the 50 percent that passed to her daughters. Her Estate ended up paying $8 million in federal estate taxes and penalties, a staggering sum considering that Matilde's modest living expenses probably never exceeded $25,000 a year.

Jean-Michel and Matilde are both buried in Green-Wood Cemetery, a sprawling resting place in Brooklyn. Established in 1838, Green-Wood is larger than the National Mall in Washington, DC. Its picturesque landscape features rolling hills, majestic trees, and tranquil ponds interconnected by winding roads and paths with names like Mulberry Avenue and Marigold Path. As the final resting place of many individuals with important historical ties to New York City, the cemetery offers a user-friendly website with a search tool to help visitors locate specific burial sites.

When I visited, the coordinates provided by the cemetery's website indicated that Matilde was buried near Jasmine Avenue, but the area is vast and lacks clear markers, making her grave near impossible to find. Further inquiries with the cemetery confirmed the grave's location, revealed that the plot was owned by one of Matilde's daughters, and led to an offer of assistance during a future visit to locate the site.

A Green-Wood Cemetery staff member later guided the way, driving to the general area of Matilde's grave before we continued on foot to the exact spot. The reason for the difficulty in locating her resting place quickly became evident: Her grave was unmarked by a headstone. The only marker was a concrete slab embedded in the grass, a standard measure used by the cemetery to designate graves. Since her burial, the sole identifying detail has been a small metal tag set into the slab stamped with "A25," her plot number.

AROUND THE TIME of Matilde's death and funeral, her oldest child's influence was extending far beyond galleries and auction houses, permeating everyday life through branded merchandise. From sneakers to designer dresses, Basquiat's imagery appeared on a wide range of consumer products. This commercialization followed the trail blazed by his close friend and fellow artist, Keith Haring, who pioneered the licensing of artwork to bridge the gap between high art and popular culture.

Keith Haring rose to prominence in the early 1980s with his bold, graphic imagery, often featuring motifs such as a barking dog or a crawling infant. Like Basquiat, he exhibited his works internationally, mingled with luminaries like Andy Warhol, and danced at the best clubs. As the value of his paintings and drawings soared beyond the reach of most people, Haring opened a downtown Manhattan store called the Pop Shop, selling affordable merchandise adorned with his recognizable images. The items flew off the shelves, prompting him to open a second location in Tokyo. Contrary to skeptics' fears, collectors continued to pay top dollar for his gallery-based works. Before Haring, visual artists generally avoided licensing their images for anything beyond books and posters, fearing it might devalue their high-end creations. Haring, however, defied this convention, demonstrating that there was more than one way to build a successful career as an artist.

Haring lived openly as a gay man and often used his art to support gay causes. In an August 1989 *Rolling Stone* interview, he revealed his AIDS diagnosis and that he was already battling Kaposi's sarcoma, a cancer often associated with the disease. Knowing that his time on the planet was limited, Haring took steps to secure the future of his Estate. In November of that year, he memorialized his wishes in a will, stipulating that most of his assets would go to fund the Keith Haring Foundation. This foundation would then dedicate its resources to supporting AIDS-related initiatives, educational institutions, and children's charities.[7] Haring died on February 16, 1990, just shy of his thirty-second birthday.

The Keith Haring Foundation received three types of assets: artworks that Haring owned at the time of his death, copyrights to all his artworks, and some financial assets. In accordance with his wishes, the Foundation kept as much of his art as possible for museum exhibitions. Earnings from the Pop Shop were directed back to the Foundation to be distributed to charitable causes. The Foundation also decided to aggressively pursue licensing deals to generate additional funds for philanthropic purposes.

While Gerard Basquiat had initially wanted to create distance between his son and Keith Haring when he had selected the Robert Miller Gallery to represent the Estate in 1989, he liked the commercial potential associated with licensing. The legal team that advised

Gerard was the same team that assisted Haring during his lifetime and later supported the Keith Haring Foundation.[8] Through these advisors, Gerard learned how licensing could generate the revenues he craved so that he could continue to own as many of his son's works as possible.

In 2006, for example, Gerard licensed images to the fashion designer Valentino for use in his fall women's collection. The runway show featured eighty-one looks, fifteen of which incorporated Basquiat-inspired fabrics. The fashion press, however, was not impressed. *Vogue* reported: "Less successful was a passage of sequined graffiti prints in jarring Easter egg colors that paid too direct an homage to the eighties art star Jean-Michel Basquiat. Valentino must know that his clients prefer their contemporary art on their walls, not on their cocktail dresses."[9]

Although this portion of the runway show was scorned, the designer's homage to Basquiat came from a genuine appreciation for his work. Valentino was a noted Basquiat collector, owning *The Nile*, a massive three-panel painting about the slave trade, which he prominently displayed in his Fifth Avenue apartment near the Frick Museum.

The Basquiat Estate also began issuing posthumous prints based on photographs of Basquiat's paintings and drawings. The company Gerard hired would take a digital image of an original artwork and print it on high-quality paper. The dimensions of the prints sometimes differed from the originals, especially for paintings, as Basquiat often worked on a large scale. To create a sense of exclusivity, Gerard would sign and number a limited edition of prints, typically eighty-five copies. This was as if Claude Monet's heirs had selected a few paintings and sold signed and numbered copies as authentic works by the artist. In reality, however, the Basquiat prints were little more than high-end posters. Nonetheless, Gerard was soon delighted to discover that Basquiat enthusiasts were willing to pay thousands of dollars for one.[10]

Gerard and his licensing team truly stepped up their game when they secured a partnership with Reebok in 2009.[11] At the time, hip-hop and Reebok were closely entwined due to a series of successful collaborations with rappers like Jay-Z, Pharrell, and 50 Cent. Basquiat's work was chosen to decorate a new line of Reebok sneakers.[12] The partnership proved to be highly lucrative for all involved and lasted for five years.

Following this success, more deals were struck with a constellation of brands. Today, it is possible to purchase a wide range of products featuring Basquiat-related imagery, including washable doormats by Ruggable; clothing from fashion retailers like Comme des Garçons, Coach, the Gap, and Uniqlo; boardshorts and other surfing paraphernalia from Billabong; porcelain plates and candles from Ligne Blanche Paris; workout clothes, including a sports bra, from Peloton; underwear for men and women by MeUndies; snow skis and helmets by Bomber; tequila by 1800 Tequila; lipsticks and other cosmetics from Urban Decay; and a Black Barbie wearing Basquiat-inspired clothing and a crown.

These licensing agreements made it possible for millions of people around the world to own a small piece of Basquiat. As with Keith Haring's example, the proliferation of Basquiat merchandise has not hurt his high-end market. In fact, the availability of such merchandise has helped validate Basquiat's importance as an artist for some new collectors.

These licensing deals have also generated significant income for the Basquiat Estate. While specific details about their licensing revenues are not publicly available, since the Estate is a private entity, the Keith Haring Foundation, a tax-exempt nonprofit, is required to disclose its financial results. The Foundation's licensing income grew from $3.8 million in 2020 to $8.8 million in 2023.[13] Considering the numerous deals struck by the Basquiat Estate and the superior pricing power it commands, as Basquiat is better known than Haring, the Estate likely earned multiples of the Haring licensing revenues each year.[14]

A natural question arises regarding the extraordinary commercial success of Basquiat-branded merchandise: How would the artist himself have felt about it? Speculation is easy, yet knowing is impossible. The pervasive world of celebrity merchandise we see today did not exist at the time of Basquiat's death. It is akin to wondering how Bob Marley, the famed Jamaican reggae singer, who died in 1981, would react to the plethora of clothes, backpacks, and other items bearing his image that are available today.

What is clear is that until the day he died, Basquiat was an intensely competitive man who wanted to be recognized as one of the great artists of his generation. He was irked, after all, to learn that paintings by his contemporary Julian Schnabel fetched substantially higher prices than his own. It is plausible that Basquiat would be pleased to know that his work now outsells Schnabel's and that there is no market for Schnabel-branded merchandise.

Basquiat relished the limelight and witnessed how his mentor, Andy Warhol, built a profitable global brand that included commercial endorsements and the sale of low-priced items featuring his artworks. The widespread availability of Basquiat-branded merchandise might be seen by the artist as affirmation of his enduring importance and popularity.

BASQUIAT'S STANDING as a notable figure in the art world, akin to the reputations of such other art-world grandees as Picasso and Modigliani, was ultimately cemented with the opening of an exhibition–in his case, in 2010. The show, however, did not take place at an iconic venue such as MoMA in New York, the Louvre in Paris, or the Tate Modern in London. Instead, it occurred at a small museum located in an industrial town in northern Switzerland. But to the art-world cognoscenti who flocked to it, the show was a status-changing event.

The little museum that punched way above its weight, like the role that Switzerland plays in the world economy, was the Beyeler Foundation. Located in a quiet suburb of Basel, Switzerland, it was founded by the legendary art dealer Ernst Beyeler and his wife, Hildy, to house their personal collection of around 180 masterpieces by Alberto Giacometti, Fernand Léger, and other twentieth-century greats. "Masterpiece" is an often-overused word thrown around indiscriminately by curators and auction house staffers. But in the case of the Beyeler collection, it aptly describes the exceptional quality of the artworks.

The foundation opened to the public in a stunning building designed by the Italian architect Renzo Piano, widely regarded as a masterpiece of Modernist architecture. It has become a destination not only for viewing highlights from the collection but also for enjoying the beautifully curated exhibitions of modern and contemporary art held annually. When Ernst Beyeler passed away in 2010, the foundation's collection was estimated to be worth approximately $3 billion, a testament to its quality. In his will, Beyeler also established an endowment to ensure the museum could continue organizing and hosting the acclaimed exhibitions that had solidified its reputation.[15]

Known for his discerning eye, Ernst Beyeler recognized Basquiat's talent early on. In 1983, he had included Basquiat in a group show at his gallery titled *Expressive Painting After Picasso*. Beyeler showed young Basquiat along with a cornucopia of art-world greats. Three Basquiat paintings were in the show, including *Philistines*, which is now regarded as one of Basquiat's finest works. Basquiat attended the show's opening, making it one of his many visits to Switzerland during his brief lifetime. All three of the works in the show sold, which must have been a heady moment for the then-twenty-two-year-old artist.

Before his death, Ernst Beyeler selected Sam Keller to be the new director of his museum. Keller was then the director of Art Basel, the Super Bowl of art fairs, which Beyeler co-founded in 1970. Each

Sam Keller, director of the Beyeler Foundation in Basel, Switzerland, co-curated the exhibition that transformed Basquiat's reputation.

June, collectors with the means and desire to spend lavishly on modern and contemporary art descend on Basel for three days to wander through a convention center filled with offerings from some two hundred of the best galleries in the world. Unlike its more party-based sister fair, Art Basel Miami, the Swiss-based event is more about the art. It consistently attracts the best collectors and curators from around the world. Most of them make it a priority to visit the Beyeler Foundation during their Basel stay so they can be sure to see the latest exhibition at the museum.

Keller's first major show as director of the Beyeler Foundation was a Basquiat retrospective, which debuted in the spring of 2010. This exhibition surpassed the Brooklyn Museum show in scale, becoming the largest display of Basquiat's works ever held in Europe. For the forty-four-year-old Keller, the show fulfilled a youthful dream. "I remember studying art history in the 1980s,"[16] he said. "Jean-Michel was one of the artists that appealed to me the most, perhaps for the wrong reason. I loved his rebellious nature. I loved graffiti art and all the Neo-Expressionist artists in that generation, including Julian Schnabel. Whenever I saw an article or a book about Jean-Michel, I read it. I probably thought of myself as having a rebellious nature, so I kind of identified with him."

Keller and his co-curator, Dieter Buchhart, saw the exhibition as an opportunity to introduce Basquiat's work to a European audience, which may have been aware of his name but had not experienced his art in person. They were also cognizant of the lingering reluctance within the museum world about recognizing Basquiat's significance as an artist. "I think some were hesitant about appreciating him for his art," remembered Keller. "His fame and infamy sometimes overshadowed his merits as an artist. I felt the Beyeler could be one mosaic stone in changing those perceptions."

The exhibition was a tremendous success and became one of the most visited exhibitions in the history of the museum. It showcased Basquiat's best work, including *Philistines*, which returned to Basel almost thirty years after Beyeler sold it.

The timing of the exhibition, which coincided with the Art Basel fair, turned this show into a market-defining moment. "Those who already loved Jean-Michel of course came to it," remembered Keller. "But those who were skeptical about his work or disliked it also came because they were in town for the fair. If the show was in a different city, they probably wouldn't have bothered to see it." Keller recounted how "dozens of curators and collectors who I respect told me the show was a revelation for them. By seeing the work in person, they were finally able to understand how great he was. The show extended beyond the Jean-Michel fan club and reached people who didn't care about his work or who had a negative impression of him."

One collector deeply moved by the show was Nicola Erni, a contemporary art and photography collector based in Zug, Switzerland. While she was aware of Basquiat's work, it was her experience at the Beyeler exhibition that sparked her profound appreciation. "I was just paralyzed," she recalled.[17] "I still remember the night after seeing the show–I couldn't sleep." Later that year, she purchased her first Basquiat painting. Like many early collectors of his work, one piece was not enough. Over the next eight years, Erni went on to assemble one of the largest Basquiat collections in private hands, encompassing works from throughout his career.

While the Beyeler Foundation show did not win over everyone, it dramatically enlarged the circle of influential collectors and curators who believed Basquiat to be one of the greats of the twentieth century. This critical apotheosis, which occurred in a small Swiss town, soon reverberated through the art world. The direction of travel for Basquiat's commercial market was clear.

CHAPTER 10

COMMERCIAL APOTHEOSIS (2011–2017)

THE MARKET FOR EXPENSIVE MODERN AND CONTEMPORARY ART WENT GLOBAL AT THE TURN OF THE DECADE.

Great wealth had been created in most corners of the world, with much of it being concentrated in the hands of the few. Many of these extravagantly wealthy individuals found art collecting to be an exciting and glamorous way to join an exclusive club. If they spent $50 million on a piece of real estate, no one in their circle would care. But if they instead invested in art, the attention they received from galleries and auction houses, as well as the parties and people they encoun-

The Basquiat market's upturn created some surprising beneficiaries.

tered along the way, were priceless. New buyers from China, Japan, Malaysia, and beyond entered the art market alongside American and European buyers, making the market for many artists more global and helping their prices to rise even further.

Two art-buying whales, one from Malaysia and the other from Japan, splashed onto the scene. Their actions would profoundly impact the Basquiat market and help turn him into a cultural icon. Both buyers amassed their wealth through their wits, although one was remarkably corrupt.

Low Taek Jho, otherwise known as Jho Low, hailed from Malaysia. Situated between Thailand and Indonesia, the small country finally gained its independence from the United Kingdom in 1957. However, elite families continued to send their male children to the United Kingdom for high school. After graduating from a posh boarding school outside of London, Jho Low ventured to the United States, where he obtained his undergraduate degree from the University of Pennsylvania's Wharton School in 2005.

During his school years, Jho Low excelled at developing relationships with the children of Malaysian and Middle Eastern business and political leaders. The most significant relationship would prove to be with Riza Aziz, the stepson of the man who would soon become the Malaysian prime minister. After college, Low returned to Malaysia and set up a financial advisory business. Through his friendship with Aziz, he met the future prime minister and began chatting him up about different ways to attract foreign capital to the country. After Najib Razak became prime minister in 2009, these discussions soon led to the creation of a Malaysian state investment company known as 1MDB (short for 1Malaysia Development Berhad).

While structurally complex, the concept behind 1MDB was straightforward. It would raise billions in the bond market using the Malaysian government's guarantee and invest the funds in joint ventures with foreign firms for much-needed infrastructure projects.

Although not an official of 1MDB, the twenty-seven-year-old Jho Low operated behind the scenes as the mastermind, orchestrating the flow of billions of dollars in and out of the organization.

Jho Low wasted no time in diverting 1MDB funds for his own purposes.[1] The first tranche of embezzled funds was transferred to a Swiss bank account he controlled in September 2009, with $400 million subsequently laundered into the United States. Additional diversions followed. The plump, baby-faced Low began using his skim to spend staggering sums on table service and parties at the best clubs in Las Vegas and New York. He paid exorbitant appearance fees to Hollywood celebrities and Playmates to join his revelries. According to calculations by *Wall Street Journal* reporters who helped expose Jho Low's 1MDB corruption, he and his entourage spent $85 million over an eight-month period, starting in October 2009, on gambling, parties, private jets, yachts, and appearance fees.[2]

Low's extravagant lifestyle allowed him to build relationships with A-list celebrities like Leonardo DiCaprio, who joined him on lavish gambling trips. Their outings often included Riza Aziz, the prime minister's stepson, who was a film buff. With little experience in the movie industry, Low funneled 1MDB funds to support a new film production company, Red Granite Pictures, helmed by Aziz. Their debut movie, *The Wolf of Wall Street*, a pet project of DiCaprio's that he had struggled to get produced, went into production with a $100 million budget, featuring DiCaprio in the lead role and directed by Martin Scorsese.

Flush with stolen funds, Low became interested in art. DiCaprio, who collected himself, likely encouraged him.[3] Jho Low's first art acquisition was a Basquiat painting, *Red Man One*, purchased for $9.4 million in October 2012. Given Basquiat's association with rebellion and unconventional creativity, it is not surprising that Low would be drawn to his work. By the end of the year, Low had bought two more high-priced artworks, by Andy Warhol and Claude Monet.

Jho Low, a Malaysian financier (seen here in October 2014), caused prices for Basquiat's work to surge.

The millions Low spent on art in late 2012 were only the beginning. Early in the new year, his art purchases included a Basquiat drawing for $4.1 million. By spring, he set his sights on a major Basquiat piece, *Dustheads*, which was featured in an evening sale at Christie's on May 15, 2013. Since it had an estimated price range of $25 to $35 million, a successful bid would set a new world record for the artist.

The night of the sale, Low and his entourage enjoyed a private skybox that overlooked the auction room. The one-way mirrored glass ensured their privacy. Low's guests included Leonardo DiCaprio and Swizz Beatz, the rapper and husband of Alicia Keys, among others.[4] Low communicated his bidding instructions by phone to a Christie's specialist who stood on a podium in the auction room.

Bidding for *Dustheads* began at $20 million and quickly escalated to $25 million. Low then began bidding wildly, often instructing the specialist to raise his bid by more than what was required, such as bidding an additional $1 million when only $500,000 was needed. Low was determined to own the painting, no matter its price. When the final bid was placed, he had committed to spending a staggering $48.8 million for it, nearly double the previous auction record for a Basquiat of $26.4 million.

After winning the auction, Low and his mates celebrated by pounding on the skybox window, causing those below to twist around and stare up at the mirrored glass quizzically. Low stuck around for the rest of the sale and spent an additional $8.3 million on two more artworks.

Jho Low reveled in sharing his ill-gotten wealth with his expanding circle of friends. His generosity reached extravagant heights when it came to his *Dustheads* skybox mates. As Basquiat's prices soared, even Leonardo DiCaprio, one of Hollywood's highest-paid actors, likely found the work to be unaffordable. Low solved this problem for his art-collecting buddy by giving him *Red Man One*, the Basquiat painting he had purchased for $9.4 million. Additionally, he gave the actor two more pieces: a Picasso painting that cost $3.3 million and an iconic work by the American photographer Diane Arbus that cost $750,000. Swizz Beatz received a painting of Jackie Kennedy by Andy Warhol, which set Low back a cool $1.1 million.[5]

After the *Dustheads* evening sale, Low continued splurging on art, spending $248 million to buy thirteen more pieces by the likes of Pablo Picasso and Vincent van Gogh over the following twelve months. Among his acquisitions was his fourth and final Basquiat, a large drawing titled *Untitled (Head of Madman)*, which set a new auction record for a Basquiat drawing when he paid $12 million for it on November 12, 2013.

Low's extravagant spending had a profound impact on the Basquiat market. The exorbitant prices he paid for *Dustheads* and *Untitled (Head of Madman)* fostered a perception in the art market that Basquiat's creations had been severely undervalued. In the peculiar dynamics of the art world, a surge in prices can sometimes boost demand for an artist's pieces. It is akin to the allure of luxury goods: The higher the price tag, the more some individuals covet it. Because of Low, Basquiat's market trajectory was now on a rocket ship that would soon attract new billionaire buyers.

The price Low paid for *Dustheads* was put to the test a few years later when another important Basquiat painting, *Untitled (The Devil)*, was slated for auction at Christie's. The art press immediately speculated that it could surpass the $48.8 million record set by *Dustheads*. Yusaku Maezawa, a forty-year-old billionaire from Japan and a first-time Basquiat buyer, paid an astonishing $57.3 million for it in May 2016. Maezawa had amassed immense wealth by creating Japan's largest online fashion mall. While he had been steadily building his art collection for a few years, the Basquiat painting marked by far his most expensive acquisition.

Yet just as this new Basquiat-buying whale splashed into the marketplace, Low made his exit. One week following the record-breaking sale of *Untitled (The Devil)*, *The Wall Street Journal* revealed that Low had offloaded *Dustheads* the month before for $35 million in a private transaction—a sum $13.8 million below what he had paid for it. The *Journal* disclosed this shocking price decline in an article that delved into Jho Low's involvement in the growing 1MDB scandal.[6] Shortly after publication of the article, US prosecutors filed a lawsuit seeking to recover more than $1 billion in assets they believed Jho Low had fraudulently paid for using funds diverted from 1MDB. Since then, Low has forfeited more than $700 million in assets, yet he remains a fugitive from US and Malaysian authorities.[7]

Jho Low's pernicious corruption as an art buyer without price-point barriers whipsawed the Basquiat market. His lavish spending using stolen funds helped dupe the art market into believing that Basquiat's work was vastly undervalued. Additionally, had the lower sale price of *Dustheads* been disclosed prior to the auction of *Untitled (The Devil)*, it would have helped temper bidder expectations for what exceptional Basquiat works should cost. Instead of another surge in Basquiat prices, they would have likely flatlined or fallen.

JHO LOW'S NEFARIOUS ACTIONS created a significant financial issue for Gerard Basquiat and his family. Two months after the record-breaking sale of *Dustheads* in May 2013, Gerard passed away, leaving behind an extraordinary legacy as the custodian of his son's Estate. However, the record price achieved for *Dustheads* meant that many of the art assets Gerard owned had surged in value. As a result, his estate now faced an estate tax bill that could be tens of millions of dollars higher than if he had passed away just one day before Jho Low's wild bidding. Unlike Jean-Michel and his mother, both of whom died without a will, Gerard had drawn one up. While he owned valuable real estate and investment accounts, his primary asset was his 75 percent interest in the Jean-Michel Basquiat Estate. The remaining 25 percent had already been distributed to his two daughters when their mother, Matilde Basquiat, passed away in 2008.

The Jean-Michel Basquiat Estate now consisted of three types of assets: artworks, royalty income from image licensing, and an apartment at 25 Fifth Avenue that Gerard had purchased to use as a place of business for the Estate. In his will, Gerard stipulated that his youngest child, Jeanine, and Gerard's long-term partner, Nora Fitzpatrick, would be the co-executors of his Estate. He also stipulated that his 75 percent interest should be divided equally, with one-third going to each daughter and one-third going to Nora.

When Jeanine and Nora filed Gerard's estate tax return with the IRS, they valued the artworks at $238.5 million and paid $29.4 million in federal estate taxes.[8] In 2008, when Matilde died, the equivalent figure had been $147 million. By their accounting, the art had risen in value 62 percent during the intervening five years.[9] This increase, while substantial, appears relatively modest considering that *Dustheads* had sold for almost twice the previous auction record.

Almost three years after Jeanine and Nora submitted Gerard's estate tax return, the IRS contested their figures, asserting that the art assets were worth almost $100 million more and demanding an *additional* $49.7 million in estate taxes.[10] The IRS was apparently unwilling to accept assertions by Gerard's co-executors that the exorbitant price Jho Low had paid for *Dustheads* was an aberration that should be discounted, if not ignored completely.

The co-executors decided to fight the assessment and filed the necessary paperwork with the US Tax Court in July 2017. Seven years later, the case remains unresolved, partly due to COVID-related delays. However, in early 2023, the parties did reach an agreement that the IRS had correctly valued the art assets, setting them at $337.3 million.[11] As of the end of 2024, they have yet to reach an agreement on the critical issue of whether Gerard's Estate can apply a blockage discount factor to the value of the art assets, suggesting the case will likely go to trial.

Shortly after Gerard's death, Nora made an important decision regarding her inheritance. She chose not to accept Gerard's bequest of a one-third interest in the Jean-Michel Basquiat Estate. Instead, she disclaimed her share, causing it to be passed on to Jean-Michel's two sisters.[12] Nora was effectively making what would be an $84 million gift to them, based upon the value of the art assets she was soon to own.[13]

Refusing an inheritance is uncommon, but Nora, who did not have biological children of her own, likely anticipated eventually passing these assets on to Jean-Michel's sisters. Rather than waiting for this to occur upon her own passing, she elected to make the transfer in 2014.[14]

Regardless of her reasons, it was a remarkably generous act that meant the entirety of the Jean-Michel Basquiat Estate was now owned and controlled by his two sisters. The baton for managing his legacy had firmly passed into their hands.

NO ONE EXPECTED IT to happen. A Basquiat painting of a grimacing skull had been hanging in the basement of a suburban home for years. The few viewers who saw it were probably shocked by its lurid colors and menacing face. Jerry and Emily Spiegel had bought it for $20,900 at an auction in 1984. Jerry, a onetime potato farmer, had built a lucrative business developing residential and commercial properties on Long Island. Emily was a sophisticated and cultured woman who was knowledgeable about art and music. While Jerry brought the business sense, it was Emily's eye for art that helped them acquire what would unexpectedly turn into their best-ever investment.

The glamorous couple lived in Kings Point, a Long Island community of stately mansions against a backdrop of rolling hills and sandy beaches, nestled on a piece of land that juts into Long Island Sound. Many of the homes in the small enclave have wonderful views of the water and the distant Manhattan skyline. During the early 1920s, F. Scott Fitzgerald lived in a neighboring community while crafting the opening chapters of *The Great Gatsby*. The fictional town of West Egg, where Jay Gatsby hosted his jazz age parties, was modeled on Fitzgerald's own experiences in the exclusive social milieu found in Kings Point.

As the Spiegels' art collection grew, so too did demands for wall space. Emily converted the basement of their home, which had no real windows in it, into an exhibition space. Over time, as their tastes in art changed, the Basquiat painting found its way down there, rarely to be seen by others. They never lent the work to an exhibition, nor was an image of it ever published in a book or magazine, except for Enrico Navarra's important

Jerry and Emily Spiegel, the owners of the mysterious Basquiat painting, October 2007.

catalog. By the time Emily and Jerry both died in 2009, the painting was more of a myth than a physical reality in the minds of the art market.

The Spiegels' daughters, Pamela Sanders and Lise Wilks, inherited their substantial art collection. Seven years after their parents' deaths, the siblings, who had a fractious relationship, reached an agreement to divide the collection. Shortly thereafter, each sister decided to sell some pieces. Lise Wilks chose to sell the Basquiat painting she now owned, and following a competitive selection process, Sotheby's secured the mandate for it, while Christie's was entrusted with selling items owned by Pamela Sanders.

When Sotheby's unveiled the lineup for its May Contemporary Art evening sale, it touted the Basquiat painting as the standout piece of the season, estimating it would fetch over $60 million. If achieved, *Untitled*, which was colloquially referred to as the skull painting, would set a new world record for the artist, surpassing the previous record set just a year earlier by the sale of *Untitled (The Devil)* for $57.3 million.

Amy Cappellazzo, the Sotheby's executive who managed the sale of the Basquiat painting.

Amy Cappellazzo, the head of Sotheby's fine art department, led the team that secured the consignment. "Part of its wonderful commerciality was that it was so good, but it was totally unknown," remembered Cappellazzo.[15] "It was in the right book, so it didn't lack documentation. But no one had seen it in the flesh because it hung in the Spiegels' basement art gallery." The painting also had a compelling narrative. "It's a skull from a great time in his career when he's finding his stride," she explained. "It was made in 1982, the preferred year, both academically and in the market. It was also a companion piece to the great skull painting owned by Eli and Edye Broad. Everybody knew that painting and coveted it, but the Broads were never going to sell it."

Asserting that a painting is a masterpiece is one thing but backing it with a financial guarantee is another. Sotheby's provided Wilks with a guarantee that ensured that she would receive a minimum payout regardless of how the painting performed at auction. While specific details of the guarantee were not publicly disclosed, the whisper number in the marketplace was that Sotheby's had promised Wilks an amount in the vicinity of $60 million. This meant that if the painting failed to sell for at least a new world record, Sotheby's would be obligated to make up the difference.[16]

Being a seasoned dealmaker, Cappellazzo was accustomed to assessing risk and return and determining where to place bets. "It wasn't like we were coming out of nowhere on that number," she shared. "The devil painting sold for $57.3 million, so we knew the market could be taken to a new level. If it's $57 million, why not $77 million or $97 million? Why does it stop there? I knew the market would be ready for it. I knew there were new buyers who would go for it."

The auction was scheduled to begin at 7 P.M. on May 18, 2017, at Sotheby's Upper East Side location, marking the culmination of a busy week of sales across various auction houses. The question remained: Did potential buyers still have enough resources left to propel the Basquiat painting into the record books?

Lot 24 hung at the front of the room, near the auctioneer. On either side of his podium, platforms were filled with auction staffers eagerly awaiting the start of the proceedings. The press was corralled into an area that allowed reporters to easily monitor the actions of the approximately seven hundred attendees. They hoped to spot notable bidders so they could include their names in the articles they would write following the sale.

The light chatter in the room wound down with the sound of a gavel tapping the rostrum. The auctioneer that night was Oliver Barker, a Sotheby's stalwart. His role was to engage the crowd with cheery exhortations that would, hopefully, stimulate incremental bids, while moving things along smartly so that energy in the room never flagged. With his sonorous voice and polyglot European accent, Barker warmly welcomed the audience and made various announcements about the sale, including that Sotheby's had sold off its Basquiat guarantee to a third party. The house apparently no longer wanted to shoulder all the price risk itself. Since it was a publicly traded company, its officers might have grown concerned about the depth of bidding for the Basquiat that night and the potentially messy story they would have to convey to shareholders if things did not go well.

The initial lots in the sale saw a flurry of bids surpassing their auction estimates, a common occurrence for evening auctions. Auction house specialists strategically set conservative estimates for these early lots to generate excitement right from the start, and tonight was no exception. Auctioneers typically take about two minutes to sell a multimillion-dollar lot in an evening sale. It would be approximately forty-five minutes before the skull painting came up for sale.

A murmur of surprise swept through the auction room when the auctioneer opened the bidding at $57 million, the previous auction record for a Basquiat. The bidding progressed steadily, with successive million-dollar increments, until reaching $68 million from a phone bidder. A quiet descended over the room when that bid went unchallenged. With buyer's fees factored in, the phone bidder's commitment now stood at $76.7 million.

The auctioneer, well aware that the lull in bidding did not automatically indicate the end of the sale, calmly surveyed the audience, seeking incremental bids, while vamping to keep a high level of suspense. A few rows ahead was Nick Maclean, a dealer he knew, who was chatting discreetly on his phone, using earbuds. Was a new bidder about to emerge, or was he simply sharing the action with a client who planned to bid on the next lot?

When Barker confidently declared his readiness to sell the painting for $68 million, Maclean entered the fray with a $69 million bid. A back-and-forth ensued between the two bidders, with bids increasing by a million dollars each time. Minutes later, the phone bidder regained the lead with a bid of $98 million. The auctioneer locked eyes with Maclean, wondering if his client would counter once more. A slight shake of the head indicated that the answer was no. Barker then brought down his gavel, selling the Basquiat painting for $98 million, or $110.5 million with fees.

This sale shattered numerous records. It was now the sixth most expensive work ever sold at auction, trailing works by artists including Pablo Picasso, Amedeo Modigliani, and Edvard Munch. It also became the most expensive painting ever sold at auction by an American artist, surpassing the previous record held by Basquiat's mentor, Andy Warhol.

The press's focus shifted immediately to uncovering the identity of the anonymous phone bidder. Many turned their attentions to Yuki Terase, Sotheby's representative who had been on the phone with the winning bidder. Would she reveal something?

Meanwhile, the new owner wasted no time in making his presence known. Yusaku Maezawa, who had bought *Untitled (The Devil)* the previous year, took to Instagram and Twitter to proudly announce that he was the new owner of the skull painting. Sharing a series of images featuring himself next to the artwork during the exhibition preview at Sotheby's, the billionaire expressed his elation and gratitude for art, writing, "I am so happy to announce that I just won this masterpiece. When I first encountered this painting, I was struck

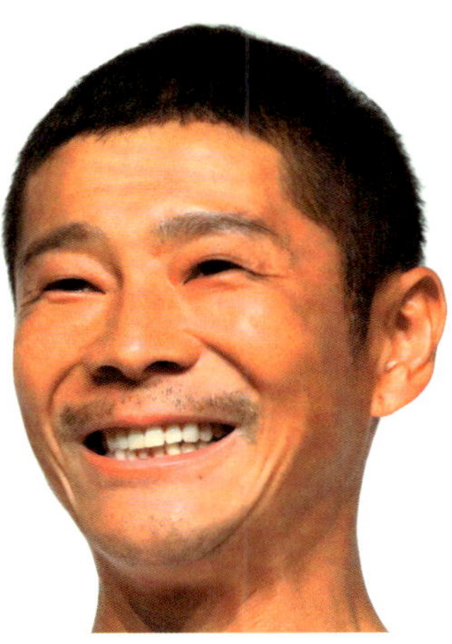

Yusaku Maezawa, the buyer of the record-setting Basquiat painting.

with so much excitement and gratitude for my love of art. I want to share that experience with as many people as possible."

The sale became a top news story around the world. The numerous articles and social media posts always emphasized the shocking $110.5 million price. For many readers, this marked their first introduction to Basquiat. Searches for his name skyrocketed on Google, reaching four times the previous five-year average. After a journey spanning decades, Basquiat became known around the world in one quick moment.

Yusaku Maezawa also rose to prominence alongside Basquiat. Major publications such as *The New York Times*, *Forbes*, and *The Wall Street Journal* featured profile pieces on the maverick e-commerce executive. He relished the attention, which the media would not have showered on him had he chosen to invest the money in a sports team or a charitable venture. Such can be the captivating power of art to command the spotlight, particularly when it involves an extraordinarily expensive work.

Frank Fertitta, the underbidder in the Sotheby's sale.

Another crucial figure in the unfolding events of that night was the underbidder, who had entered the bidding late in the sale. His participation drove up the price and compelled Maezawa to spend an additional $34 million to secure the painting. The underbidder was Frank Fertitta III, a Las Vegas casino operator and former owner of the Ultimate Fighting Championship (UFC), a mixed martial arts business.[17]

To art-world insiders, Fertitta was a well-known collector, having amassed a large collection that included multiple works by Basquiat. His willingness to splurge on the skull painting may have been influenced by the previous year's sale of the UFC business, which he co-owned with his brother, for $4 billion.[18] Unlike the fake underbidder on the Basquiat painting that broke the million-dollar barrier in 1998, Fertitta was the real deal.

The morning after the night before, Basquiat's journey from young artist seeking recognition in the early 1980s to being a global cultural icon was complete.

CHAPTER 11

AFTERMATH (2018–2024)

UNEXPECTEDLY LARGE NUMBERS, LIKE THE PRICE OF TAYLOR SWIFT CONCERT TICKETS, IVY LEAGUE TUITION, OR SILICON VALLEY REAL ESTATE, CAPTURE ATTENTION AND MAKE HEADLINES.

Four months after the May 2017 sale of the Basquiat painting at Sotheby's, a London museum opened the first large-scale UK exhibition of Basquiat's work. Long lines soon snaked around the Barbican Center, as thousands waited to see his work in person. Glowing reviews and rapturous social media posts predominated throughout the exhibition's run.

The following year, a larger retrospective of Basquiat's work opened at the Fondation Louis Vuitton in Paris, a museum housed in

Jean-Michel's sisters, Jeanine Heriveaux (left) and Lisane Basquiat (right), September 2017.

a striking building designed by Frank Gehry. The VIP preview period coincided with Paris Fashion Week, an event that serves as one of the most influential platforms for fashion brands, some owned by LVMH, to showcase their latest collections to buyers and the press. Many attendees were invited to glittering events tied to the Basquiat exhibition. After the retrospective closed in January 2019, a slightly smaller version traveled to New York City, where it was shown at the Brant Foundation, a grand new exhibition space in the East Village created by Peter Brant, one of Basquiat's earliest and most fervent supporters. Tickets for the exhibition quickly sold out.

While museum-goers clamored to see Basquiat's work, there was now a potential market split: Those who owned his pieces now believed their value had significantly increased, but potential buyers questioned whether the record-breaking price for the skull painting truly reflected the artist's broader market value. Was the Sotheby's sale simply the result of two overly eager bidders, both potentially unique in the marketplace, or did it genuinely establish a new benchmark? This highlights an important dichotomy in the art world: Fame and market value can run on separate tracks rather than converging as one might expect. The fame that drives museum attendance, for instance, does not always translate into higher prices.

This dynamic can be especially pronounced at the very top end of the market. "You've got a $100 million price tag, but there are plenty of Basquiats out there just as good," explained an auction house specialist active in the Basquiat market.[1] "Yet the higher price didn't bring any of these great works into the market because every owner now wants $100 million. The reality is, there aren't many buyers at that level. Occasionally, you might find a billionaire—maybe a Saudi—willing to pay a crazy price for the right Basquiat. But owners hold on, waiting for that perfect moment." He went on to reveal, "Collectors of his top works have always been greedy, and that greed helps keeps the market intact—they wouldn't dream of selling for a dime less than a significant premium on the last record price. You try to find that person and if you do, you hit pay dirt. But if you don't, the price is 50 percent less. So the supply at the top end remains very tight."

A year after the Sotheby's sale, another significant Basquiat work came to auction. Consigned by Basquiat's two sisters, the nearly ten-foot-tall 1984 painting *Flexible* featured an elongated figure with a skeletal face, rib-like torso, and outstretched arms. After spirited bidding, it sold for $45.3 million, reinforcing the idea that the record price paid for the skull painting leaned more toward being an outlier than a new benchmark of value. It would take a several years before the astronomical price paid for the skull painting was validated by another billionaire buyer—and it was not a Saudi prince.

IN EARLY 2020, the COVID-19 pandemic upended the global order. As infections spread across the United States, the government took the unprecedented step of shutting down large portions of the economy in March. This triggered a swift economic downturn, with unemployment soaring to levels not seen since the Great Depression. In response, the federal government implemented massive fiscal stimulus measures while the Federal Reserve slashed interest rates to near zero. Amid this turmoil, another event shook the nation. On May 25, 2020, George Floyd was murdered by a police officer in Minneapolis. His death became a catalyst for widespread protests under the banner of Black Lives Matter, a movement that had been building since the police killing of Michael Brown in 2014.

The murder of George Floyd and the ensuing Black Lives Matter marches pushed conversations about race to the forefront of corporate boardrooms, union halls, and family dinner tables. The art world—spanning museums, galleries, auction houses, and artists—also aligned itself with the movement. Their collective actions led *ArtReview*, an industry publication, to rank Black Lives Matter at the top of its

Power 100 list of the most influential figures (or in this case, organizations) in the art world in 2020.

The art world's swift embrace of the Black Lives Matter movement reminded many of Basquiat's singular role nearly forty years earlier, when he first emerged as an artist. Much of his work addressed the history and treatment of Black people, making him especially relevant during this period of racial reckoning. His influence continues to resonate with the next generation of Black creatives—artists, filmmakers, and performers—who find inspiration from his tenacity and work as they forge their own paths. Notable figures include playwright Jeremy O. Harris, best known for *Slave Play*, and filmmaker Julius Onah, director of the Marvel movie *Captain America: Brave New World*.

BEAUTIFUL THINGS in robin's-egg-blue boxes have been a hallmark of the Tiffany's brand for over a century. The company even trademarked the instantly recognizable color to prevent its use by competitors. Despite this and many other important corporate assets, Tiffany had been in decline for most of the decade leading up to the COVID pandemic. The causes were various, including not enough new products, a boring online experience, a dowdy flagship store in midtown Manhattan, and being slow to capitalize on the burgeoning luxury market in China. As a result, the company's stock consistently underperformed the S&P 500 and other key market indexes.

Recognizing an opportunity to revitalize the brand, LVMH acquired Tiffany in a $16 billion deal in early 2021, even as the pandemic continued to impact the global economy.[2] This acquisition, the largest in the history of the luxury sector, added Tiffany to LVMH's portfolio of more than seventy-five brands, including Louis Vuitton, Dom Pérignon, and Sephora.

Bernard Arnault, the long-serving CEO of LVMH, is renowned for using art and culture to shape the Louis Vuitton brand. Under his leadership, collaborations with leading artists, designers, and architects have made art a cornerstone of the brand's identity. Partnerships with figures like Yayoi Kusama and Takashi Murakami have positioned LVMH not just as a seller of luxury goods, but as a cultural leader, blending high art with luxury craftsmanship. A prominent art collector, Arnault has acquired major works by numerous blue-chip artists, including Basquiat.

Alexandre Arnault, the mastermind behind Tiffany's collaboration.

Arnault's five children are all actively involved in different parts of the LVMH business empire, and within days of finalizing the acquisition, he appointed one of them to become the new head of products and communications at Tiffany. Alexandre Arnault quickly set about revamping the brand to make it more relevant to today's customers. In the fall of 2021, the company unveiled a global advertising campaign that featured Jay-Z, Beyoncé, and a Basquiat painting.[3]

The centerpiece of the promotion was a photograph of Jay-Z, seated in a chair, dressed in a black tuxedo, with dreadlocks reminiscent of Basquiat's signature hairstyle. Jay-Z gazes up at Beyoncé, who stands nearby in a body-hugging black evening gown with a statement necklace featuring a large, dangling yellow diamond pendant. Nonchalantly leaning against a wall behind them is a six-foot-square Basquiat painting from 1982, titled *Equals Pi*, filled with his signature motifs, including crowns, text, and a masklike face. What made the artwork particularly relevant in this context was that Basquiat's marks were painted atop a blue background that looked eerily similar to Tiffany's signature blue. Tiffany announced that it had acquired the Basquiat painting from a private collector and would permanently display it in the company's flagship store in a few years once renovations were completed. The company likely paid around $20 million for the artwork.[4]

The simplicity of the photograph vividly demonstrated just how far the Basquiat brand had traveled since his death in 1988. The image lacked any descriptive text and did not showcase any products for sale. It simply presented three icons hanging out together. No explanations were needed, as the viewer was presumed to understand what they were looking at. Basquiat's global identity had grown to such an extent that it was now in the same league as Jay-Z and Beyoncé.

Campaigns like this are extremely expensive. Tiffany's substantial investment in these three brand ambassadors aligned with an important reality transforming the luxury goods industry: Its customers are getting younger. According to Bain, a management consulting firm, the "under forty" crowd increased its share of global luxury spending from 44 percent to 63 percent during the period from 2019 to 2021. The firm anticipates that this figure will rise further, to 75 percent, by 2025.[5] Tiffany's campaign was a bold effort to modernize the brand by associating it with three iconic brands relevant to Millennial and Gen Z buyers.

The campaign garnered a tremendous amount of attention, along with some controversy. Shortly after it debuted, some people complained that Beyoncé was wearing a "blood diamond," as the yellow pendant had been mined in South Africa in the late 1800s.[6] Others objected when Alexandre Arnault, the mastermind behind the campaign, suggested in an interview that Basquiat might have selected the blue color as a type of homage to Tiffany.[7] Stephen Torton, who had been working in the studio with Basquiat when this painting was made, ridiculed this possible association, saying on Instagram, "The idea that this blue background, which I mixed and applied was in any way related to Tiffany Blue is so absurd that at first I chose not to comment. But this very perverse appropriation of the artist's inspiration is too much."

While Alexandre Arnault may have overreached, the campaign was intended as a celebration of love, creativity, and diversity, aimed to make the Tiffany name and its signature blue color feel fresher and more relevant in a post–George Floyd world. The controversy over the color, however, did not deter the company from incorporating the Basquiat painting into an unusual product for the Christmas season. In November 2021, Tiffany unveiled a Basquiat-themed Advent calendar priced at $150,000—a four-foot-tall white oak cabinet with doors covered by a reproduction of *Equals Pi*. Inside, shelves held twenty-four ribbon-wrapped gift boxes in the brand's signature robin's-egg blue, each tagged with a number corresponding to the day it should be opened to discover Tiffany jewelry and objects. Despite being a remarkably ostentatious and vulgar object, this collaboration with the Basquiat Estate must have resonated with some luxury buyers, as the following year, Tiffany introduced an equally extravagant Warhol-themed Advent calendar.

Tiffany reopened its Manhattan store in April 2023 after a nearly four-year renovation. The interior design was overseen by Peter Marino, the go-to designer for luxury brands such as Chanel, Louis Vuitton, Dior, Valentino, and Fendi, who have relied on him for decades to shape their retail boutiques and flagship stores around the world. To celebrate the store's reopening, Tiffany hosted a high-profile party for top clients, celebrities, and prominent influencers, featuring performances by the Radio City Rockettes and Katy Perry. As guests explored the renovated main floor, admiring the dramatically lit display cases filled with beautiful jewelry, one striking object was impossible to miss. Hung high on a wall, where everyone had to pass to reach the upper floors, was Basquiat's painting, now in its new permanent home. Since that party, hundreds of thousands of people have visited the store, some no doubt, just to see this painting. Given the scarcity of Basquiat works on public display worldwide, it is nice one of his finer paintings is available for all to see in his hometown.

AFTER A TWO-YEAR EXHIBITION LULL during the pandemic, global interest in Basquiat again ignited with several major shows. These included a retrospective at the Albertina Museum in Vienna, Austria, an exhibition at the Montreal Museum of Fine Arts exploring the role of music in his work, and a show of the *Collaboration* paintings Basquiat created with Andy Warhol, which was featured at both the Fondation Louis Vuitton and the Brant Foundation.

These exhibitions, along with those held before COVID, were organized by museum curators or independent scholars, in partnership with the Basquiat Estate. To complement these efforts, Basquiat's sisters and Nora Fitzpatrick curated their own exhibition which opened in New York City in April 2022, before traveling to Los Angeles. Although Gerard had always been secretive about the hoard of artworks he and Matilde inherited after their son's death, the sisters and Nora chose to display the pieces still owned by the Estate, paired with their personal memories of Jean-Michel. The paintings and drawings were displayed alongside ephemera from his life, including books and album covers found in his studio after his death, as well as furniture from Gerard's brownstone, where Jean-Michel had lived before leaving home. Highlights of the show included the two monumental paintings that once hung in the Mike Todd VIP Room at the Palladium. This room was recreated with mirrors and chandeliers to display these rarely seen paintings, last exhibited in 1992 when Gerard lent them to the Metropolitan Museum of Art to coincide with the Whitney Museum's retrospective.

Also prominently featured in the exhibition was Andy Warhol's *Piss* portrait of Basquiat, with ghostly green splotches marking his face—an effect created when urine was splashed onto a canvas primed with metallic paint, causing it to oxidize. Gerard disliked this painting, as the green splotches were reminiscent of the scars and blotches that many people with AIDS developed in the 1980s. He kept the painting rather than sell it alongside other Warhol works owned by the Estate when he urgently needed funds in 1989 to cover legal fees and estate taxes. The context surrounding this painting has shifted dramatically since Basquiat's death, with HIV/AIDS increasingly becoming a chronic, manageable illness for many due to advances in antiretroviral therapy. Whatever Gerard's initial reasons for keeping the painting, it turned out to be an extraordinarily astute financial decision; another version of the portrait, owned by Peter Brant, sold for $40.1 million at Christie's in November 2021.

While these exhibitions celebrated Basquiat's legacy, another show exposed a darker facet of the art world: the persistent issue of forgery and the lengths some will go to exploit his name. Secondary museums, rather than major institutions, can sometimes become vehicles for displaying forged artworks by artists like Picasso, Modigliani, and Basquiat. Unlike major institutions which typically have rigorous authentication protocols and access to leading experts (which still does not always protect them), smaller museums often lack the resources or expertise to thoroughly verify the provenance of works. For forgers, these institutions offer an opportunity to showcase fake pieces in a seemingly credible setting, lending them an air of legitimacy. In such instances, museum exhibitions shift from cultural showcases to strategic tools in the forger's arsenal.

In early 2022, the Orlando Museum of Art in Florida opened *Heroes and Monsters: Jean-Michel Basquiat*, an exhibition featuring twenty-five works purportedly created by the artist in 1982. Painted on salvaged cardboard, the pieces were said to have been discovered in a Los Angeles storage unit in 2012. The exhibition attracted significant attention, not only for the works themselves but also for mounting questions about their authenticity. The controversy came to a head in June 2022 when the FBI's Art Crime Team raided the museum and seized all twenty-five artworks, alleging they were forgeries. Legal proceedings followed, and in April 2023, Michael Barzman, a Los Angeles auctioneer, admitted to collaborating with an associate to create the fakes. The pair spent as little as five minutes on each piece, weathering them outdoors to mimic age. Barzman also fabricated false documents to market the works as authentic Basquiats, which were sold to buyers who then arranged for them to be featured at the museum.[8]

Shortly after the FBI's June 2022 raid, the Orlando Museum of Art's director, Aaron De Groft, was dismissed from his position. In August 2023, the museum filed a lawsuit against De Groft, alleging fraud, conspiracy, and breach of fiduciary duty related to the exhibition of the disputed artworks. In November 2023, De Groft countersued the museum, claiming wrongful termination and defamation, while maintaining that the artworks in question are authentic. As the lawsuits progressed, De Groft passed away on January 18, 2025, at the age of fifty-nine. His wife stated that he had died after a brief illness. The following month, the Orlando Museum and De Groft's estate announced they had agreed to drop their lawsuits against each other, bringing an end to the legal battle over the fake Basquiat paintings.

THE PANDEMIC did not dampen collectors' interest in buying great works of art. If anything, being stuck at home with time on their hands led many to ponder whether they truly loved the art on their walls and to explore opportunities to upgrade or refine their collections. Early in the pandemic, an important Basquiat painting that had been included in the Fondation Louis Vuitton and Brant Foundation retrospectives sold privately for $115 million, setting a new world record for the artist.[9] Painted in 1982 with colors reminiscent of a hot summer day, *Boy and Dog in a Johnnypump*, at almost fourteen feet by eight feet, depicts a Black youth with outstretched hands standing next to a dog while enjoying the spray from a fire hydrant ("Johnny pump" being New York slang for an open hydrant). Billionaire financier and art collector Ken Griffin purchased the painting from Peter Brant, who had acquired it from Bruno Bischofberger in the late 1990s for $1 million. Other significant Basquiat paintings also fetched exceptional prices; in the period from 2020 to 2024, seventeen of his paintings sold for $20 million or more.

An important driver behind this demand for Basquiat's art was the tremendous amount of wealth created during the pandemic. While many suffered devastating losses of family members and friends, governments and central banks around the world took aggressive steps to bolster their national economies, leading to the rise in value of equities, bonds, and real estate globally. More people than ever before became extraordinarily wealthy.

According to UBS's Global Wealth Report, there were 79,490 individuals around the world with a net worth of at least $100 million in 2022, up 42 percent from 2019, the year before the pandemic. The same was true higher up the wealth pyramid. The number of individuals with a net worth of at least $500 million grew by 45 percent, to 7,020 individuals, in 2022. Most of them were concentrated in either the United States or China.

Basquiat's sisters, taken together, are members of this elite group. The Basquiat Estate assets they own are now worth well in excess of $500 million.[10] Jean-Michel's fame has bestowed on them dynastic wealth that they and their families will be able to enjoy for generations to come.

CHAPTER 12

LEGACY

IN ONE OF THE MOST CELEBRATED SCENES IN *THE DEVIL WEARS PRADA*, Meryl Streep's character, Miranda Priestly, delivers a masterclass in how cultural hierarchies shape individual choices. When her assistant, Andy Sachs, dismisses a debate over two nearly identical belts as irrelevant, Priestly zeroes in on the cerulean blue sweater Andy is wearing. She explains, with surgical precision, that the color was first introduced by Oscar de la Renta before being championed by other designers and eventually trickling down through countless iterations to the bargain-bin sweater Andy chose, believing it to be the product of her own taste. Priestly's point is clear: The decisions of a powerful elite cascade through the fashion industry to shape even the choices of those who think they exist outside its influence.

A tattoo inspired by Basquiat's iconic crown images.

This scene is a parable for how judgments are made across cultural domains, including the world of fine art. In this sphere, a small group of influential tastemakers—curators, critics, gallerists, auction house specialists, and top collectors—act as arbiters of value. Their decisions determine which artists are showcased, which works are deemed significant, and ultimately, which names ascend to the canon. These choices filter down to institutions, publications, and collectors at every level, influencing what is bought, displayed, and discussed.

Like the cerulean sweater, the art that ends up in a living room or museum (or on a pair of sneakers) often carries the invisible weight of decisions made in boardrooms and private viewing rooms. Consumers may believe their purchases or favorite art works reflect personal taste, but those tastes are also often shaped by the narratives, trends, and hierarchies constructed by a relatively small group of people. Yet, as Priestly's monologue implies, this system is not inherently flawed. It creates coherence in a fragmented landscape, providing frameworks for value and meaning. In both fashion and art, the challenge lies in recognizing these structures without succumbing to cynicism. The mechanisms that shape taste can be exclusionary, but they also hold the potential to amplify voices and styles that might otherwise remain obscure.

Art is about far more than aesthetics; it serves as a vessel for identity, values, and personal meaning. Basquiat's legacy, in particular, extends beyond his artwork, embodying powerful narratives that continue to captivate and inspire admirers. Five key elements define his enduring appeal, each highlighting why his work occupies such a distinctive place in contemporary culture.

Basquiat embodies the allure of the tortured artist. His meteoric rise—from leaving home to achieving acclaim by the age of twenty-four—followed by his untimely death, weaves a poignant narrative. His struggles with mental health and addiction reinforce the image of a brilliant yet fragile talent whose life was tragically cut short. For many admirers, Basquiat's personal challenges hint at their own tribulations, creating a bond that transcends aesthetic appreciation and deepens their connection to his work.

Themes of racial identity in Basquiat's art resonate deeply with audiences, particularly those who have faced marginalization. As a Black artist navigating a predominantly white art world, Basquiat confronted issues of race and identity with courage and creativity. His exploration of these themes strikes a chord with admirers who see parallels in their own experiences. In an era where cultural leaders in music, fashion, and film champion diversity and social justice, Basquiat's work feels strikingly ahead of its time, offering inspiration through his early defiance of societal norms.

The enigmatic nature of Basquiat's art adds to his mystique. His use of cryptic symbols and fragmented text invites viewers to interpret his work in deeply personal ways. This ambiguity fosters a unique connection, as admirers uncover meanings that resonate with their own lives. Basquiat's refusal to over-explain his creations leaves room for endless reinterpretation, giving his art a timeless, almost intimate, quality that keeps it relevant across generations.

Basquiat's status as a pop-culture icon further amplifies his reach. His relationships with figures like Andy Warhol and Madonna, combined with posthumous tributes from the likes of U2 and David Bowie have cemented his place in the cultural pantheon. This dual identity as both artist and celebrity broadens his appeal, making him a symbol not just of artistic genius but also of cultural cool.

Finally, Basquiat's legacy is deeply tied to nostalgia for 1980s New York City. The city's raw, gritty vibrancy in that era contrasts sharply with its gentrified present. For those who came of age at that time, Basquiat epitomizes the rebellious spirit and creative ferment of a bygone New York. For younger generations, he represents an idealized vision of the city as a crucible of innovation in art, music, and fashion. His trajectory—from street artist to international sensation—captures the energy and audacity of a cultural moment that continues to inspire today.

AS DETAILED IN THIS BOOK, Basquiat's rise to cultural icon status was driven in part by the art market's aggressive embrace and promotion of his extraordinary talents. For some readers, learning the mechanics of this process—how the sausage was made—may temper their enthusiasm. Nothing dampens the appetite, as they say, quite like understanding the machinery behind the product. Yet this interplay of admiration and market forces reveals the mechanisms that not only elevated Basquiat but also shape the broader criteria for artistic greatness. It is at this intersection of cultural reverence and commercial promotion that the art market and its key players come sharply into focus.

The art market and the realm of curators and critics represent two distinct mechanisms for assessing artistic achievement, each with its strengths and shortcomings. The marketplace, for all its imperfections, offers immediacy and clear financial signals. Auction prices and gallery sales provide quantifiable indicators of demand, with buyers effectively putting their money where their taste is. This financial commitment subjects decisions to scrutiny. However, the market is far from a perfect gauge of merit. Speculation, branding, and trend-following often skew evaluations, elevating works that are visually striking or culturally fashionable over those with more enduring qualities. In this way, the market sometimes prioritizes spectacle over substance, exposing its reliance on marketing theatrics and herd behavior.

Critics and curators, by contrast, operate outside the financial pressures of the marketplace. Their reputations rest on their ability to shape intellectual discourse and influence cultural perception. This independence allows them to champion overlooked or experimental artists who may lack immediate commercial appeal. Yet their detachment from financial stakes introduces its own challenges. If their judgments fail to sway public opinion or influence the market, why should they be regarded as cultural barometers? Their authority risks becoming self-referential, confined to academic or institutional echo chambers without capturing broader societal engagement. The strength of critics and curators lies in their ability to mediate over time. While the market captures the tastes of the moment, these gatekeepers can contextualize art within historical, social, and cultural frameworks, ensuring its significance endures beyond fleeting trends.

An ideal system would balance these two forces. The market delivers immediacy and financial validation, while critics and curators offer perspective and intellectual rigor. Each serves as a check on the other's excesses.

Basquiat's rise is all the more remarkable because, after his death, both the art market and the critical establishment—the very forces that determine artistic legacy—initially dismissed his work. Despite his success during his lifetime, many influential critics wrote him off as a passing fad, while the market, hesitant and uncertain, failed to sustain its enthusiasm. Yet his art prevailed. Over time, both spheres reversed course, with critics reevaluating his significance and the market driving his prices to unprecedented heights.

Between the forces of the art market and the critical establishment, a third figure played a decisive role in shaping Basquiat's posthumous reputation: his father, Gerard Basquiat, who oversaw his Estate. For every deceased artist, someone must take charge of their legacy—whether a spouse, children, or a trusted individual, ideally chosen before their passing. Those who assume this responsibility for an artist of significance often find themselves navigating unfamiliar and, at times, overwhelming territory. Gerard Basquiat played his hand with remarkable skill and foresight. While his response to the trauma of losing his son ultimately led him to chart a course that elevated Jean-Michel's commercial legacy to unprecedented heights, he was also a controlling presence when it came to the critical contexts in which his son's work was presented. Without his decades-long stewardship, that work's posthumous path would almost certainly have been a different one.

One goal of this book was to look beyond the familiar narratives and examine the deeper forces that shaped Jean-Michel's ambition and artwork—factors that have often been overlooked or simplified. His traumatic childhood, struggles with addiction, and questions around his sexuality were not just aspects of his personal life, they influenced his creative vision. By acknowledging these complexities, we can gain a fuller understanding of Basquiat—not just as an art market phenomenon, but as an artist whose work was deeply tied to his lived experience. One hopes that future generations will be able to approach his legacy with this broader perspective, appreciating his art in all its depth and raw intensity—just as he intended.

ACKNOWLEDGMENTS

I AM ESPECIALLY GRATEFUL to the more than one hundred individuals interviewed for this book, who generously shared their time and insights. In alphabetical order, they are: Nancy Abraham, Reuben Andrades Jr., Reuben Andrades Sr., Sylvie Ball, Mary Bartow, Alex Berggruen, Jim Billipp, Bruno Bischofberger, Victor Bockris, David Bowes, Sara Jane Boyers, Peter Brant, Kathy Brew, Romain Brun, Dieter Buchhart, Amy Cappellazzo, Emmanuelle Chapoulie-Danjean, John Cheim, Adam Clayton, Maureen Cohn, Marquitos Corvalán, Tamra Davis, Beth Rudin DeWoody, Al Diaz, Maureen Dorment, Geoff Dunlop, Cliff Einstein, Philip Elmer-DeWitt, Marcel Erni, Nicola Erni, James Fanelli, Sara Fitzmaurice, Carter Foster, Sara Friedlander, Valentina Frutig, Christopher Gaillard, Vincent Gallo, Anthony Grant, Ronnie Greenberg, Bobby Grossman, Roland Hagenberg, Jeremy Hodkin, Michael Holman, Bradley Hope, Nicole Horowitz, Koji Inoue, Louis Jammes, Stéphane Janssen, Jonathan Katz, Sam Keller, Michael Kline, Hannah Kurnit, Suzanne Landau, Joe La Placa, Arnold Lehman, Hal Ludacer, Lawrence Luhring, Nicholas Maclean, Lio Malca, Robert Manley, Don Marron, Andy Massad, Atreya Mathur,

Jean Minguet, Sebastien Moreu, Caroline Moustakis, Jose Mugrabi, Gina Nanni, Doriano Navarra, Maureen Neihart, Annina Nosei, Curtis Nowosad, Paula Olszewski-Kubilius, Julius Onah, Anna O'Sullivan, Francis Outred, Catherine Owens, Francesco Pellizzi, Boris Pevzner, Géraldine Pfeffer-Lévy, Laurence Poggi, Paige Powell, Nathalie Prat-Couadau, Lee Quiñones, Jeremy Rhodes, John Rivera-Irizarry, Richard Rodriguez, Perry Rubenstein, Jérôme Schlomoff, Barbara Schwartz, Philippe Ségalot, Silvia Sokalski, Michael Stout, Nicholas Taylor, Stephen Torton, Tracy Williams, Wendy Williams, Martin Wilson, Irving Zucker, and five individuals who preferred to remain anonymous.

I am particularly grateful to Reuben Andrades Sr.—Matilde Basquiat's youngest brother and Jean-Michel's uncle—and his son, Reuben Andrades Jr.—Jean-Michel's eldest cousin—for sharing their personal recollections of Jean-Michel, Matilde, Gerard, and their wider family circle. During multiple interviews between 2020 and 2022, they provided invaluable insights that deepened my understanding of Matilde's pivotal influence on Jean-Michel's life. Matilde was never interviewed prior to her death in 2008, and Gerard never spoke publicly about her before his death in 2013. Through their testimony, Reuben Sr. and Reuben Jr. have rightfully ensured that Matilde takes her place in the historical account of her son.

I also owe special thanks to Maureen Neihart, a clinical psychologist and researcher, and Paula Olszewski-Kubilius, a professor in the School of Education and director of the Center for Talent Development at Northwestern University, for their invaluable guidance in helping me navigate the extensive literature on gifted children.

Unfortunately, I was unable to interview Enrico Navarra, who passed away from emphysema on July 21, 2020. However, his family and friends, generously shared their memories with me. I am grateful to Doriano Navarra (Enrico's son) and Lio Malca (one of Enrico's business partners) for their time and for introducing me to Nathalie Prat-Couadau (project director for the Basquiat catalog); Géraldine

Pfeffer-Lévy, Emmanuelle Chapoulie-Danjean, and Sebastien Moreu (who worked closely with Enrico in the gallery); and Laurence Poggi (Enrico's companion, with whom he created a fashion label).

I am deeply indebted to my agent, Carol Mann, for recognizing the potential of this project and offering steadfast support throughout the writing process. My sincerest gratitude goes to Will Balliett at Thames & Hudson for believing in this book and for the countless hours he devoted to making it the best it could be. I was fortunate to have Tom Dyja as my editor—his keen insights helped me see where the manuscript could be improved. Neil Mann did an excellent job copyediting the text. I am especially grateful to Beth Tondreau for designing an elegant cover and interior for the book, as well as to Adam Ellis for his handwriting. Additionally, I want to thank Vicky Wilson, Ben Shields, Lisa Lucas, and Bonnie Thompson for their guidance and comments while I was writing this book. Several friends also took the time to review early drafts of various chapters, and I am particularly appreciative of Alex Herzan and Vicky Weber for their thoughtful feedback.

Finally, I want to express my deepest gratitude to my wife, Dalya, and our daughters, Abby and Lizzy, for their patience and support throughout the five years I spent writing this book—many evenings and weekends—while also managing my art-related financial advisory practice. Their unwavering encouragement made this endeavor possible.

NOTES

CHAPTER 1. EARLY YEARS (1960–1978)

1 **"For being a Puerto Rican…":** This and all subsequent comments attributed to him are drawn from both phone interviews and in-person meetings with Reuben Andrades Sr. at his Brooklyn home, conducted between 2020 and 2022.

2 **At just twenty years old:** According to Gerard's death certificate, he was born on September 29, 1935, in Port-au-Prince, Haiti. Passenger lists from the National Archives, accessible via Ancestry.com, indicate that he arrived in the United States on December 10, 1955. These records confirm that Gerard was twenty years old at the time of his immigration.

3 **It was Matilde's second marriage:** According to Matilde's death certificate, she was born on July 28, 1934. The date of her marriage to Gerard is listed in the program from her funeral service, confirming that she was twenty-four years old at the time of their wedding. Additionally, Reuben Andrades Sr. confirmed that Matilde had been married once before her marriage to Gerard.

4 **Through hard work:** The purchase of their home in April 1956 is documented in the deed of sale on file at the Brooklyn City Register.

5 **The extensive literature:** See the work by Maureen Neihart, Paula Olszewski-Kubilius, Tamra Stambaugh, and Rene Subotnik. See the bibliography for a

selection of material by Maureen Neihart, Paula Olszewski-Kubilius, Tamra Stambaugh, and Rene Subotnik.

6 **The neighborhood was known:** The brownstone is located at 347 East Thirty-Fifth Street in Brooklyn. Gerard and Matilde bought it on April 14, 1966, as confirmed by the deed and mortgage documents available at the Brooklyn City Register. According to Reuben Andrades Sr., shortly before they purchased it, Gerard and Matilde moved from the 36 Covert Street home to a rental building in Prospect Heights, Brooklyn. While Reuben could not recall the address, the mortgage and deed agreements for the East Thirty-Fifth Street purchase indicate that the Basquiat family lived in a rental building at 180 Prospect Place.

7 **Believing that education:** Hannah Kurnit, director of alumni relations at Saint Ann's, confirmed that Jean-Michel attended the school for three years, from the fall of 1967 through the summer of 1970.

8 **"He was a total wreck…":** After our second phone interview, Reuben Andrades Sr. asked me to meet with his son, Reuben Andrades Jr. The three of us first met at Reuben Sr.'s Brooklyn home in the fall of 2020. We subsequently met there twice more. I also conducted phone interviews with Reuben Jr. All comments attributed to Reuben Andrades Jr. are drawn from these meetings and conversations.

9 **A few years later:** For more on Boerum Hill at the time Gerard bought the brownstone, see Jervis Anderson, "The Making of Boerum Hill," *The New Yorker,* November 6, 1977.

10 **At the time:** According to records from the Brooklyn City Register, Gerard purchased the 553 Pacific Street residence on May 23, 1972. He and Matilde continued to own the East Flatbush brownstone, which they eventually sold on July 1, 1976.

11 **In March of 1974:** While in Puerto Rico, they lived in an apartment at 656 Calle Estado, in the Miramar section of San Juan.

12 **As part of the enrollment:** Information about the schools Jean-Michel attended was gathered by John Rivera-Irizarry, a researcher based in Puerto Rico. Rivera-Irizarry collaborated with the Episcopal Cathedral School and the Academia San Jorge to assemble various school-related documents. Rivera-Irizarry shared these materials on his "All About Art" Facebook page.

13 **He later confided:** Suzanne Mallouk, who had an on-again, off-again relationship with Basquiat in the early 1980s, shared what Basquiat told her about his time in Puerto Rico in *Widow Basquiat: A Love Story* (New York: Broadway Books, 2014), 41.

14 **"I became an early graffiti fanatic...":** These and all subsequent comments attributed to him are taken from three interviews with Al Diaz that took place from mid-2021 to mid-2022.

15 **During this period:** For examples of his early figure drawings see Lisane Basquiat, Jeanine Heriveaux, and Nora Fitzpatrick, *Jean-Michel Basquiat: King Pleasure* (New York: Rizzoli Electa, 2022), 38.

16 **Jean-Michel, however, viewed:** Accounts of Gerard's use of corporal punishment can be found in chapter 3 of Phoebe Hoban's book *Basquiat: A Quick Killing in Art* (Penguin Books, 1999).

17 **"I was smoking pot...":** Jean-Michel spoke about his father in a video interview he did with Becky Johnston and Tamra Davis in 1985. The clip where Jean-Michel talks about his father stabbing him is included in the first part of *Shooting Star Basquiat*, a documentary directed by Geoff Dunlop, released in 1990 and currently available on Vimeo.

CHAPTER 2. ART MAKING (1979–1982)

1 **"For sheer kinkiness...":** "The Most Outrageous Disco in America," *People Weekly*, July 16, 1979.

2 **"We were on the grimier side...":** These comments are taken from an interview with Hal Ludacer on February 10, 2023.

3 **Holman remembers Basquiat's request:** These and all subsequent comments attributed to him are drawn from three phone interviews with Michael Holman conducted in October 2021.

4 **By this time:** From my interview with Al Diaz.

5 **Brian Eno:** "A Tribute to Diego Cortez (1946–2021)," in the September 2021 issue of *The Brooklyn Rail*, edited by Raymond Foye.

6 **Another friend:** Sylvère Lotringer's tribute to Diego Cortez in the magazine *Paris LA*.

7 **"He looked very unusual...":** Thierry Somers, "Jean-Michel Basquiat / Diego Cortez Interview," *200%* (magazine), 2018.

8 **Gael Greene**, "Eat and Be Seen: Odeon, Joanna, Nuccio," *New York Magazine*,

August 3, 1981; cf. *Insatiable: Tales from a Life of Delicious Excess* (New York: Warner, 2006), 273.

9 In the evening: The exhibition ran from February 15 through April 5, 1981. Alanna Heiss, the director of PS1 at the time, when reflecting on the show and Cortez's role in it, noted that "Doing an exhibition with the young Diego was not for the faint-hearted. He was completely uninterested in the process of assembly, transport, shipping, insurance, and labels, which are the scaffolding of any large group show. He was a consummate liar, and frequently misrepresented crucial details that he either hoped would come true or didn't care about. In this, he was more similar to the manager of a rock band (Diego successfully acted in this role several times) than the curator of an art exhibition." From Alanna Heiss's essay in "A Tribute to Diego Cortez (1946–2021)," in the September 2021 issue of *The Brooklyn Rail*, edited by Raymond Foye.

10 While critics were largely: *Artforum*, an influential art publication, published a press summary about the show. See "Skied and Grounded in Queens: 'New York/New Wave' at P.S. 1," in the Summer 1981 issue.

11 These works, along with: Basquiat's show at Mazzoli's gallery ran from May 23 to June 20, 1981.

12 "I believed they were...": These and all subsequent comments attributed to Annina Nosei are drawn from phone interviews and in-person meetings held between May 2020 and December 2022 at her apartment and the former location of her gallery.

13 Windows that looked: The space that once housed Nosei's SoHo gallery is now occupied by Miu Miu, a high-fashion brand owned by Prada. The stairwell leading from the first floor to the basement remains hidden behind a closed door. The basement area, formally used for private viewings and art storage, is now lined with shelves holding store inventory. The section where Basquiat once worked is still framed by the same walls and windows but is now cluttered with boxes and assorted paraphernalia.

14 The six other artists: The group show ran from October 31 to November 19, 1981.

15 "I would buy large rolls...": These comments are taken from two interviews with Joe La Placa that took place on December 14, 2022, and February 21, 2023.

16 **"I had no clear direction…":** These and all subsequent comments attributed to him are taken from an interview with Perry Rubenstein on July 14, 2020.

17 **He set the record straight:** Marc H. Miller interview with Basquiat in 1982, as transcribed in *The Jean-Michel Basquiat Reader: Writings, Interviews, and Critical Responses*, edited by Jordana Moore Saggese (Oakland: University of California Press, 2021), 26.

18 **"I remember the day…":** These and all subsequent comments attributed to him are taken from an interview with Vincent Gallo on February 6, 2023.

19 **"Black people are never…":** Geoff Dunlop's and Sandy Naire's 1985 interview with Basquiat as published in the exhibition catalog *Basquiat: Boom for Real* (London: Barbican Centre, 2017).

20 **In this context:** For more information on crowns and their significance in graffiti culture, see Norman Mailer and Jan Naar's *The Faith of Graffiti* (New York: Praeger, 1974). The first part of the book includes photos that show how crowns were incorporated into graffiti pieces. Another valuable resource for exploring the history of graffiti and crowns is *Subway Art* by Martha Cooper and Henry Chalfant (New York: Thames & Hudson, 2016).

21 **"Jean-Michel was fascinated…":** These and all subsequent comments attributed to him are taken from three interviews with Lee Quiñones that took place from December 2021 to August 2022.

22 **"He had a sort of silver Mohawk…":** Glenn O'Brien's essay "Who Was That Masked Man?," included in the catalog that accompanied the Beyeler Foundation's Basquiat retrospective that opened in 2010.

23 **Although the film:** One of the film's backers withdrew from the project, preventing its completion during Basquiat's lifetime. Years later, O'Brien acquired the rights and released a version titled *Downtown 81* in 2000. While the original music was preserved, Basquiat's voice had to be dubbed due to the loss of his original recordings. The film serves as an intriguing historical artifact of the Downtown scene; however, it had little impact on the market for Basquiat's work, as it was released well after his market had already surged.

24 **"Before I met Jean-Michel…":** These and all subsequent comments attributed to him are drawn from a phone interview with David Bowes on July 8, 2021, and an in-person meeting in Turin, Italy, on August 9, 2021.

25 **Mallouk arrived in New York City:** See Jennifer Clement's and Suzanne Mallouk's accounts, 3–22.

26 **"It was clear that...":** Jennifer Clement, a close friend of Suzanne Mallouk, wrote a book about Mallouk's tumultuous relationship with Basquiat, *Widow Basquiat: A Love Story*. In it, Clement complements her prose with passages provided by Mallouk, including the one used here, which appears at the end of the section titled "Jean-Michel Basquiat."

27 **"he basically did everything...":** These comments come from an interview with a close friend of Basquiat who wished to remain anonymous.

28 **"He was an amazing man...":** Madonna's March 11, 2015, interview with Howard Stern is available online.

29 **"He started surrounding...":** John Lurie, *The History of Bones: A Memoir* (New York: Random House, 2021), 162 and 164.

30 **"I would go there...":** Comments from an interview with an art dealer who bought many works directly from Basquiat who wished to remain anonymous.

CHAPTER 3. EARLY COLLECTORS (1981–1982)

1 **"He had this bug...":** These and all subsequent comments attributed to her are taken from an interview with Maureen Dorment on February 23, 2023.

2 **"We sent the monthly...":** These and all subsequent comments attributed to her are taken from an interview with Barbara Schwartz on July 24, 2020.

3 **Gene never received:** Stephen Torton, who became Basquiat's studio assistant in the middle of 1982, discussed Cortez's dubious sale practices in a piece he wrote for *The Brooklyn Rail* about Cortez after he died in 2021. According to Torton, "Diego was beginning to be persona non grata around Jean's studio. Jean was pretty pissed with him because when he started showing with Annina Nosei, Diego had refused to return a bunch of work he'd had on informal consignment." Torton went on to say "Diego played with ethics sort of like a beach ball, and he kind of laughed at lesser people. I think he was quite an elitist, an intellectual elitist, and he didn't apologize for that."

4 **Back in late 1982:** Suzanne Landau was appointed curator of international contemporary art at the Israel Museum in 1982. That summer, she attended the Venice Biennale, where she had an extensive conversation with Annina Nosei about Basquiat's work. Intrigued by what she learned, Landau made a point of visiting Nosei's gallery during a November trip to New York. It was

there that she acquired *Agony of the Feet*, making it her first acquisition for the museum.

5 **The proceeds from the sale:** Works purchased with the assistance of the Barbara and Eugene Schwartz Contemporary Art Acquisition Endowment Fund include *Palast*, by Tacita Dean, a 16mm color film; *Western Union: Small Boats*, by Isaac Julien, a three-screen projection; and *In the Between*, by Darren Almond, a three-channel video projection.

6 **However, in the early 1980s:** For more information on the Schorrs, see Thessaly La Force, "Learn About a Couple That Collected Jean-Michel Basquiat—and Became His Friend, Too," *Vogue*, May 15, 2014, and the essay by Fred Hoffman in the catalog accompanying an exhibition of the Schorr's Basquiat drawing collection at the Acquavella Gallery in 2014. The account of the Schorrs here draws on information from both articles.

7 **By the time of Basquiat's death:** Other paintings in their collection include *Piscine Versus the Best Hotels*, *Leonardo da Vinci's Greatest Hits*, and an eleven-painting cycle titled the *Blue Ribbon* paintings.

8 **He bought a painting:** This painting, *Untitled (Black Figure)*, is now in the collection of Leeum, Samsung Museum of Art in Seoul, Korea.

9 **"It was exactly…":** These and all subsequent comments attributed to him are taken from two interviews with Stéphane Janssen during July 2020.

10 **He then stopped:** The other Basquiat works in his collection included *Versus Medici*, *Red Man One*, *Santo 1*, *Santo 4*, *Evil Thoughts*, *Self Portrait as a Heel, Part Two*, and *The Year of the Boar*.

11 **If hung together:** All these works are included on The Broad museum's website. The one missing painting of the fourteen they purchased, titled *Moon View*, was sold by the couple.

CHAPTER 4. FAME (1983–1985)

1 **"She was the one…":** These comments are taken from a phone interview with Anthony Grant on July 16, 2020.

2 **"I became an art dealer…":** These and all subsequent comments attributed to him are drawn from in-person meetings with Bruno Bischofberger at his gallery in Männedorf, Switzerland, on August 13, 2021, and March 8, 2022.

3 **The resulting exhibition:** The show at Bischofberger's gallery included work by John Chamberlain, Jim Dine, Roy Lichtenstein, Claes Olden-

burg, Robert Rauschenberg, James Rosenquist, Andy Warhol, and Tom Wesselmann.

4 **Using borrowed funds:** The works included hand-painted images of Superman, Batman, and a colored Coca-Cola, large double-panel silk-screened works from the *Death and Disaster* series, and multiple portrait paintings that Warhol made between 1961 and 1963.

5 **Their collaboration extended:** Bischofberger sold his 25 percent share in the magazine to Warhol in 1986 in exchange for a group of Warhol paintings.

6 **By the late 1970s:** Bischofberger also represented the American artist George Condo and the Spanish artist Miquel Barceló.

7 **Before the article:** Gina Nanni, Glenn O'Brien's wife, shared this story during an interview on March 15, 2023.

8 **Warhol's active social life:** Warhol and his business team utilized various strategies to secure portrait commissions, one notable method being a promotion in the Neiman-Marcus Christmas Book. This Dallas-based department store, known for its lavish holiday gift offerings, such as "his and hers" hot-air balloons, distributed its annual Christmas Book to hundreds of thousands of households globally. The 1986 Christmas Book featured a Warhol collaboration with Aramis, a fragrance company. This package included first-class flights to New York for a couple to meet Warhol in his studio for a private photo session. Warhol would then make a forty-inch-square portrait painting, with delivery promised within two months. Factory staffers would also escort the couple for a glamorous night out and, the following day, give them a tour of *Interview* magazine's editorial offices. The price for this exclusive offering: $35,000.

9 **He had it delivered:** Basquiat titled his five-foot-square double portrait *Dos Cabezas*, which is Spanish for "Two Heads."

10 **"I saw him in Andy's studio...":** These and subsequent comments attributed to her are taken from interviews with Paige Powell on July 6, 2020, and July 29, 2021.

11 **She had a talent:** Powell's relationships with advertisers led her to encourage Warhol to do commissioned art projects for consumer brands and corporations. These would become an important source of revenue for the Factory. Warhol, for example, was the first artist Absolut Vodka commissioned to create an artwork using the Absolut Vodka bottle.

Warhol's piece appeared in numerous magazine, newspaper, and billboard ads, above a simple line of text saying, "Absolut Warhol." An immediate hit, it prompted the company to commission other artists, based on recommendations from Warhol and Powell. These ads helped transform an otherwise obscure Swedish vodka into the top-selling imported brand by the end of 1989.

12 **Powell and Warhol became:** Powell discussed her special relationship with Warhol in "Paige Powell on Andy Warhol, Fashion and America's Art Scene," *Spear's* magazine, January 9, 2013.

13 **Paige is upset:** Andy Warhol and Pat Hackett, *The Andy Warhol Diaries* (New York: Warner Books, 1989), 502, 520, 522.

14 **Warhol, who loved real estate:** At the time, Warhol also owned a single-family town house at 57 East Sixty-Sixth Street, his primary residence; a seaside compound on the eastern tip of Long Island; and another carriage house near the Great Jones studio.

15 **Keith wanted to go to Rounds:** *The Andy Warhol Diaries*, 594, 605, 650.

CHAPTER 5. ENDGAME (1986–1988)

1 **Basquiat would then respond:** These paintings marked the second collaboration between the two artists. In 1984, at the suggestion of Bruno Bischofberger, Andy Warhol, Jean-Michel Basquiat, and Francesco Clemente created a series of paintings and drawings that blended their distinctive styles. Bischofberger showed fifteen pieces from the series at his Zurich gallery, from September 15 to October 13, 1984. Basquiat and Warhol greatly enjoyed the experience, and sometime after this exhibition, they embarked on the much larger series of paintings now known as the *Collaboration* paintings.

2 **"[The collaboration] looks like one of Warhol's…":** Vivien Raynor, "Art: Basquiat, Warhol," *The New York Times*, September 20, 1985.

3 **Basquiat arrived at the gallery:** This account is based on an interview with Jérôme Schlomoff conducted on November 23, 2021, in Amsterdam.

4 **The Italian Neo-Expressionists:** Bruno Bischofberger provided the prices used in this section.

5 **Baghoomian enticed:** Several individuals knowledgeable about the situation talked about the financial considerations that influenced Basquiat's

decision to work with Vrej Baghoomian. Baghoomian had passed away by the time this book was being written, making it impossible to confirm these details with him. However, given the backgrounds of the sources, their accounts appear credible.

6 **Basquiat struggled:** The invitation and poster for the show were designed using Schlomoff's portrait of Basquiat holding the Kerouac book, rather than showcasing artwork from the exhibition. When Baghoomian first showed Basquiat designs using artworks, he rejected them, saying he had a much better idea for how he wanted the show to be memorialized. Basquiat returned to the gallery with his copy of the Schlomoff photograph, which Baghoomian then agreed to use.

7 **"It was painted…":** Glenn O'Brien in his essay "Who Was That Masked Man?"

8 **Inspired by a drawing:** The painting is thought to be inspired by Leonardo da Vinci's drawing titled *Illustration for His Thoughts on Virtue and Envy*, which depicts a naked woman sitting on a crawling skeleton.

9 **From Hawaii:** Matilde regularly walked around her neighborhood with her brother, Reuben Andrades, Sr., who lived nearby. During these walks, she shared updates with Reuben about her latest phone calls or letters from Jean-Michel, including this letter from Hawaii, that may have been his final communication with her.

10 **"the last few years…":** As reported in David Sheff, "Keith Haring: An Intimate Conversation," *Rolling Stone*, August 1989.

11 **One of his earliest cover stories:** Greg Tate, "Flyboy in the Buttermilk: The Crisis of the Black Artist in White America," *The Village Voice*, November 14, 1989.

12 **In doing so:** Tate wrote, "It is easier for a rich white man to enter the kingdom of heaven than for a Black abstract and/or Conceptual artist to get a one-woman show in lower Manhattan, or a feature in the pages of *Artforum*, *Art in America*, or *The Village Voice*. The prospect that such an artist could become a bona fide art-world celebrity (and at the beginning of her career no less) was, until the advent of Jean-Michel Basquiat, something of a fucking joke."

13 **The accompanying book:** Robert Hughes, *The Shock of the New* (New York: Alfred A. Knopf, 1981).

14 **Hughes's assessment:** Robert Hughes, "Requiem for a Featherweight: The Sad Story of an Artist's Success," *The New Republic*, November 21, 1988.

CHAPTER 6. POSTHUMOUS MAELSTROM (1988–1989)

1 **He discovered a checking account:** The figures in this section are from Basquiat's estate tax return, which was submitted to the IRS on May 11, 1989.

2 **Stout also found:** Bischofberger told me that in the spring of 1988, a year after Warhol died, Basquiat asked him to meet with Fred Hughes, from the Andy Warhol Foundation for the Visual Arts, to select Basquiat's half of the remaining *Collaboration* paintings that Basquiat and Warhol jointly owned. Basquiat delegated this task, as he did not feel up to it. Subsequently, Basquiat sold his share of the works to Bischofberger and another gallerist, Thomas Ammann, who agreed to make scheduled payments for them. When Basquiat died in August 1988, some of these payments had not yet come due. They were later remitted to the Jean-Michel Basquiat Estate.

3 **No one knew:** One storage facility was located in Manhattan (Hahn Brothers, at 571 Riverside Drive), while the other was in Long Island City (Ollendorff Fine Arts, at 21–44 Forty-Fourth Road).

4 **Basquiat had kept:** Christie's was hired to appraise the artworks in the Estate, which included, in addition to the Basquiat pieces mentioned, twenty-five sketchbooks and eighty-five prints. The appraisal document had details on each artwork, such as dimensions, media, and title, and was included with the tax return.

5 **Additionally, there were:** For example, Basquiat owned two works by Keith Haring and a few pieces by artists whose work often explored Black identity, such as Alison Saar, Sam Doyle, and James Van Der Zee.

6 **Basquiat exhibited canny forethought:** Among the 171 paintings he kept were fifteen works from 1981–82, including *Charles the First, Self Portrait as a Heel*, and *Jawbone of an Ass*. These works were made before he became friends with Andy Warhol, who also encouraged him to preserve his early work: "I think Jean Michel's early stuff is sort of better, because then he was just painting, and now he has to think about stuff to paint to sell. And how many screaming Negroes can you do?" Warhol went on to say, "But what he should do—and I've told him this—is keep his early paintings and store them so that he'll have them to sell later on. Because Bruno just buys up everything and then sells them off slowly. But Jean Michel really should be keeping them for a nest egg" (October 31, 1984, *The Andy Warhol Diaries*, 611).

7 **Matilde agreed:** Technically speaking, because there was no will, Gerard Basquiat requested the New York Surrogate's Court for "Letters of Administration." These letters appointed Gerard the executor of the estate in the absence of a will. Gerard was then responsible for locating and securing all his son's assets, paying off his debts, filing required income and estate tax returns, and performing various other tasks, big and small. Once Gerard completed these duties, he would be obligated to distribute the remaining assets equally between himself and Matilde.

8 **Among the pieces he decided:** Gerard chose to keep one additional work by Warhol: a print of a cow.

9 **Gerard chose to keep:** It was only after Gerard's death in 2013 that his Estate decided to sell the painting, which they did anonymously, in a Sotheby's auction in 2014.

10 **However, the judge ruled:** The timeline presented here is based on an affidavit filed by Joseph Kartiganer, the lawyer representing Christie's in the dispute.

11 **Despite the successful sale:** As detailed in Kartiganer's affidavit, sixteen of the nineteen lots sold for $477,455 (including a 10 percent buyer's premium). Net proceeds to the Estate after fees and commissions amounted to $390,645. Two low-value Warhol lots—wigs that Warhol wore that were framed in Plexiglas boxes—were removed from the sale when the auction house discovered that they would not be included in the forthcoming Warhol catalogue raisonné.

12 **John Cheim, a senior director:** This account comes from an interview conducted with John Cheim on October 26, 2021.

13 **Gerard was forced:** The court lifted the restraint on the Robert Miller Gallery and the Estate selling Estate assets on December 7, 1989. However, it required the Estate to deposit 50 percent of the sale proceeds into an escrow account, where it would be held until the court ruled on Baghoomian's claims.

14 **"People took advantage . . .":** Grace Glueck, "The Basquiat Touch Survives the Artist in Shows and Courts," *The New York Times*, July 22, 1991.

15 **They reached out to his galleries:** For example, Basquiat was paying $4,000 a month to rent his Great Jones loft from Andy Warhol. Since he both lived and worked there, his Estate likely deducted some of this rent against his business income to lower his estimated income tax payments.

16 **Based on this analysis:** This figure is derived from $412,731 in taxes, $14,023 in penalties, and $66,518 in interest payments.

17 Rough calculations suggest: I estimated this figure as follows: Focusing first on his 1988 income, the Estate paid $53,387 in federal income taxes, $19,276 in New York State and New York City income taxes, and $4,083 in New York City UBT (unincorporated business tax). These figures do not include penalties or interest. The federal income tax amount likely includes taxes on his business income as well as self-employment taxes on the first $45,000 of income. Considering his city and state income tax liabilities, the Estate would have itemized rather than taken the standard deduction. Based on these estimates and using IRS Form 1040 (Individual Income Tax Return), Schedule A (Itemized Deductions), Schedule SE (Social Security Self-Employment Tax), and Schedule C (Profit or Loss from Business) from 1988, his estimated business income was $228,646. Calculating business income for the period 1985 through 1987 is more complex because tax rates changed in each of these years and the Estate only reported total federal, state, and city income taxes for the period, rather than by year. Assuming the business income was spread evenly across the three years, and using average federal income tax rates by year, the federal income tax payment made by the Estate implies that the artist earned on average around $250,000 a year from 1985 through 1987. This estimate is likely conservative because Basquiat also sold paintings for cash, and it is unlikely that all these cash payments were included in the earnings used by Gerard's advisors to calculate Basquiat's delinquent taxes.

18 To establish the fair market value: "Fair market value" has a specific definition: It refers to the price at which an artwork would likely change hands between a willing buyer and a willing seller, with neither being under any compulsion to buy or sell, and both having reasonable knowledge about the market. Each object is also valued as if it were the only work for sale, rather than if many works were on the market at the same time. For purposes of the estate tax filing, the price needs to reflect what a piece of art would have likely sold for on or about the time of Basquiat's death.

19 The concept can be understood: Bernstein Research, a top Wall Street research firm, estimates that Hermès makes about twelve thousand Birkin bags a year. As reported by Robert Frank, "Handbags Were the Hottest Investment for the Rich Last Year," CNBC, March 4, 2020.

CHAPTER 7. MORE FAMOUS THAN RESPECTED (1990-1996)

1 **Fortunately, when he passed:** For more on the painting and what happened to it after Saito died, see Martin Bailey, "Where is the Portrait of Dr Gachet? The Mysterious Disappearance of Van Gogh's Most Expensive Painting," *The Art Newspaper*, November 15, 2019.

2 **The recovery would be:** Clare McAndrew, a leading art market economist, estimates that global art market sales were $27.2 billion in 1990, falling to $9.7 billion in 1991. It took fourteen years before sales recovered to their previous peak. McAndrew shared these figures in a public webinar hosted by UBS and Art Basel about the impact of COVID-19 on the art market.

3 **Yet in 1991:** In 1989, one hundred works by Basquiat were offered for sale at auction. All but one of them sold. Total sale proceeds equaled $9,870,805, or $99,705 on average. Contrast that with 1991, when forty-one works were included in auction sales, with only twenty-eight finding buyers. Total sale proceeds dropped to $786,060 because fewer lots sold, and the average sale price fell to $28,074.

4 **"I never lived with art...":** These and all subsequent comments attributed to him are drawn from an interview with Jose Mugrabi at his New York City office on July 2, 2021.

5 **A few months later:** Painted in 1962, *Marilyn Monroe (Twenty Times)* was estimated at between $1.25 and $1.75 million. With fees, it sold for $3.96 on November 1, 1988, at Sotheby's.

6 **His involvement in the market:** Basquiat made about one thousand paintings and two thousand drawings. To get to the available market, I netted out what the Estate owned, which reduces the object count to 1,912. I then subtracted an estimate of the number of works owned by collectors and institutions that were not available for sale, for example, works owned by Eli and Edye Broad. There are probably five hundred objects in this category, which takes the available object count down to 1,412. Based on this estimate, Mugrabi has owned, or still has in his collection, 30 percent of the available market.

7 **"I became interested in art...":** These and all subsequent comments attributed to him are taken from two phone interviews with Peter Brant on July 16, 2021, and February 10, 2022.

8 **"From 1990 to about 1995...":** He bought, for example, *Arroz con Pollo*, another Basquiat painting from 1981. It had sold previously at auction for

$440,000, the year after Basquiat died. Brant bought it for less than half that amount in 1991, a reminder of the sharp repricing that took place during the art market's downturn.

9 **"He'd meet someone...":** These and all subsequent comments attributed to her are drawn from an interview with Géraldine Pfeffer-Lévy, conducted at the Navarra Gallery in Paris on August 31, 2021.

10 **Before Basquiat died:** In one of his exhibition catalogs, Enrico shared the story of how he came to buy these works: "The person who introduced me to Basquiat was the lawyer Pierre Hebey, in 1988. He'd bought one of Basquiat's paintings from Yvon Lambert [Gallery], but it didn't fit in his house, so I ended up buying it. I was in New York a month later and bought another two there." *Basquiat–Château La Coste en Provence* (Paris: Galerie Enrico Navarra, 2019), 9.

11 **Prat, known for his role:** Enrico became acquainted with Prat, who, in addition to his Maeght Foundation role, was the head of the Marc Chagall Committee, which the artist's family had created to oversee his Estate.

12 **With forty-six solo exhibitions:** This accounting was calculated using the Basquiat exhibition history as reported on the Gagosian Gallery website.

13 **Enrico relied on:** It is important to note, however, that a work's presence in the book did not require a certificate from the committee. Gerard knew that well-documented works, such as the fourteen paintings Eli and Edye Broad bought, were genuine. He did not want to force collectors with obviously authentic paintings to go through the committee process.

14 **"I traveled a lot...":** These comments are drawn from an interview with Sebastien Moreu, conducted on August 8, 2021, at the Navarra residence in the south of France.

15 **"I remember sitting...":** These and all subsequent comments attributed to him are drawn from an interview with Lio Malca, conducted on July 7, 2021, at his residence in New York.

16 **Weighing in at twelve pounds:** Gerard gave Navarra's editorial team permission to include some of the works owned by the Estate in the two-volume catalog. But he held back most of them, choosing, for whatever reason, to keep them private. This is the primary reason why the publication covers about 80 percent of the known paintings. The figures cited in the text refer to the third edition, which had the largest print run.

17 The elegant Navarra catalog: Enrico Navarra, like Jose Mugrabi, organized numerous Basquiat exhibitions. In 1997, works from his collection were shown at the Kaohsiung Museum of Fine Arts in Taiwan; the Fondation Dina Vierny–Musée Maillol in Paris; the Gallery Hyundai in Seoul, South Korea; Art Beatus Gallery in Vancouver, Canada; Mitsukoshi Museum of Art in Tokyo, Japan; and the Museo Nacional de Bellas Artes in Buenos Aires, Argentina. Navarra would go on to organize many more exhibitions, including taking a large show of works to Cuba in November 2000.

18 His retrospective debuted: For more on the funders, see David D'Arcy, "Whitney Compares Basquiat to Leonardo da Vinci in New Retrospective: Music Television and Madonna Sponsor Her Late Lover," *The Art Newspaper*, November 1, 1992.

19 These works had once adorned: The larger of the two works, titled *Nu-Nile*, is approximately seven and a half by forty feet. The second, *Untitled (Palladium Painting),* is almost nineteen by sixteen feet. Christie's experts valued the two works at $12,500 and $10,000 in their estate tax appraisal.

20 The Palladium: The club was located at 126 East Fourteenth Street. After the nightclub closed in 1997, NYU bought and tore down the building and replaced it with student housing.

21 The Met Museum: Museum officials reported to me that the murals were installed on the second floor in Gallery 920 at the end of October 1992. This area was typically devoted to showing modern and contemporary art.

22 But in the final analysis: Roberta Smith, "Basquiat: Man for His Decade," *The New York Times*, October 23, 1992.

23 Yet other important institutions: The exhibition traveled to three institutions: the Des Moines Art Center, in Des Moines, Iowa; the Montgomery Museum of Fine Arts, in Montgomery, Alabama; and the Menil Collection, in Houston, Texas.

24 "One morning, I woke up...": These and all subsequent comments attributed to her are taken from a phone interview with Sara Jane Boyers on June 4, 2020.

25 Next, she acquired: The Basquiat Estate, Maya Angelou, and Sara Jane Boyers agreed to share the book royalties equally.

26 A notable feature of the book: The seventy-two-inch-square painting was made in 1984. On November 8, 1989, during the height of the Basquiat euphoria, it sold for $170,500 at Christie's. Enrico Navarra bought the painting after the Basquiat market declined in the early 1990s.

27 **The court ordered:** The $209,000 penalty is from Robert Atkins, "Baghoomian: It's Only Money," *The Village Voice*, October 25, 1994.

28 **The taint surrounding:** This was one of two lawsuits between the cousins as per Elizabeth Hess, "Family Feud," *The Village Voice*, June 13, 1995.

CHAPTER 8. CREATIVE EMBRACE (1996–2000)

1 **"I'd been in this amazing U2 bubble...":** These and all subsequent comments attributed to him are taken from a phone interview with Adam Clayton on July 27, 2021.

2 **These works resonated:** For more about Ulrich's art collection, see *Metallica: Some Kind of Monster*, a 2004 documentary, in which he discusses selling a large portion of it at Christie's.

3 **"a very difficult result..."**: Johnny Depp, "Basquiat Paintings–for Enrico–under the influence of pork," in ed. Enrico Navarra, *Jean-Michel Basquiat*, 16–17.

4 **Even the one hundredth:** The ticket sales figures are from the website The Numbers, self-described as "where data and the movie business meet."

5 **"Hoban leaves little to the imagination..."**: Patricia Bosworth, "Hyped to Death," *The New York Times*, August 9, 1998.

6 **Seven of these images:** Gerard listed the copyrighted images used by Hoban in his complaint filed with the US District Court for the Southern District of New York. They were *Made in Japan I* (1982), *Quality Meats for the Public* (1982), *Untitled (Head)* (1987), *Man from Naples* (1982), *Eroica* (1988), *Fats II* (1987), and *Unbreakable* (1987).

7 **Given Gerard's tenacious pursuit:** For more on the intersection of art and copyright law, the Center for Art Law is an excellent resource. This nonprofit organization is dedicated to research, education, and public programming, frequently publishing articles and hosting seminars on the topic.

8 **One curator who worked:** Comments from an interview with a curator who wished to remain anonymous.

9 **"You need to have...":** These and all subsequent comments attributed to him are taken from a phone interview with Victor Bockris on March 1, 2022.

10 One scholar who: Fred Hoffman, *The Art of Jean-Michel Basquiat* (New York: Enrico Navarra Gallery, 2017), 157.

11 "Johns is a highly intelligent...": These and all subsequent comments attributed to him are taken from a phone interview with Jonathan Katz on October 3, 2023.

12 Yet time and again: The extensive body of literature applying queer theory to Jasper Johns is summarized in the catalog for his 2021 retrospective co-hosted by the Whitney Museum and the Philadelphia Museum of Art. See Drew Sawyer's "Once More, with Feeling: Jasper Johns and Queer Art Histories," in *Jasper Johns: Mind/Mirror*, ed. Carlos Basualdo and Scott Rothkopf (New York: Whitney Museum of American Art, 2021).

13 The Basquiat Estate refused: The Estate maintains a formal application and review process that all potential licensees are required to follow. This process is overseen by Artestar, a licensing agency and creative consultancy. In May 2021, I applied to use images of eight artworks. I also provided supplementary information about my book, including an executive summary, in response to questions raised by the Estate. On June 21, 2022, Natalie Bryt, the director of strategy and marketing at Artestar, conveyed via email that she had "been able to formally review this with the Estate and they do not wish to proceed with permissions and this project is not authorized by the Estate of Jean-Michel Basquiat as they wish to limit the proliferation of Basquiat imagery in this manner."

14 They quickly became friends: Thompson's painting was composed of nine Xerox copies of drawings that Basquiat had pasted onto a canvas. He applied white paint to cover the edges of the drawings and added a blue border around the perimeter of the canvas. After owning the painting for over thirty-five years, Thompson sold it for $1,351,000 at Sotheby's in May 2021.

15 Thompson's essay: Robert Farris Thompson's "Activating Heaven: The Incantatory Art of Jean-Michel Basquiat" is in the exhibition catalog published by the Mary Boone Gallery and Michael Werner Gallery in 1985. The essay is also reprinted in Jordana Moore Saggese's *The Jean-Michel Basquiat Reader*.

16 "Happy days are here...": As quoted in Carol Vogel, "A de Kooning 'Woman' Tops the Year's Art Sales," *The New York Times*, November 21, 1996.

17 The Ganzes bought: It was purchased by Phyllis C. Wattis, a San Francisco–

based philanthropist, who then donated the piece to the San Francisco Museum of Modern Art.

18 Yet shortly thereafter: For more on the deal, see Amy Barrett, "France's Pinault Bids $1.2 Billion for U.K. Auction House Christie's," *The Wall Street Journal*, May 19, 1998.

19 "We changed everything...": These and all subsequent comments attributed to him are taken from a phone interview with Philippe Ségalot on March 7, 2022.

20 One of Basquiat's best: The other Basquiat painting in the sale was *Untitled (Chinese Man, Orange)* from 1981.

CHAPTER 9. CRITICAL APOTHEOSIS (2001–2010)

1 "We had a very dynamic...": These and all subsequent comments attributed to him are taken from a phone interview with Arnold Lehmann on July 16, 2020.

2 "One critic said about Basquiat...": Jay-Z, *Decoded* (New York: Spiegel & Grau, 2010), 95.

3 Matilde's daughters: This is the account of Reuben Andrades, Sr.

4 This is especially noteworthy: Because Matilde and Gerard never divorced, New York State law stipulated that he was automatically entitled to one-third of her Estate. If she had had a will, she could have distributed the remaining two-thirds however she wanted, whether to her daughters, siblings, friends, or charities. However, since she died without a will, New York State law once again stepped in and stipulated that 50 percent of her Estate must go to Gerard, with the balance automatically split between her two daughters.

5 While Gerard and the IRS: When Matilde's estate tax return was filed in 2010, the appraisers Gerard hired believed that the art assets Matilde jointly owned with him were worth $127.2 million at the time of her death. The Estate also believed they were entitled to a 45.96 percent blockage discount factor on these assets. The IRS sent a notice of deficiency to the Estate in February 2013, stating its agents believed the art assets were worth $157.3 million and that the correct blockage discount factor was 16.42 percent. In 2014, the parties agreed to a settlement whereby the art assets were valued at $147 million, and that the Estate could use a 40 percent blockage discount factor. These figures were included in the petition the co-executors for Gerard Basquiat's Estate filed with the US Tax Court in July 2017, pp. 10–12.

6 **This was a sharp increase:** The increase was even greater than these figures imply because some artworks from the Estate were sold between Jean-Michel Basquiat's death and that of his mother.

7 **This foundation would then:** Haring not only signed the document at the end but also added his initials and an iconic crawling baby figure at the bottom of each page.

8 **The legal team:** The law firm of Stout Thomas & Johnson represented both the Basquiat and the Haring Estates.

9 **"Less successful...":** Nicole Phelps, "Valentino Fall 2006 Ready-to-Wear," *Vogue*, March 4, 2006.

10 **Nonetheless, Gerard was soon:** For example, the Estate issued in 2001 what is now known as *Portfolio 1*, comprising four screenprints of artworks that Basquiat created in 1982 and 1983: *Untitled (Per Capita)*, *Untitled (Ernok)*, *Untitled (Head)*, and *Untitled (Rinso)*. The portfolio was published by De Sanctis Carr Fine Art in an edition of 85, along with 15 artist's proofs. Each print was signed and dated in pencil by Gerard Basquiat, with the Estate stamp on the reverse. Ten years after its publication, one copy resold for $86,600 at Phillips New York on June 28, 2011. Since then, its value has soared, with the highest auction price of $604,800 achieved at Phillips New York on April 20, 2021.

11 **Gerard and his licensing team:** Artestar, a licensing agency and creative consultancy, assisted Gerard with the licensing deals. To learn more about the company, see Alec Banks, "Meet the Company Responsible for Some of Fashion's Biggest Collabs," *Highsnobiety*, July 14, 2016.

12 **At the time:** For more on these early deals, see Joseph Pereira and Stephanie Kang, "Phat News: Rappers Choose Reebok Shoes," *Wall Street Journal*, November 14, 2003.

13 **The foundation's licensing income:** As a tax-exempt organization, the Keith Haring Foundation must file reports with details about their revenues, grants, and operating costs to the IRS via Form 990. The figures cited are royalty income for the fiscal year ending in September, which are payments for the use of trademarks, trade names, service marks, and copyrights.

14 **Considering the numerous deals:** Data from Google Trends, which tracks how often particular words are entered into its search engines, is a useful tool for measuring popularity. Over the last decade, web searches for Basqui-

at ran about 50 percent higher than those for Haring. For YouTube searches, Basquiat searches were three times higher.

15 **In his will, Ernst:** The Beyelers continued to donate works to the museum after it opened in 1997. By the time Ernst died in 2010, the couple had donated around 220 works. The value of these works then was approximately $3 billion, as shared by Sam Keller, the director of the foundation.

16 **"I remember studying...":** These and subsequent comments attributed to him are taken from a phone interview with Sam Keller on July 20, 2020.

17 **"I was just paralyzed...":** These comments are taken from a phone interview with Nicola Erni on August 24, 2020.

CHAPTER 10. COMMERCIAL APOTHEOSIS (2011–2017)

1 **Jho Low wasted no time:** Beginning in 2009 and continuing for approximately five years, Jho Low and his co-conspirators fraudulently diverted billions of dollars from 1MDB. How they did this is detailed in civil forfeiture complaints the US Justice Department started filing in 2016. The names, dates, and actions of Jho Low and others mentioned in this section were taken from the Justice Department's July 1, 2020, filing.

2 **According to calculations:** Tom Wright and Bradley Hope, the *Wall Street Journal* reporters who helped expose Jho Low, detailed his corruption in *Billion Dollar Whale: The Man Who Fooled Wall Street, Hollywood, and the World* (New York: Hachette Books, 2018). Jho Low's partying behavior is covered in chapter 10.

3 **DiCaprio, who collected himself:** For more on DiCaprio's tastes in art, see Daria Daniel, "Take a Look Inside Leonardo DiCaprio's Growing Art Collection," *Artnet News*, March 11, 2015.

4 **Low's guests:** The names of Low's skybox entourage were included in *Billion Dollar Whale*, chapter 31.

5 **Swizz Beatz received a painting:** The US Justice Department's civil forfeiture complaint indicates that Low made these gifts to Leonardo DiCaprio and Swizz Beatz in the first quarter of 2014.

6 **The Journal disclosed:** Kelly Crow and Bradley Hope, "1MDB Figure Who Made a Splash in Art Market Becomes a Seller," *The Wall Street Journal*, May 19, 2016.

7 **Since then, Low has forfeited:** Najib Razak, the Malaysian prime minister, was voted out of office in 2018 due in part to the 1MDB scandal. He was found guilty of abuse of power, criminal breach of trust, and money laundering by a Malaysian court in July 2020. He received a twelve-year prison sentence but appealed the verdict. After losing his appeal, he was jailed in August 2022. Goldman Sachs, the primary investment bank advising 1MDB, agreed to pay more than $2 billion in fines to settle various lawsuits. Leonardo DiCaprio and Swizz Beatz also resolved issues related to their relationship with Low when they voluntarily surrendered the artworks they had received from Low to the Justice Department.

8 **When Jeanine and Nora:** These figures were taken from the petition Gerard's co-executors filed with the US Tax Court on July 21, 2017. The $238.5 million figure refers to 100 percent of the value of the art assets in the Jean-Michel Basquiat Estate, not Gerard's 75 percent interest in them. Furthermore, because Gerard and Nora never married, the portion of his Estate that she inherited would be subject to estate taxes.

9 **By their accounting:** The 62 percent figure understates the increase because Gerard likely sold some assets during this five-year period. But as this sale information is not publicly available, I was unable to adjust the calculation.

10 **Almost three years after:** Gerard's federal estate tax return was submitted in October 2014. The IRS sent the co-executors a demand letter in April 2017. The issues in the case are numerous and complex and fall into three categories: (1) the fair market value of artworks and real estate owned by the Estate when Gerard died; (2) the extent to which two types of discounts (a blockage discount and a fractional share discount) should be applied to the fair market value estimates; and (3) the value of the licensing rights business.

11 **However, in early 2023:** The IRS and the Estate reached agreements on two issues in February 2024: the value of the licensing rights business and the value of the 25 Fifth Avenue apartment.

12 **Instead, she disclaimed:** Nora filed her disclaimer with the Surrogate's Court in Brooklyn on April 2, 2014. In the opening paragraph, she states: "I, A. NORA FITZPATRICK, residing at 553 Pacific Street, Brooklyn, New York 11217, do hereby irrevocably renounce, disclaim and refuse to accept my one-third (1/3) share of the residuary estate of GERARD BASQUIAT (the "Decedent"),

to which I am entitled under Article THIRD of the Decedent's Last Will and Testament, as a result of his death." The residuary estate she refers to includes the Jean-Michel Basquiat Estate assets.

13 **Nora was effectively:** The IRS and Gerard's co-executors agreed that the Jean-Michel Basquiat Estate art assets were worth $337.3. Gerard's Estate owned 75 percent of them, or $253 million. Nora's one-third interest was therefore worth $84.3 million.

14 **Rather than waiting:** This also means that her Estate will be vastly smaller when she dies and, as a result, may not be subject to federal estate taxes at that time.

15 **"Part of its wonderful commerciality...":** These and all subsequent comments attributed to her are taken from phone interviews with Amy Cappellazzo conducted in July 2021.

16 **This meant that if the painting:** For more on how guarantee deals work, see the appendix in my book *Art Collecting Today: Market Insights for Everyone Passionate about Art* (New York: Allworth Press, 2017).

17 **The underbidder was:** Fertitta's identity as the underbidder was first reported in Motoko Rich and Robin Pogrebin, "Why Spend $110 Million on a Basquiat? 'I Decided to Go For It,' Japanese Billionaire Explains," *The New York Times*, May 26, 2017.

18 **His willingness to splurge:** See Noah Kirsch, "UFC Sale Officially Closes for $4 Billion, Fertitta Brothers Earn Huge Payday," *Forbes*, August 22, 2016.

CHAPTER 11. AFTERMATH (2018–2024)

1 **"You've got a $100 million price tag...":** Comments from an interview with a senior auction house specialist who wished to remain anonymous.

2 **Recognizing an opportunity:** LVMH announced an agreement to acquire Tiffany & Co. for $16.2 billion (or $135 per share) on November 24, 2019. Over the next nine months, as the pandemic reduced sales at Tiffany, LVMH tried to renegotiate the purchase agreement. Its executives first announced they were backing out of the merger on September 9, 2020, which led Tiffany to sue the conglomerate. Over the next month, the two parties negotiated a revised agreement and announced on October 24 that the purchase price had been reduced to $131.50 per share. LVMH completed its acquisition of the company on January 7, 2021.

3 In the fall of 2021: For more about the Jay-Z, Beyoncé, and Basquiat campaign, see Rory Satran, "How Alexandre Arnault Is Shaking Things Up at Tiffany & Co.," *The Wall Street Journal*, February 8, 2022.

4 The company likely paid: It is unclear from press reports who purchased the Basquiat painting. Possible buyers include Bernard Arnault for his personal collection, a Tiffany corporate entity for the company's art collection, an LVMH entity for the parent company's collection, or the Fondation Louis Vuitton. The painting's first owner was Anne Dayton, who bought it for $7,000 around the time it was first exhibited in 1982, as reported by *The New York Times* in their September 1, 2021, article "The Mystery of That Basquiat Painting—and Its Tiffany Blue." Seven years later, amid the surge in Basquiat's market following his death, Dayton sold it at Sotheby's on May 3, 1989, for $220,000. The buyer was likely a speculator, as the painting reappeared a year later at a Sotheby's in London but failed to sell, making it an early casualty of the art market downturn. Its third and final appearance at auction was in 1996, when it was purchased by Alberto and Stefania Sabbadini, owners of a family-run luxury jewelry company in Milan, for $253,000. The painting hung in their penthouse living room, as shown in the *W Magazine* article "Go Inside the Understated Yet Eccentric Milan Home of the Fabulous Sabbadini Family," published on April 14, 2018, before being purchased by Tiffany.

5 The firm anticipates: These figures are from Claudia D'Arpizio and Federica Levato, "Luxury Is Back . . . to the Future," *Bain-Altagamma Luxury Goods Worldwide Market Study*, 20th ed. (Bain & Company, 2021).

6 Shortly after it debuted: For example, see Karen Attiah, "Sorry, Beyoncé, but Tiffany's Blood Diamonds Aren't a Girl's Best Friend," *The Washington Post*, August 26, 2021.

7 Others objected: See Miles Socha, "Beyoncé and Jay-Z Meet a Blue Basquiat in Tiffany's New Campaign," *Women's Wear Daily*, August 23, 2021. For more on the controversy his comments engendered, see Vanessa Friedman, "The Mystery of That Basquiat Painting—and Its Tiffany Blue," *The New York Times*, September 1, 2021.

8 Barzman also fabricated: *The New York Times* played a pivotal role in uncovering the scandal surrounding the fake Basquiat works exhibited at the Orlando Museum of Art. In May 2022, the newspaper published an investigative report that raised serious questions about the authenticity of the works.

This reporting brought national attention to the controversy and set the stage for the FBI's subsequent investigation and raid of the museum.

9 **Early in the pandemic:** Jose Mugrabi shared that his son (Alberto Mugrabi) and Larry Gagosian jointly represented Peter Brant in the sale of this painting to Ken Griffin for $115 million, for which they received a 3 percent commission.

10 **The Basquiat Estate assets:** The value of the Jean-Michel Basquiat art assets owned by his sisters was estimated as follows: First, the Gerard Basquiat Estate and the IRS agreed in February 2023 that the art assets owned by Basquiat's sisters and Nora Fitzpatrick totaled $337.3 million at the time of Gerard's death in July 2013. As Nora Fitzpatrick had disclaimed her interest in them, her share passed to Jean-Michel's sisters. Second, Basquiat prices have increased significantly since Gerard's death. A handful of firms offer art price indexes for specific artists based on factors such as the performance of artworks that sold repeatedly at auction. The Basquiat price index calculated by LiveArt, an art-trading platform, rose 147 percent over the period from Gerard's death through the first half of 2024. These figures imply that a Basquiat painting valued at $5 million in the first half of 2013 would, a decade later, fetch around $12.25 million. Based on this, Basquiat's sisters own art worth roughly $826 million. Third, this figure needs to be adjusted for estate taxes. Negotiations between Basquiat's sisters and the IRS are ongoing, but the IRS believes that the Gerard Basquiat Estate owes $79.1 million in federal estate taxes. Deducting this tax liability, the post-tax value of the art assets stands at $747 million. Fourth, the value of the Estate's licensing business would likely push this number back above $800 million.

BIBLIOGRAPHY

Abrams, Nora Burnett, ed. *Basquiat Before Basquiat: East 12th Street, 1979–1980*. Denver, CO: Museum of Contemporary Art Denver, 2017.

Anderson, Jervis. "The Making of Boerum Hill." *The New Yorker*, November 6, 1977.

Angelou, Maya, and Sara Jane Boyers. *Life Doesn't Frighten Me*. New York: Stewart, Tabori & Chang, 1993.

Atkins, Robert. "Baghoomian: It's Only Money." *The Village Voice*, October 25, 1994.

Attiah, Karen. "Sorry, Beyoncé, but Tiffany's Blood Diamonds Aren't a Girl's Best Friend." *The Washington Post*, August 26, 2021.

Bailey, Martin. "Where Is the Portrait of Dr. Gachet? The Mysterious Disappearance of van Gogh's Most Expensive Painting." *The Art Newspaper*, November 15, 2019.

Banks, Alec. "Meet the Company Responsible for Some of Fashion's Biggest Collabs." *Highsnobiety*, July 14, 2016.

Barrett, Amy. "France's Pinault Bids $1.2 Billion for U.K. Auction House Christie's." *The Wall Street Journal*, May 19, 1998.

Basualdo, Carlos and Scott Rothkopf, eds. *Jasper Johns–Mind/Mirror*. New York: Whitney Museum of American Art, 2021.

Basquiat, Jean-Michel. *Basquiat-isms*. Edited by Larry Warsh. Princeton, NJ: Princeton University Press, 2019.

Basquiat, Lisane, Jeanine Heriveaux, and Nora Fitzpatrick. *Jean-Michel Basquiat: King Pleasure*. New York: Rizzoli Electa, 2022.

Bischofberger, Bruno. "Collaborations–Reflections on the Experiences with Basquiat, Clemente and Warhol." In *Collaborations: Warhol, Basquiat, Clemente*, edited by Tilman Osterwold. Ostfildern-Ruit, Germany: Cantz, 1996.

Brick, John, and Carlton K. Erickson. *Drugs, the Brain, and Behavior: The Pharmacology of Drug Use Disorders*. New York: Routledge, 2013.

Buchhart, Dieter, and Sam Keller, eds. *Jean-Michel Basquiat*. Berlin: Hatje Cantz, 2010.

Buchhart, Dieter, ed. *Jean-Michel Basquiat*. Paris: Fondation Louis Vuitton and Éditions Gallimard, 2018.

Buchhart, Dieter, and Eleanor Nairne, eds. *Basquiat: Boom for Real*. Munich: Prestel Verlag, 2017.

Clement, Jennifer. *Widow Basquiat: A Love Story*. New York: Broadway Books, 2014.

Cooper, Martha, and Henry Chalfant. *Subway Art*. New York: Thames & Hudson, 2016.

Crow, Kelly, and Bradley Hope. "1MDB Figure Who Made a Splash in Art Market Becomes a Seller." *The Wall Street Journal*, May 19, 2016.

Daniel, Daria. "Take a Look Inside Leonardo DiCaprio's Growing Art Collection." Artnet News, March 11, 2015.

D'Arcy, David. "Whitney Compares Basquiat to Leonardo da Vinci in New Retrospective: Music Television and Madonna Sponsor Her Late Lover." *The Art Newspaper*, November 1, 1992.

D'Arpizio, Claudia, and Federica Levato. "Luxury Is Back . . . to the Future." *Bain-Altagamma Luxury Goods Worldwide Market Study*. 20th ed. Bain & Company, 2021.

Dávila, Arlene M. *Latinx Art: Artists, Markets, and Politics*. Durham, NC: Duke University Press, 2020.

Desmarais, Mary-Dailey, Vincent Bessières, and Dieter Buchhart. *Music and the Art of Jean-Michel Basquiat*. Paris: Éditions Gallimard, 2022.

Faflick, Philip. "SAMO© Graffiti: BOOSH-WAH or CIA?" *The Village Voice*, December 11, 1978.

Flood, Richard. "Skied and Grounded in Queens: 'New York/New Wave' at P.S. 1." *Artforum*, July 1981.

Fondation Beyeler. *Basquiat.* Ostfildern: Hatje Cantz, 2010.

Foye, Raymond, ed. "A Tribute to Diego Cortez (1946–2021)." *The Brooklyn Rail*, September 2021.

Friedman, Vanessa. "The Mystery of That Basquiat Painting—and Its Tiffany Blue." *The New York Times*, September 1, 2021.

Glueck, Grace. "The Basquiat Touch Survives the Artist in Shows and Courts." *The New York Times*, July 22, 1991.

———."A Huge Exhibition at Broadway Terminal." *The New York Times*, September 30, 1983.

Greene, Gael. "Eat and Be Seen: Odeon, Joanna, Nuccio," *New York Magazine*, August 3, 1981.

——. *Insatiable: Tales from a Life of Delicious Excess* (New York: Warner, 2006).

Hermann, Michael Dayton, ed. *Warhol on Basquiat: The Iconic Relationship Told in Andy Warhol's Words and Pictures.* Köln: Taschen, 2019.

Hess, Elizabeth. "Family Feud." *The Village Voice*, June 13, 1995.

Hoban, Phoebe. *Basquiat: A Quick Killing in Art.* New York: Penguin Books, 1999.

Hoffman, Fred. *The Art of Jean-Michel Basquiat.* New York: Enrico Navarra Gallery, 2017.

Hoffman, Fred, and Acquavella Galleries. *Jean-Michel Basquiat—Drawing: Work from the Schorr Family Collection.* New York: Rizzoli, 2014.

Hughes, Robert. "Requiem for a Featherweight: The Sad Story of an Artist's Success." *The New Republic*, November 21, 1988.

——. *The Shock of the New.* New York: Alfred A. Knopf, 1981.

Jay-Z. *Decoded.* New York: Spiegel & Grau, 2010.

Kirsch, Noah. "UFC Sale Officially Closes for $4 Billion, Fertitta Brothers Earn Huge Payday." *Forbes*, August 22, 2016.

Kolk, Bessel van der. *The Body Keeps the Score: Brain, Mind, and Body in the Healing of Trauma.* London: Penguin Books, 2014.

La Force, Thessaly. "Learn About a Couple That Collected Jean-Michel Basquiat—and Became His Friend, Too." *Vogue*, May 15, 2014.

Lambarelli, Roberto. *Annina Nosei.* Rome: Arte e Critica, 2023.

Lotringer, Sylvère. "Diego Cortez." *Paris LA Magazine*, September 2021.

Lurie, John. *The History of Bones: A Memoir.* New York: Random House, 2021.

Mailer, Norman, and Jan Naar. *The Faith of Graffiti.* New York: Praeger, 1974.

Marshall, Richard, ed. *Jean-Michel Basquiat.* Whitney Museum of American Art, 1992.

Mayer, Marc, ed. *Basquiat.* New York: Brooklyn Museum, 2005.

Munsell, Liz, and Greg Tate, eds. *Writing the Future: Basquiat and the Hip-Hop Generation.* Boston: MFA Publications, Museum of Fine Arts, 2020.

Navarra, Enrico, ed. *Jean-Michel Basquiat.* Paris: Galerie Enrico Navarra, 2000.

——, ed. *Basquiat–Château La Coste en Provence.* Paris: Galerie Enrico Navarra, 2019.

Neihart, Maureen. "Building Resilience in Gifted Children: Can Resiliency Be Taught or Is It Innate?" *Understanding Our Gifted* 18, no. 2 (2006).

——. "Creativity, the Arts, and Madness." *Roeper Review* 21, no. 1 (September 1998).

Neihart, Maureen, Steven I. Pfeiffer, and Tracy L. Cross. *The Social and Emotional Development of Gifted Children: What Do We Know?* Waco, TX: Prufrock Press, 2016.

O'Brien, Glenn. "Who Was That Masked Man?" In *Jean-Michel Basquiat*, edited by Dieter Buchhart and Sam Keller. Berlin: Hatje Cantz Press, 2010.

O'Flaherty, Mark. "Paige Powell on Andy Warhol, Fashion and America's Art Scene." *Spear's*, January 9, 2013.

Olszewski-Kubilius, Paula M., Marilynn J. Kulieke, and Noma Krasney. "Personality Dimensions of Gifted Adolescents: A Review of the Empirical Literature." *Gifted Child Quarterly* 32, no. 4 (October 1988).

People Weekly. "The Most Outrageous Disco in America." July 16, 1979.

Pereira, Joseph, and Stephanie Kang. "Phat News: Rappers Choose Reebok Shoes." *The Wall Street Journal*, November 14, 2003.

Ricard, Rene. "The Radiant Child." *Artforum* 20, no. 4 (December 1981).

Saggese, Jordana Moore, ed. *The Jean-Michel Basquiat Reader.* Oakland: University of California Press, 2021.

Satran, Rory. "How Alexandre Arnault Is Shaking Things Up at Tiffany & Co." *The Wall Street Journal*, February 8, 2022.

Sheff, David. "Keith Haring, an Intimate Conversation." *Rolling Stone*, August 1989.

Smith, Roberta. "Basquiat: Man for His Decade." *The New York Times*, October 23, 1992.

Socha, Miles. "Beyoncé and Jay-Z Meet a Blue Basquiat in Tiffany's New Campaign." *Women's Wear Daily*, August 23, 2021.

Somers, Thierry. "Jean-Michel Basquiat/Diego Cortez Interview." *200%* (magazine), December 18, 2017.

Spunt, Barry. *Heroin and Music in New York City*. New York: Palgrave Macmillan, 2014.

Stambaugh, Tamra, and Paula Olszewski-Kubilius. *Unlocking Potential: Identifying and Serving Gifted Students from Low-Income Households*. Waco, TX: Prufrock Press, 2020.

Subotnik, Rena F., Paula Olszewski-Kubilius, and Frank C. Worrell. "Rethinking Giftedness and Gifted Education." *Psychological Science in the Public Interest* 12, no. 1 (January 2011).

Tate, Greg. "Flyboy in the Buttermilk: The Crisis of the Black Artist in White America." *The Village Voice*, November 14, 1989.

Thompson, Robert Farris. "Activating Heaven: The Incantatory Art of Jean-Michel Basquiat." In *The Jean-Michel Basquiat Reader*, edited by Jordana Moore Saggese. Oakland: University of California Press, 2021.

———. *Flash of the Spirit: African and Afro-American Art and Philosophy*. New York: Vintage Books, 1984.

Vogel, Carol. "A de Kooning 'Woman' Tops the Year's Art Sales." *The New York Times*, November 21, 1996.

———."Prices and Hopes Rise as Spring Art Auctions Reveal a Robust Market." *The New York Times*, May 10, 1996.

Warhol, Andy, and Pat Hackett. *The Andy Warhol Diaries*. New York: Warner Books, 1989.

Woodham, Doug. *Art Collecting Today: Market Insights for Everyone Passionate About Art*. New York: Allworth Press, 2017.

Wright, Tom, and Bradley Hope. *Billion Dollar Whale: The Man Who Fooled Wall Street, Hollywood, and the World*. New York: Hachette Books, 2018.

ILLUSTRATION CREDITS

Every reasonable effort has been made to supply complete and correct credits; if there are errors or omissions, please contact Thames & Hudson Inc.

Page numbers in brackets refer to full page illustrations without a printed page number.

Front cover: Jean-Michel Basquiat, ca. 1981. © Edo Bertoglio

[p. 8] Jean-Michel Basquiat, ca. 1981 (detail). © Edo Bertoglio

[p. 14] Jean-Michel Basquiat, 1962. Courtesy of Reuben Andrades, Sr.

p. 16 Matilde Basquiat with her mother, late 1950s. Courtesy of Reuben Andrades, Sr.

p. 17 The Andrades family townhouse in Bushwick. Courtesy of Reuben Andrades, Sr.

p. 22. The Basquiats' brownstone in Boerum Hill. Courtesy of Lizzy Woodham, 2021

p. 23 Jean-Michel Basquiat in Brooklyn, 1975. Courtesy of Reuben Andrades, Sr.

p. 25 Al Diaz, 1975. © Flint Gennari

p. 27 Basquiat with a SAMO© tag, 1978. © Jim Billipp

p. 28 Diaz's receipt for interview, 1978. Courtesy of Philip Elmer-DeWitt, otherwise known as Philip Faflick.

p. 31 Gerard Basquiat and Nora Fitzpatrick, 1978. © Dinanda Nooney, courtesy of the Photography Collection, the Miriam and Ira D. Wallach Division of Art, Prints and Photographs, the New York Public Library.

[p. 32] Jean-Michel Basquiat, 1979. © Nicholas Taylor

p. 34 The Mudd Club, 1979. © Bob Gruen

p. 35 Iggy Pop and David Bowie. © Bobby Grossman

p. 37 Michael Holman, 1981. Courtesy of Michael Holman

p. 38 Basquiat with the band Gray, October 1979. © Nicholas Taylor

p. 39 Diego Cortez, 1977. © Bobby Grossman

p. 40 Basquiat dancing, 1979. © Marcia Resnick

p. 45 Annina Nosei. © Michel Delsol via Getty Images

p. 50 Basquiat, ca. 1981. © Edo Bertoglio

p. 53 Basquiat in the Crosby Street loft, 1982. © Roland Hagenberg

p. 54 Vincent Gallo. © Andrew Buurman/ Alamy Stock Photo

p. 62 Glenn O'Brien interviewing Basquiat, 1979. © Bobby Grossman

p. 65 David Bowes. © Bernard Warkentin

[p. 69] SoHo architecture. © Patti McConville/ Alamy Stock Photo

p. 76 Gene and Barbara Schwartz, 1990. © Timothy Greenfield-Sanders

p. 79 Stéphane Janssen, 2017. © Daniel Swadener

[p. 84] Basquiat in Tokyo, 1985. © Ikeda Gallery,

photo by Yoshitaka Uchida
p. 92 Bruno Bischofberger, Brook Bartlett, and Basquiat in St. Moritz, 1983. © Christina Bischofberger, Courtesy of Galerie Bruno Bischofberger
p. 94 Andy Warhol and Basquiat, 1982. © 2024 The Andy Warhol Foundation for the Visual Arts, Inc./ Licensed by Artists Rights Society (ARS), New York
p. 95 Basquiat and Paige Powell, 1984. Courtesy of the Paige Powell Archives
p. 97 Basquiat and Andy Warhol, 1984. © Richard Schulman
p. 100 Gerard, Jean-Michel, and Jeanine Basquiat, 1985. © 2024 The Andy Warhol Foundation for the Visual Arts, Inc./ Licensed by Artists Rights Society (ARS), New York
p. 101 Jean-Michel and Matilde Basquiat, 1984. © 2024 The Andy Warhol Foundation for the Visual Arts, Inc./Licensed by Artists Rights Society (ARS), New York
p. 102 Basquiat at Dallas Museum of Art, 1985. © Dallas Museum of Art Archives, photo by Andy Hanson
[p. 104] Keith Haring and Basquiat, 1987. © Irving Zucker
[p. 110] Jean-Michel Basquiat, 1988. © Jérôme Schlomoff
[p. 111] Jean-Michel Basquiat, 1988. © Jérôme Schlomoff
p. 113 Vrej Baghoomian, 1990. © Sylvie Ball, 1990
p. 116 Jean-Michel Basquiat's grave, 2021. Courtesy of Lizzy Woodham
p. 118 Greg Tate, 2013. © Janette Beckman
[p. 120] The entrance to Green-Wood Cemetery in Brooklyn. Courtesy of Lizzy Woodham
[p. 132] Maya Angelou, ca. 1988. © Stephen Parker/ Alamy Stock Photo
p. 138 Jose and Mary Mugrabi, 1982. Courtesy of Jose Mugrabi
p. 143 Peter Brant and Stephanie Seymour. © CelebrityArchaeology.com/Alamy Stock Photo
p. 146 Enrico Navarra. © Raul Higuera/Galerie Enrico Navarra,
[p. 160] Debbie Harry and Basquiat dancing, December 1987. © Irving Zucker
p. 165 Adam Clayton, 2016. © Sam Jones
p. 166 U2 in Tangier, 1991. © Anton Corbun
p. 168 Lars Ulrich, 1996. © Alamy Stock Photo
p. 172 Jeffrey Wright in Basquiat, 1996. © Moviestore Collection/Alamy Stock Photo
p. 173 Poster for *Basquiat*. © Alamy Stock Photo
p. 179 Basquiat and William Burroughs, December 1986. © Victor Bockris
p. 186 Thelma Golden. © ZUMA Press/Alamy Stock Photo
p. 193 Philip Niarchos, ca. 1970. © Keystone Pictures USA/Alamy Stock Photo
[p. 194] Paige Powell and Gerard Basquiat, 2005. © Patrick McMullan via Getty Images
p. 199 Matilde Basquiat's funeral program, November 2008. Courtesy of Reuben Andrades, Sr.
p. 207 Sam Keller. © Wenn/Alamy Stock Photo
[p. 210] Jerry and Emily Spiegel, 2007. © Patrick McMullan via Getty Images
p. 214 Jho Low, 2014. © Wenn/Alamy Stock Photo
p. 219 Jerry and Emily Spiegel, 2007. © Patrick McMullan via Getty Images
p. 220 Amy Cappellazzo. © Sean Zanni/Patrick McMullan via Getty Images
p. 223 Yusaku Maezawa. © Nippon News/Alamy Stock Photo
p. 224 Frank Fertitta. © Image Press Agency/ Alamy Stock Photo
[p. 226] Jeanine Heriveaux and Lisane Basquiat, 2017. © Londonphotos/Alamy Stock Photo
p. 231 Alexandre Arnault. © Abaca Press/Alamy Stock Photo
[p. 238] A crown tattoo. Courtesy of Marquitos Corvalán and Motorra Tattoo, Argentina
Back cover: Basquiat in the Crosby Street loft, 1982. © Roland Hagenberg
Inside flap: Doug Woodham. Photo by Drew Massangkay

INDEX

Page numbers in italics indicate an illustration and brackets indicate the number is not printed.

This book is set in Richmond Text, created by the eminent type designer Matthew Carter, whose decades-long experience in the typographic arts ranges from hand-cut punches for hot metal to fonts designed for screen legibility on the computer, such as Verdana and Georgia.